# *The* STUDENT BIBLE DICTIONARY

# *The* STUDENT BIBLE DICTIONARY

*A complete learning system to help you understand
words, people, places, and events of the Bible*

KAREN DOCKREY
JOHNNIE & PHYLLIS GODWIN

BARBOUR
PUBLISHING

Published by Barbour Books, an imprint of Barbour Publishing, Inc., P.O. Box 719, Uhrichsville, OH 44683, www.barbourbooks.com

 Member of the
Evangelical Christian
Publishers Association

Printed in China.

# TABLE OF CONTENTS

## Major Charts

## Full Page Maps

# PREFACE

*The Student Bible Dictionary* was written with your needs in mind. We know you basically want to look up a Bible word only once and in one place, find exactly the information you need to make the Bible passage clear, and then return to your Bible study. Because of this, we have defined words quickly and precisely in the first line or two and then added details in later sentences. Cross-references are rare. When we could, we added an illustration or tiny map to help you know just what the item looked like or just where the place was. We've told you what people did what and who was related to whom, so you could understand some of the whys and wherefores of their actions and keep Bible families straight. We've added easy-to-read pronunciations for proper names so you'll know just how to say the names.

Why a student Bible dictionary? Because you as a Bible student have special study needs. You have a curiosity that is ready for more specific information. You have an aptitude that lets you build on what you have learned during your childhood years.

You may be older than the teen years but be young in your Christian faith. This Bible dictionary is for you and for any Christian who wants clear, concise, need-meeting definitions. *The Student Bible Dictionary* puts Bible terms into language that will help the faith of the Bible become yours and will help you honor God in your life.

In *The Student Bible Dictionary* you'll find words defined in the way they are used in the Bible rather than the way they might be used today in another context. For example, *conversation* in the King James Version of the Bible means "behavior, conduct, manner of life" rather than a talk between two people. You'll usually find primary meanings rather than remote or exhaustive ones. Though true to the original languages, the definitions use Hebrew and Greek references sparingly.

Each entry is organized so that the further you read the more detail you will find. If you want a simple definition of the word/person/place/idea, read the first word or sentence only. Many entries include only this basic information.

Special entries include features that will help you understand a word more thoroughly:

- ■ **Requested Word:** This symbol indicates a high-frequency word, requested by a group of over five hundred student leaders participating in leadership conferences. These leaders identified this word as one students need to understand and consider in living their Christian faith.
- ▼ **Greater Detail:** This paragraph includes details that help you understand a specific usage of the word, aids you in completing a Bible study challenge, gives you information not available in other dictionaries, or provides fascinating facts.
- ● **Curriculum Hooks:** This question or thought-provoker helps you think further about the word, discuss it in class, or apply it to daily life. Bible study teachers or curriculum writers may use this added thought for a curriculum hook in identifying, clarifying, or forming convictions and in guiding students to make applications to their lives.

Throughout *The Student Bible Dictionary* you'll find interesting lists and charts such as **Names of God** (page 103), **Titles for Jesus in Scripture** (page 130), **Table of Weights and Measures** (pages 244–245), and **Feasts and Festivals** through which believers celebrated (page 92). You'll also find summaries of all Bible books and definitions of theological words such as *millennium* and *plenary verbal inspiration*. Though the dictionary is compatible with other Bible translations, the King James Version of the Bible is the base. The English language is steeped in the language of the King James Version; and since this most-used translation is nearly four hundred years old, it requires the most definitions for readers of the Bible. Other versions are referenced as appropriate.

To save space, we refer to the New Testament with NT and the Old Testament with OT. Abbreviations for Bible versions are:

KJV=King James Version
NASB=New American Standard Bible
NIV=New International Version
NRSV=New Revised Standard Version
GNB=Good News Bible, also called The Bible in Today's English

You'll find evangelistic inroads when defining such key words as "believe," "repent," "confess," and "salvation." These key words help you understand your salvation as well as guide you to lead your friends to Jesus Christ.

This Bible dictionary is unapologetically student-oriented and conservative in nature. Words selected for definition are those the authors and their research showed were most needed for students. The factors determining the length and detail of definitions are accuracy, clarity, and developmental needs. The authors have attempted to create a unique and user-friendly student Bible dictionary both for students and their leaders. Because it is directed toward young people, it does not focus on critical problems or peripheral matters that dictionaries intended for adults might include. It focuses on central meanings of Bible words and helps students apply those meanings in their lives.

You'll find approximately twenty-five hundred entries in *The Student Bible Dictionary,* chosen because of their appeal to or importance for students. We've aimed for strong, quick definitions that are accurate and clear. We hope you'll find this Bible dictionary different from the usual dictionary. We intend for this to be an inviting and usable tool that meets your needs and interests, spiritually, intellectually, and developmentally.

# CONTRIBUTORS

## Authors
Karen Dockrey

Johnnie Godwin                    Phyllis Godwin

## Editorial Staff
Trent C. Butler, General Editor

Forrest W. Jackson                    Jean Jenkins

Melody McCoy                    Marsha A. Ellis Smith

June Swann

## Artists
Ernie Couch / Consultx

Gene Elliott                    Jack Jewell

Ed Maksimowicz                    Tom Seale

## Production Staff
Joyce Anderson                    Daniel Halpin

Marc McDougan                    Bob Morrison

# TIME LINE

## BIBLICAL HISTORY

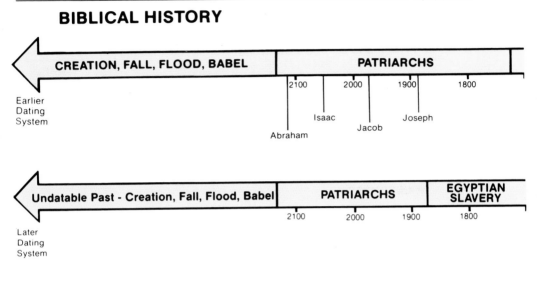

CREATION, FALL, FLOOD, BABEL | PATRIARCHS

2100    2000    1900    1800

Earlier
Dating
System

Isaac    Joseph

Jacob

Abraham

Undatable Past - Creation, Fall, Flood, Babel | PATRIARCHS | EGYPTIAN SLAVERY

2100    2000    1900    1800

Later
Dating
System

---

ANCIENT HISTORY

## WORLD HISTORY

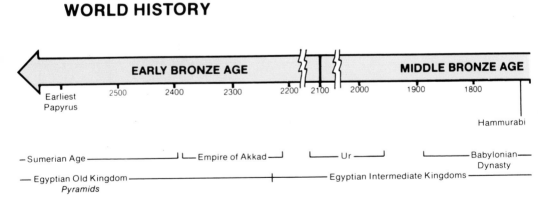

EARLY BRONZE AGE | MIDDLE BRONZE AGE

2500   2400   2300   2200   2100   2000   1900   1800

Earliest
Papyrus

Hammurabi

— Sumerian Age —————⏌ ⌐— Empire of Akkad —⏌ ⌐— Ur —⏌ ⌐— Babylonian — Dynasty

— Egyptian Old Kingdom ————————— Egyptian Intermediate Kingdoms —
Pyramids

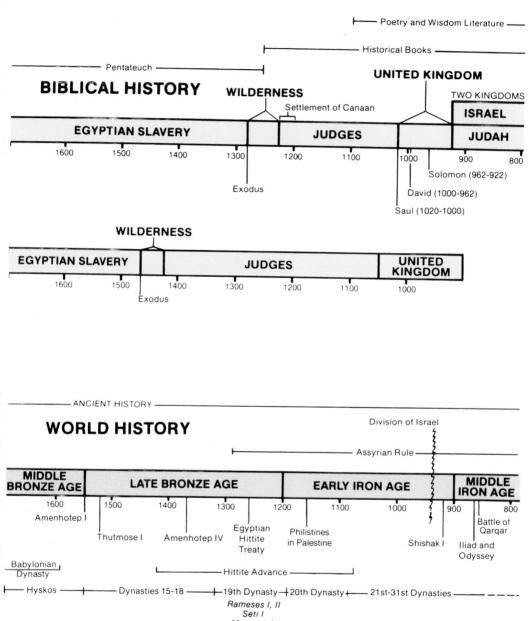

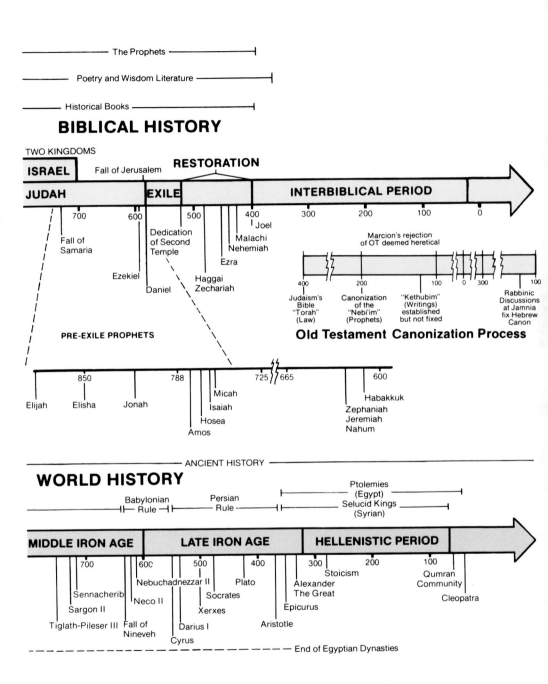

The Prophets

Poetry and Wisdom Literature

Historical Books

# BIBLICAL HISTORY

TWO KINGDOMS

**ISRAEL**    Fall of Jerusalem    **RESTORATION**

**JUDAH**    **EXILE**    **INTERBIBLICAL PERIOD**

700    600    500    400    300    200    100    0

Fall of Samaria

Dedication of Second Temple

Joel

Malachi
Nehemiah

Ezra

Ezekiel

Haggai
Zechariah

Daniel

**PRE-EXILE PROPHETS**

Marcion's rejection of OT deemed heretical

400    200    100    0    300    100

Judaism's
Bible
"Torah"
(Law)

Canonization
of the
"Nebi'im"
(Prophets)

"Kethubim"
(Writings)
established
but not fixed

Rabbinic
Discussions
at Jamnia
fix Hebrew
Canon

**Old Testament Canonization Process**

850    788    725 // 665    600

Elijah    Elisha    Jonah

Micah

Isaiah

Hosea

Amos

Habakkuk

Zephaniah
Jeremiah
Nahum

ANCIENT HISTORY

# WORLD HISTORY

Ptolemies
(Egypt)

Babylonian    Persian    Selucid Kings
Rule    Rule    (Syrian)

**MIDDLE IRON AGE**    **LATE IRON AGE**    **HELLENISTIC PERIOD**

700    600    500    400    300    200    100

Sennacherib

Nebuchadnezzar II

Plato

Stoicism

Qumran
Community

Neco II

Socrates

Alexander
The Great

Cleopatra

Sargon II

Xerxes

Epicurus

Tiglath-Pileser III    Fall of
Nineveh

Darius I

Aristotle

Cyrus

End of Egyptian Dynasties

# CHURCH HISTORY

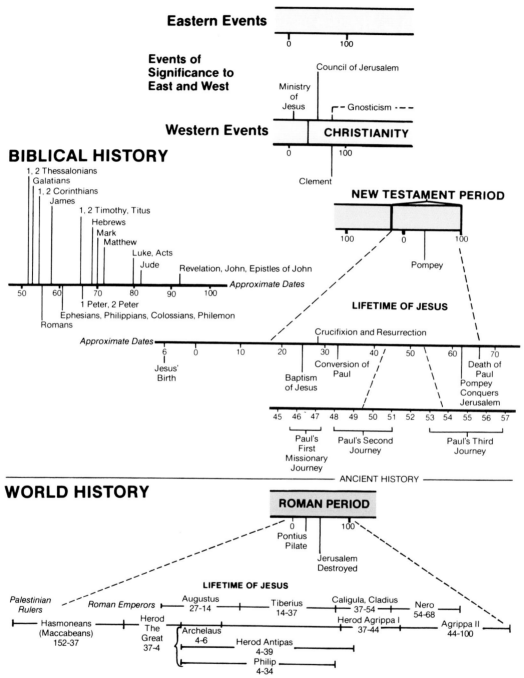

Eastern Events

0          100

Events of
Significance to
East and West

Council of Jerusalem

Ministry
of
Jesus

- - Gnosticism - - -

Western Events

**CHRISTIANITY**

0          100

# BIBLICAL HISTORY

1, 2 Thessalonians
Galatians
1, 2 Corinthians
James
1, 2 Timothy, Titus
Hebrews
Mark
Matthew
Luke, Acts
Jude
Revelation, John, Epistles of John

Clement

**NEW TESTAMENT PERIOD**

100          0          100

Pompey

*Approximate Dates*

50     60     70     80     90     100

1 Peter, 2 Peter
Ephesians, Philippians, Colossians, Philemon
Romans

**LIFETIME OF JESUS**

*Approximate Dates*

Crucifixion and Resurrection

6     0     10     20     30     40     50     60     70

Jesus'
Birth

Baptism
of Jesus

Conversion of
Paul

Death of
Paul
Pompey
Conquers
Jerusalem

45   46   47   48   49   50   51   52   53   54   55   56   57

Paul's
First
Missionary
Journey

Paul's Second
Journey

Paul's Third
Journey

———— ANCIENT HISTORY ————

# WORLD HISTORY

**ROMAN PERIOD**

0          100

Pontius
Pilate

Jerusalem
Destroyed

**LIFETIME OF JESUS**

| Palestinian Rulers | Roman Emperors | Augustus 27-14 | Tiberius 14-37 | Caligula, Cladius 37-54 | Nero 54-68 |
| --- | --- | --- | --- | --- | --- |

Hasmoneans
(Maccabeans)
152-37

Herod
The
Great
37-4

Archelaus
4-6

Herod Antipas
4-39

Philip
4-34

Herod Agrippa I
37-44

Agrippa II
44-100

# CHURCH HISTORY

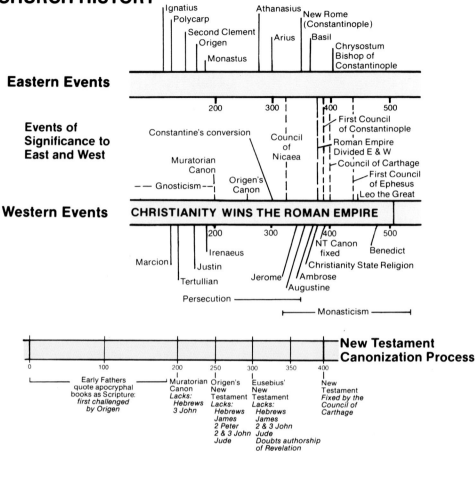

Ignatius
Polycarp
Second Clement
Origen
Monastus

Athanasius
Arius

New Rome
(Constantinople)
Basil
Chrysostum
Bishop of
Constantinople

## Eastern Events

200    300    400    500

## Events of Significance to East and West

Constantine's conversion

Muratorian Canon

— — Gnosticism — —

Origen's Canon

Council of Nicaea

First Council of Constantinople
Roman Empire Divided E & W
Council of Carthage
First Council of Ephesus
Leo the Great

## Western Events

### CHRISTIANITY WINS THE ROMAN EMPIRE

200    300    400    500

Marcion
Irenaeus
Justin
Tertullian

Jerome

NT Canon fixed
Benedict
Christianity State Religion
Ambrose
Augustine

Persecution ⟶

⊢ Monasticism ⟶

## New Testament Canonization Process

0    100    200   250   300   350   400

Early Fathers quote apocryphal books as Scripture: *first challenged by Origen*

Muratorian Canon
*Lacks:*
Hebrews
3 John

Origen's New Testament
*Lacks:*
Hebrews
James
2 Peter
2 & 3 John
Jude

Eusebius' New Testament
*Lacks:*
Hebrews
James
2 & 3 John
Jude
*Doubts authorship of Revelation*

New Testament *Fixed by the Council of Carthage*

⸻ ANCIENT HISTORY ⸻⊦⊦ MEDIEVAL HISTORY ⸻

# WORLD HISTORY

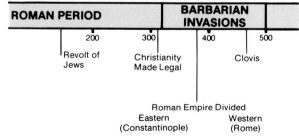

| ROMAN PERIOD | BARBARIAN INVASIONS | |

200    300    400    500

Revolt of Jews

Christianity Made Legal

Clovis

Roman Empire Divided
Eastern                     Western
(Constantinople)            (Rome)

# CHURCH HISTORY

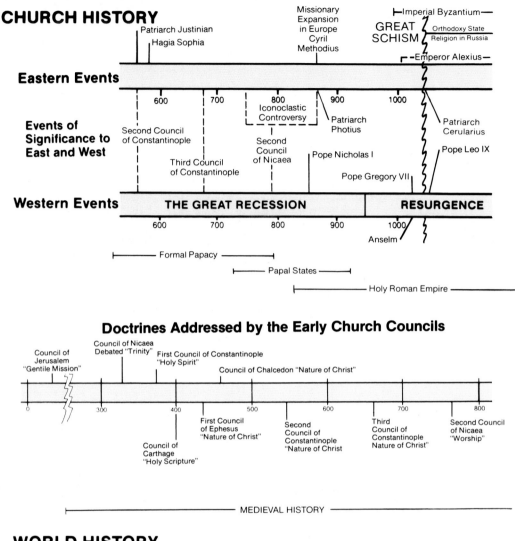

**Eastern Events**

Patriarch Justinian
Hagia Sophia

Missionary Expansion in Europe
Cyril
Methodius

Imperial Byzantium

**GREAT SCHISM**
Orthodoxy State
Religion in Russia

Emperor Alexius

600  700  800  900  1000

Iconoclastic Controversy

**Events of Significance to East and West**

Second Council of Constantinople

Third Council of Constantinople

Second Council of Nicaea

Patriarch Photius

Pope Nicholas I

Pope Gregory VII

Patriarch Cerularius

Pope Leo IX

**Western Events**

**THE GREAT RECESSION**   **RESURGENCE**

600  700  800  900  1000

Anselm

Formal Papacy

Papal States

Holy Roman Empire

## Doctrines Addressed by the Early Church Councils

Council of Jerusalem "Gentile Mission"

Council of Nicaea Debated "Trinity"

First Council of Constantinople "Holy Spirit"

Council of Chalcedon "Nature of Christ"

0   300   400   500   600   700   800

First Council of Ephesus "Nature of Christ"

Second Council of Constantinople "Nature of Christ"

Third Council of Constantinople Nature of Christ"

Second Council of Nicaea "Worship"

Council of Carthage "Holy Scripture"

MEDIEVAL HISTORY

# WORLD HISTORY

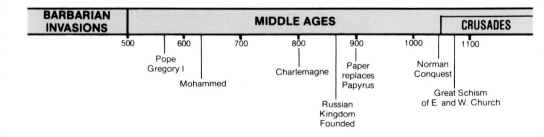

**BARBARIAN INVASIONS**   **MIDDLE AGES**   **CRUSADES**

500   600   700   800   900   1000   1100

Pope Gregory I

Mohammed

Charlemagne

Paper replaces Papyrus

Norman Conquest

Great Schism of E. and W. Church

Russian Kingdom Founded

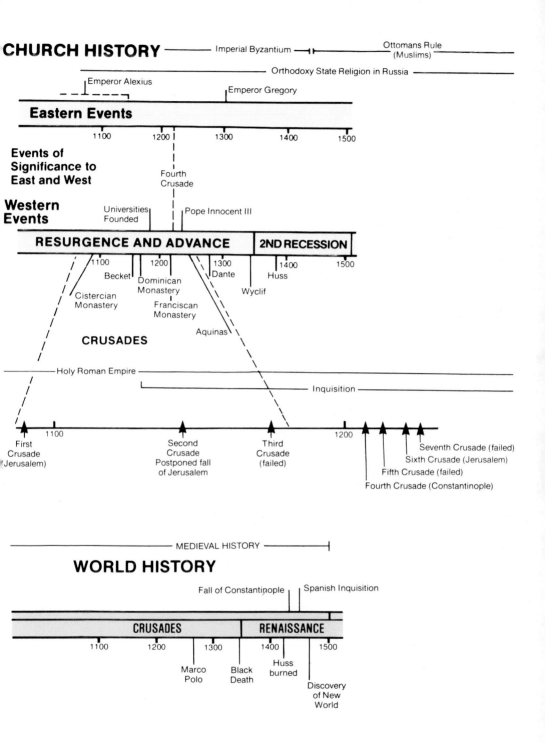

# CHURCH HISTORY
Imperial Byzantium
Ottomans Rule (Muslims)

Orthodoxy State Religion in Russia

Emperor Alexius
Emperor Gregory

## Eastern Events

1100　1200　1300　1400　1500

**Events of Significance to East and West**

Fourth Crusade

**Western Events**

Universities Founded
Pope Innocent III

## RESURGENCE AND ADVANCE　　2ND RECESSION

1100　1200　1300　1400　1500

Becket
Dante
Huss

Cistercian Monastery
Dominican Monastery
Wyclif

Franciscan Monastery

Aquinas

### CRUSADES

Holy Roman Empire

Inquisition

1100　　1200

First Crusade (Jerusalem)
Second Crusade Postponed fall of Jerusalem
Third Crusade (failed)
Seventh Crusade (failed)
Sixth Crusade (Jerusalem)
Fifth Crusade (failed)
Fourth Crusade (Constantinople)

MEDIEVAL HISTORY

# WORLD HISTORY

Fall of Constantinople
Spanish Inquisition

## CRUSADES　　RENAISSANCE

1100　1200　1300　1400　1500

Marco Polo
Black Death
Huss burned
Discovery of New World

# CHURCH HISTORY

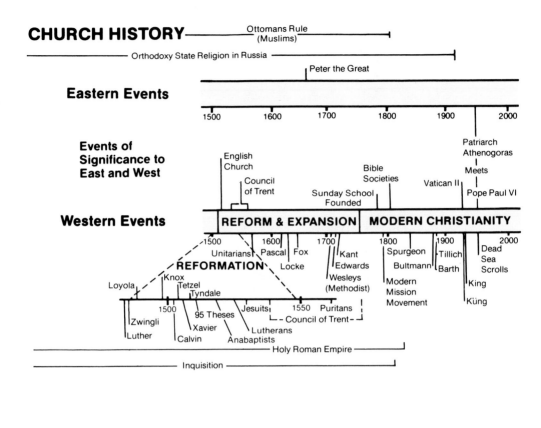

Ottomans Rule
(Muslims)

Orthodoxy State Religion in Russia

Peter the Great

## Eastern Events

1500  1600  1700  1800  1900  2000

## Events of Significance to East and West

English Church

Council of Trent

Bible Societies

Sunday School Founded

Patriarch Athenogoras

Meets

Vatican II

Pope Paul VI

## Western Events

REFORM & EXPANSION    MODERN CHRISTIANITY

1500  1600  1700  1800  1900  2000

Unitarians  Pascal  Fox

Kant

Spurgeon  Tillich  Dead Sea Scrolls

REFORMATION   Locke

Edwards

Bultmann  Barth

Wesleys (Methodist)

Modern Mission Movement

King

Küng

Loyola

Knox

Tetzel

Tyndale

1500

95 Theses

Jesuits

1550  Puritans

Council of Trent

Zwingli

Luther

Xavier

Calvin

Lutherans

Anabaptists

Holy Roman Empire

Inquisition

# WORLD HISTORY

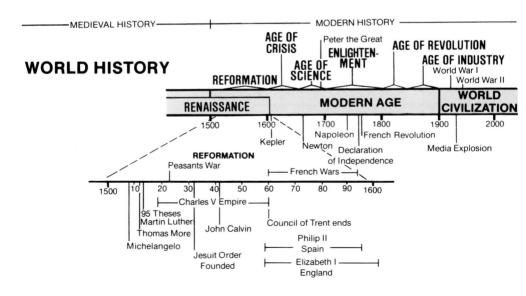

MEDIEVAL HISTORY          MODERN HISTORY

AGE OF CRISIS

Peter the Great

AGE OF REVOLUTION

ENLIGHTEN-MENT

AGE OF INDUSTRY

AGE OF SCIENCE

World War I

World War II

REFORMATION

RENAISSANCE          MODERN AGE          WORLD CIVILIZATION

1500  1600  1700  1800  1900  2000

Kepler

Napoleon  French Revolution

Newton  Declaration

Media Explosion

REFORMATION

Peasants War

French Wars

1500  10  20  30  40  50  60  70  80  90  1600

Charles V Empire

95 Theses

Martin Luther

Thomas More

John Calvin

Council of Trent ends

Michelangelo

Philip II

Spain

Jesuit Order Founded

Elizabeth I England

**AARON** (AIRn). Older brother of and early spokesman for Moses (Ex. 4:14-16). Became Israel's first high priest. The Aaronic priesthood (priests of the tribe of Levi) was named for him (Ex. 28:1; 29; Lev. 8; Num. 18). See **HIGH PRIEST.**
▼ *Early spokesman for Moses who helped him in battle (Ex. 17:9-12), but also made an idol (Ex. 32) and criticized Moses for his choice of a wife (Num. 12:1-2). Parents were Amram and Jochebed; sister was Miriam (Num. 26:59). Aaron lived until age 123 and died without entering the Promised Land because of his lack of faith in God (Num. 20:12).*

**AARON'S ROD.** Walking stick used by Aaron to carry out God's commands. The rod played a part in several miracles that resulted in Pharaoh's letting the Jewish slaves go. It became a serpent that swallowed the serpents from the rods of the Egyptian magicians (Ex. 7:8-13) and was used to bring about the first three plagues (Ex. 7:19-21; 8:5-7,16-19).

Later in Aaron's life, the rod sprouted, budded, and blossomed to signal Aaron as God's choice for the head of a priesthood (Num. 17:1-11). It was displayed before (and later in) the ark of the covenant as a warning to those who rebelled against the Lord (Heb. 9:4; Num. 17:10).

**AB.** Fifth Hebrew month (Num. 33:38). Matches part of our July and August. See the **date chart** following **TIME.**

**ABASE.** To humble oneself or be humbled; to get the right view of oneself by choice or by force (Dan. 4:37; 2 Cor. 11:7; Phil. 4:12).

**ABATE.** Decrease or withdraw (Gen. 8:8; Lev. 27:18).

**ABBA.** *Father* in Aramaic; much like our word *Daddy.* All three NT references are to God (Mark 14:36; Rom. 8:15; Gal. 4:6). Shows that God is a loving, approachable Father.

**ABEDNEGO** (uh BED nih go). New name given to Azariah, friend of Daniel (Dan. 1:6-7). Abednego survived the fiery furnace along with Shadrach and Meshach (Dan. 3:16-30).

**ABEL** (AY bel). Second son of Adam and Eve. A shepherd who pleased God with his worship. His brother Cain's sacrifice did not please God, and so Cain murdered Abel (Gen. 4:2-8; Heb. 11:4; 1 John 3:12).

**ABHOR.** Hate, repel, reject, shrink from in horror (Deut. 7:26; Rom. 12:9).

**ABIATHAR** (uh BIGH uh thar). A high priest during David's time. Served after his father Ahimelech but was later thrown out of the priestly office by Solomon because Abiathar favored Adonijah over Solomon (see 1 Sam. 22:20-22; 23:6,9; 1 Kings 1:24-25; 2:26-27).

**ABIDE.** Remain, live, continue, persist (1 Sam. 1:22; John 15:4; Phil. 1:25). Forbear (Jer. 10:10).

**ABIGAIL** (AB ih gayl). Beautiful, wise, and poised wife of David, who married him after her first husband, Nabal, died (1 Sam. 25). Another Abigail was a sister of David who married Jether and became the mother of Amasa (1 Chron. 2:16-17).

**ABIHU** (uh BIGH hyoo). The second son of Aaron and a priest (Ex. 6:23; 28:1). Went with Moses, Aaron, and others toward Mount Sinai to worship God (Ex. 24:1,9). Later he died a fiery death with his brother Nadab after they had displeased God (Lev. 10:1-2; Num. 3:4).

**ABIMELECH** (uh BIM eh lek). A son of Jerubbaal (Gideon) who became king after killing his brothers (except Jotham who escaped). Abimelech ruled Israel for three years until he attacked Thebez where his skull was crushed by a stone in battle (Judg. 8:29—9:57). Also a line of kings (Gen. 20—21; 26:1).

**ABLUTIONS.** Ceremonial washings for the purpose of religious purity (Heb. 6:2; 9:10, RSV).

**ABNER** (AB nur). Saul's cousin and commander of Saul's army. Later served under Saul's son Ishbosheth and favored David. David's commander, Joab, was suspicious of Abner and murdered him (1 Sam. 14:50-2 Sam. 3:30).

**ABODE.** Home, place to stay (John 14:23). Also, past tense of *abide* (Num. 9:17).

**ABOLISH.** Put to an end (2 Tim. 1:10); remove (Heb. 10:9, RSV).

**ABOMINABLE.** See **ABOMINATION.**

**ABOMINATION.** A horrible foul thing to God or man. The adjective *abominable* describes something hateful, loathsome, putrid, sickening, awful, disgusting, evil (Matt. 24:15; Gen. 43:32). Abominations are connected with idolatry (Rev. 17:4-5; 21:27), disrespect for God (Ezek. 7:3-4), ceremonial uncleanness (Lev. 7:21), and sexual sins (Rev. 17:4-5).

**ABOMINATION OF DESOLATION.** An indescribably evil, horrible, detestable thing to occur in the last days (see Dan. 9:27; 11:31; 12:11; Matt. 24:15; Mark 13:14). Scholars differ on whether the term refers to a person called the Antichrist (see 1 John 2:18-22) or a profane symbol, event, or act.

▼ *The evil represented by this abomination always wants to make a desert of one's spiritual life. To keep this from happening, recognize the danger of evil and run or resist in the power of God (Matt. 24:15-16; 1 Cor. 10:13).*

**ABOUND.** Overflow, increase, grow have abundance (1 Thess. 3:12; Prov. 28:20).

**ABRAHAM** (AY bruh ham). The first Hebrew (Gen. 14:13). God promised the childless Abraham that he would make him the father of a great nation. God was faithful to his promise (Gen. 12:1-2) and gave the almost one hundred year-old Abraham and his ninety-year-old wife Sarah a baby named Isaac (Gen. 17:1-8). During the many years between the promise and the baby of promise, Abraham and Sarah got tired of waiting on God, so Abraham fathered Ishmael by the handmaid Hagar and gave birth to another nation.

Despite Abraham's weakness, God's promise unfolded like a drama. Read Genesis 11:26-25:ll for the full story of Abraham and his faith in God. (Compare Heb. 11:8-12).

The name Abraham is the longer form of Abram and means *exalted father* or *father of a multitude* (Gen. 17:1-8). He lived in Ur, Haran, Egypt, and Canaan. He died at age 175 and was buried in a cave at Hebron (Gen. 13:18; 25:7-10).

▼ *Abraham's experience teaches us that God's calling is worth responding to, and His promises are worth working toward and waiting on.*

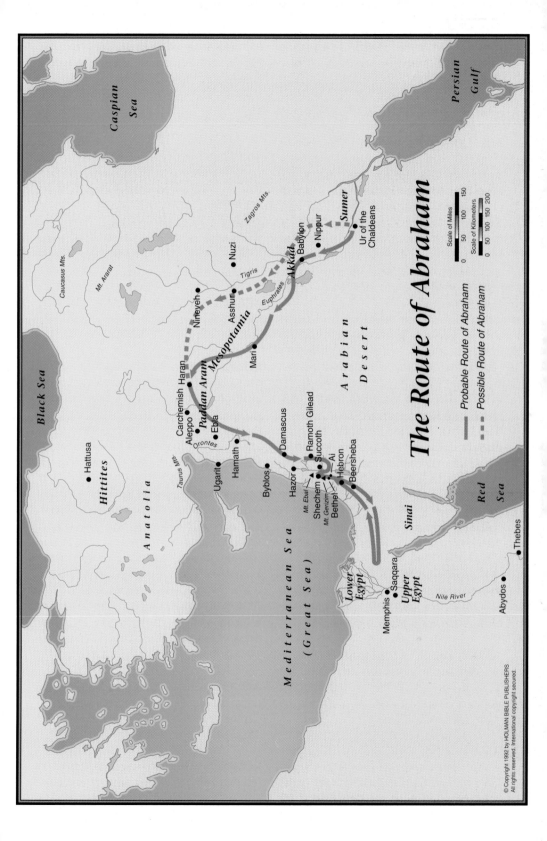

# The Route of Abraham

Probable Route of Abraham

Possible Route of Abraham

Scale of Miles
0  50  100  150

Scale of Kilometers
0  50  100  150  200

**ABRAHAM'S BOSOM**. Term that described blessing after death (Luke 16:22-23).

**ABRAM**. See **ABRAHAM**.

**ABSALOM** (AB suh luhm). Third son of David (2 Sam. 3:2-5). Absalom means *father in peace,* but his name did not fit his personality. He arranged his half brother Amnon's murder (2 Sam. 13) and rebelled against his father, King David, to make himself king (2 Sam. 15). Absalom was murdered against his father's wishes and much to his father's sadness (2 Sam. 18:5-17,31-33).

**ABSTAIN**. Avoid or keep away from. Examples of acts to abstain from include idols, sex outside marriage, and evil in general (Acts 15:20; 1 Thess. 5:22).

**ABUNDANCE**. A multitude, plenty, fullness, more than enough (Deut. 28:47; Rom. 5:17). The true abundant life is not made up of money or possessions but of such riches as commitment to God, love, joy, peace, and friendship (John 10:10; Luke 12:15).

**ABUSE**. Mistreat, misuse, damage physically or emotionally (1 Chron. 10:4; Prov. 22:10, RSV; Heb. 10:33; 1 Cor. 9:18).
● *Could it be that what we say to or about each other is the most frequent abuse that occurs? Also, how might we abuse blessings by misusing them?*

**ABYSS**. Literally, *the deep* or *bottomless pit* (compare KJV and RSV Rev. 9:1-2,11; 11:7; 17:8; 20:1). Place of torment for demons (Luke 8:31, RSV); place of the dead (Rom. 10:7, RSV).

**ACACIA** (uh KAY shuh). Large tree whose hard wood was excellent for making furniture. Used to make the ark of the covenant and other wooden objects for the tabernacle (RSV: Deut. 10:3; Ex. 25-27; 30; 37-38). Same as shittim wood from the shittah tree (KJV).

*Acacia tree growing in the Sinai desert.*

**ACCEPTABLE**. Pleasing, receivable, welcome, adequate (Ps. 51:17, RSV; Isa. 61:2; Eph. 5:8-11; Heb. 11:4, RSV).

**ACCESS**. Ability to come into the presence. Qualified to approach. Most often used of the Christian's access to God. Accepting Jesus Christ, who died for us, is the sole requirement for access to God. Jesus' death has removed all barriers between God and people. Jesus enables believers to draw near with confidence to God (Rom. 5:2; Eph. 2:18, 3:12).
● *Ponder about people you feel comfortable approaching and people you do not. What makes the difference? What about God makes it easy/hard to approach Him?*

**ACCOMPLISH**. Fulfill, complete, succeed in doing, express (Isa. 55:11; Jer. 44:25; Ezek. 20:8; Luke 2:22; John 19:28).

**ACCORD**. Like-mindedness, harmony, unity, singleness of purpose, agreement. Can be with good or evil (Acts 2:46, 7:57; 15:25).

**ACCOUNT**. Reckon, calculate, consider, let your mind dwell on, give reasons for; accept responsibility for (Matt. 12:36;

| LIFE OF ABRAHAM | | |
|---|---|---|
| EVENT | OLD TESTAMENT PASSAGE | NEW TESTAMENT REFERENCE |
| The birth of Abram | Gen 11:26 | |
| God's call of Abram | Gen 12:1-3 | Heb 11:8 |
| The entry into Canaan | Gen 12:4-9 | |
| Abram in Egypt | Gen 12:10-20 | |
| Lot separates from Abram | Gen 13:1-18 | |
| Abram rescues Lot | Gen 14:1-17 | |
| Abram pays tithes to Melchizedek | Gen 14:18-24 | Heb 7:1-10 |
| God's covenant with Abraham | Gen 15:1-21 | Rom 4:1-25 Gal 3:6-25 Heb 6:13-20 |
| The birth of Ishmael | Gen 16:1-16 | |
| Abraham promised a son by Sarah | Gen 17:1-27 | Rom 4:18-25 Heb 11:11-12 |
| Abraham intercedes for Sodom | Gen 18:16-33 | |
| Lot saved and Sodom destroyed | Gen 19:1-38 | |
| The birth of Isaac | Gen 21:1-7 | |
| Hagar and Ishmael sent away | Gen 21:8-21 | Gal 4:21-31 |
| Abraham challenged to offer Isaac as sacrifice | Gen 22:1-19 | Heb 11:17-19 Jas 2:20-24 |
| The death of Sarah | Gen 23:1-20 | |
| The death of Abraham | Gen 25:1-11 | |

Luke 16:2; Rom. 14:12). When something is accounted, it is credited to or recognized as belonging to someone (Gal. 3:6; Luke 22:24). Also, an account is a detailed record, count, or credit (Deut. 2:11; Ps. 144:3).

● *God knows all about every person and holds us accountable. How do you think this should affect your thoughts and actions?*

**ACCURSED.** Under a curse, set aside for condemnation or destruction (Rom. 9:3; Gal. 1:8-9; 1 Cor. 12:3; Josh. 6:17).

**ACCUSE.** Charge, credit with undesirable action (Prov. 30:10; Acts 25:11; Luke 11:54). Accusation can be true or false (John 8:6; Luke 3:14). Satan is sometimes called the accuser (Rev. 12:10).

**ACHAIA** (uh KAY yuh). A Roman province in the southern portion of Greece. Corinth was its capital (2 Cor. 1:1; Acts 19:21; Rom. 15:26).

**ACHAN** (AY kuhn), also called **ACHAR.** Israelite who stole items dedicated to God from the city of Jericho after its destruction. He hid what he stole and his sin threatened the security of the entire Israelite community. The Israelites put him to death in the valley of Achor after his sin was discovered (Josh. 7:1-26).

**ACKNOWLEDGE.** Admit, recognize, give attention to, agree with, accept, respond to. Opposite of *ignore*. When a person acknowledges transgressions or wrongs, that confession opens the door to repentance and change. To acknowledge God is to agree with Him in attitude and to respond to Him in action (Jer. 24:5; Deut. 21:17; Ps. 51:3; 1 Cor. 14:37).

● *Can you think of one wrong in your*

*life? How would acknowledging it free you from its burden?*

**ACTS, BOOK OF.** New Testament book written by Luke as continuation of the Gospel of Luke. Acts traces the birth and growth of the Christian church. Acts shows how the early church carried out Jesus Christ's command to make disciples of all nations (Matt. 28:18-20). Peter, a disciple, and Paul, a powerful convert to Christianity, served as significant leaders in the growth of the Christian church. Acts tells about the unique coming of the Holy Spirit upon Christians and His work in the growth of the church.

The first half of Acts focuses on the Jerusalem church, and the last half tells about efforts of Paul and other missionaries to spread Christianity to surrounding areas such as Samaria, Damascus, Antioch, Cyprus, Asia Minor, Europe, and Rome. The Book of Acts ends with an unhindered sharing of the gospel (Acts 28:31). Acts is the first book of church history and colorfully depicts both the joys and growing pains of the first century church.

▼ *Acts' teachings for today include examples of (1) how to present the gospel (Acts 2:14-21), (2) demonstrations of refusal to let physical, economic, or social barriers prevent us from sharing the message of Christ (Acts 10-11), and (3) encouragement to keep on obeying God even in the worst of persecution (Acts 5:27-32).*

**A.D.** Latin abbreviation for *Anno Domini* meaning in the year of our Lord. Popularly, "after death"-the time since Jesus Christ's death.

Jews use C. E. for common era.

**ADAM** (AD duhm). First man. God created Adam in His image (Gen. 1:27; 2:7). Adam (and Eve) chose to mar God's image by disobeying Him. This sin plunged the human race into sin (Gen. 3; Rom. 5:12-21). Jesus Christ, the second Adam, came to deliver us from sin and transform us into His perfect image (1 Cor. 15:45,49; Rom. 8:29). See **EVE**.

▼ *Self-image improves as one moves toward the God-image of creation. What kind of an image do you have of yourself?*

**ADAR** (AD ahr). Twelfth Hebrew month. Corresponds to our mid-February to mid-March (Esther 3:7). See **Calendar Chart** pages 228 & 229.

**ADDER.** Snake (Gen. 49:17; Prov. 23:32). See **SERPENT**.

**ADHERE.** Attach, stick, be loyal (2 Kings 17:34, NIV).

**ADJURE.** Plead, beg, command, appeal in the most persuasive manner. Cause to take an oath. The goal of those who adjure is to make sure the information given is correct (1 Kings 22:16; Matt. 26:63; Mark 5:7; Acts 19:13).

**ADMONISH.** Recommend, suggest, show, encourage to do right, warn, advise, counsel, correct or praise to motivate obedience to God. Those who admonish are usually more mature believers. Those who admonish are always to be motivated and guided by Jesus Christ (Rom. 15:14; Col. 3:16; 1 Thess. 5:12; 2 Thess. 3:15).

● *What has admonished you to obey God? With what words might you admonish a fellow believer?*

**ADONIJAH** (ad oh NIGH juh). Name meaning *My Lord is Yaweh*. 1. Fourth son of David who tried without success to take over his throne. When Solomon inherited the throne after his father

*Adam and Eve being banished from the garden of Eden.*▶

David's death, he had Adonijah killed (2 Sam. 3:4; 1 Kings 1:5—2:25). 2. A Levite sent by Jehosaphat to teach about God in the cities of Judah (2 Chron. 17:8-9). 3. One of Nehemiah's chiefs who sealed the covenant (Neh. 10:16).

**ADOPT**. 1. Choose to become a parent of a child you did not bear. Legally make a child of other parents your child (Esther 2:15, RSV). Every person who trusts God becomes a child of God by adoption and inherits His resources (Rom. 8:15,23; Gal. 4:5; Eph. 1:5). 2. Choose an action or item as your own (NIV: Job 15:5; Ps. 106:35).
● *How does God's adoption of you demonstrate His love for you?*

■ **ADULTERY**. Voluntary sexual intercourse of a married person with someone besides his mate (Heb. 13:4). Spiritual adultery occurs when believers turn their love from God to someone or something else (Jer. 3:9; Ezek. 23:37). Both sexual and spiritual adultery are forbidden in the Ten Commandments (Ex. 20:3,14).

Jesus explained that looking lustfully at someone is an act of adultery (Matt. 5:27-30).

Adultery also is the generic term for many sexual sins including incest and fornication (sex before marriage).
▼ *Adultery continues to be one of the more enticing sins. Many feel that saving sex for marriage is out of date, obsolete, but the Bible explains that sex outside of marriage is wrong. Why? It distorts God's design for marriage and sexual happiness. God designed sex to be best when it is an expression of unique love between husband and wife in marriage.*

**ADVERSARY**. 1. Enemy. One who is against a person or thing. May be a personal enemy, a national enemy, or a spiritual enemy (Num. 22:22; Matt. 5:25; Esther 7:6; 1 Sam. 1:6; 1 Kings 5:4; 1 Pet. 5:8; 1 Tim. 5:14). 2. Satan. A literal translation of the Hebrew *Satan* (1 Pet. 5:8). See **SATAN**.
▼ *God is His people's protector against their adversaries (Ex. 23:22; Luke 18:3).*

**ADVERSITY**. Trouble, hard times (2 Sam. 4:9; Prov. 17:17; Prov. 24:10).
● *Name a way God has helped or could help you through adversity.*

**ADVOCATE**. One called alongside to help (1 John 2:1). Helper, comforter, intercessor-one who takes our side, speaks on our behalf, pleads our case. In the NT both Jesus Christ and the Holy Spirit are our advocates (1 John 2:1; John 14:16,26; 15:26; 16:7). In the Gospel of John, *comforter* translates the same Greek word that *advocate* translates in 1 John 2:1.
● *How does it feel to have someone on your side? What thoughts and feelings do you have about knowing Jesus is on your side?*

**AFFECTION**. Feeling, passion, or thought. The KJV setting determines whether it is good or bad (Rom. 12:10; Rom. 1:26). Colossians 3:2 focuses on thought.

**AFFLICTION**. State or cause of pain, distress, grief, or misery. Generally, these English definitions can serve for the Bible use of *affliction,* but the OT Hebrew and the NT Greek shades of meaning are worth noting:

1. The OT Hebrew word usually means oppressed or humbled—a sense of helplessness or defenselessness. If the affliction is perceived as coming comes from God, it is a punishment for sin that comes to bless people by leading them to turn back to God (2 Kings 15:5; Ps. 119:71). However, Isaiah also used the word to refer to the forthcoming affliction of Christ for our sins (Isa. 53:4,7).

2. The NT Greek word literally means pressure but also carries the thought of oppression or tribulation. The idea is most often that the distress comes upon a person from someone else because he or she follows Christ and not because of personal sin (Col. 1:24).

● *Where does most of your misery come from? From within as you choose your will instead of God's? or from without as others pressure you because of your choice to follow Christ as Lord and Savior? In either case, the way to deal with affliction is to turn to God for relief or strength to endure for His glory.*

**AGABUS** (AG uh buhs). New Testament prophet from Jerusalem who foretold a great famine and the imprisonment of Paul (Acts 11:28; 21:10-11).

**AGAPE**. A Greek word for self-giving *love.* See **LOVE.**

**AGE**. Period of time. Can be past or future and is often unlimited. *Ages* often means eternity or immeasurable time. God is the King of all ages (NIV: Col. 1:26; Rom. 16:25; Joel 2:2; Rev. 15:3; Isa. 45:17; RSV: 1 Tim. 1:17).

**AGRIPPA** (uh GRIP uh). Herod Agrippa I was known in the NT as Herod (Acts 12:1-23). Herod Agrippa II (in NT, just Agrippa) was the Jewish king who listened to Paul's legal defense and found him innocent. Agrippa said Paul almost persuaded him to became a Christian (Acts 25:13-26:32). Paul was on trial because jealous Jews had him arrested for preaching what they considered heresy (Acts 21-23).

**AHAB** (AY hab). Powerful but evil king who reigned over Israel for twenty-two years. Heavily influenced by his Baal worshiping wife Jezebel. Failed to stand up for justice and true worship even though

God's prophets warned him (1 Kings 16:28—22:40). See **JEZEBEL** and the **King Chart** page 141. Another Ahab was false prophet (Jer. 29:20-21).

**AHASUERUS** (uh haz you EE russ). A king of Persia. Mentioned in three OT books (Ezra 4:6; Dan. 9:1; Esther 1:1, 10:3). In the Book of Esther, he chose Esther as his new queen. In the Book of Daniel, he was the father of Darius the Mede.

**AHAZ** (AY haz). Twelfth king of Judah. He was very wicked and promoted idolatry (2 Kings 16; 2 Chron. 28). See **King Chart** page 141.

**AHAZIAH** (ay huh ZIGH uh). 1. Eighth king of Israel. Son and successor of Ahab. Like his mother Jezebel, he trusted pagan gods rather than the true God (1 Kings 22:51-53; 2 Kings 1:2-3). 2. Sixth king of Judah who practiced idolatry (2 Kings 8:24). See **King Chart** page 141.

**AI** (AY igh). Small city east of Bethel that Joshua conquered after he and his men conquered Jericho. Achan's sin led to an initial setback. Then God said He had given Ai, its people, and its king over to Joshua. Ai's destruction demonstrated God's power (Josh. 7:2-5, 8:1-29, 10:1-2).

**ALABASTER**. Smooth cream colored stone used to make containers for perfume and ointment. The alabaster box in the Bible was a flask with a long, thin neck that was broken to release the contents (Matt. 26:7; Mark 14:3; Luke 7:37).

**ALAS**. Oh no! Pay attention! An expression of sorrow, fear, complaint, grief, or warning. (Josh. 7:7; Judg. 6:22; 1 Kings 13:30; Jer. 30:7; Rev. 18:10).

**ALEXANDER** (al eg ZAN dur). 1. Member of high priestly family (Acts 4:6). 2. Jewish speaker (Acts 19:33). 3. False teacher (1 Tim. 1:20). 4. Enemy of Paul (2 Tim. 4:14). 5. Alexander the Great probably the king described in Daniel 8.

**ALLELUIA**. Praise God! Same as *Hallelujah*. Invitation to praise God. A part of many Psalms and an element of worship in Revelation (Ps. 104:35; 105:45; Rev. 19:1,3-4,6).

**ALIEN**. Stranger, traveler, person away from home. Someone unknown to the area. Someone or something foreign (Eph. 2:12). God cares for aliens, and He encourages His people to do the same (Ex. 18:3; Gen. 21:23, NIV; Job 19:15; Deut. 10:18-19, NIV).

**ALLOTMENT**. Portion, part of land, assigned amount (NIV: Deut. 14:27; Deut. 18:1; Ezek. 48:13).

**ALMIGHTY**. All powerful, completely powerful, in control. Name for God. A reason to praise and worship God (Gen. 17:1; 2 Cor. 6:18; Rev. 11:17). See **Names of God Chart** page 103.
● *The Almighty God wants a close relationship with every person. How does His "almightiness" affect the way you relate to Him?*

**ALMS**. 1. Offering, portion of one's possessions given to the poor (Acts 3:2-3). For an OT application, see Leviticus 19:9. 2. Kind act. Act of compassion motivated by wanting to please God (Acts 9:36). Guidelines for almsgiving include give privately, give so only God can see, and give from what you have (Matt. 6:1-4; Luke 11:41).

**ALPHA AND OMEGA** (AL fuh) (oh MEG uh). First and last letters of the Greek alphabet. A name for Christ. Means *beginning and end* or *first and last*. Jesus is both first and last in time and in importance. Used by Christ of Himself in the Book of Revelation (1:8,11; 21:6; 22:13).

Alpha and Omega.

**ALPHAEUS** (al FEE uhs). 1. Father of James the apostle (Matt. 10:3: Acts 1:13). 2. Father of Levi the tax collector (Mark 2:14).

**ALTAR**. Place of worship. Place where animal sacrifices were slaughtered and presented to God (Gen. 8:20; Ex. 29:10-14). Also a place to burn incense for God (Ex. 30:1). Altars in the Bible ranged from piles of stones to intricately constructed structures (Josh. 8:30-31; Ex. 27:1-8).

Old Testament blood sacrifices pictured repentance and forgiveness. After the death and resurrection of Jesus, animal sacrifices were no longer needed. God welcomes a different type of offering at the altar: praise, confession, and good actions (Heb. 13:15-16). See **SACRIFICE**.

**AMALEK** (AM uh lek). Descendant of Esau (twin of Jacob). His descendants,

*Altars for burnt offering.*

called Amalekites, tried to keep the Israelites from entering the Promised Land. Following this, the Amalekites and the Israelites remained enemies (Gen. 36:12; Ex. 17:8-16; Deut. 25:17; 1 Sam. 15:2-3).

**AMBASSADOR.** Agent, messenger, interpreter, representative. Christians are ambassadors for Christ: They help others to understand Him and encourage their reconciliation with Him (Josh. 9:4; Prov. 13:17; 2 Cor. 5:20; Eph. 6:19-20).

▼ *In the OT ambassadors were sent to other nations for such purposes as congratulations, to ask favors, to make alliances or to protest wrongs (1 Kings 5:1; Num. 20:14; Josh. 9:4; Judg. 11:12).*

● *Name a situation in which an ambassador for Christ might serve as a messenger or interpreter for Him today.*

**AMEN.** Well said. I agree! Let what you said, happens. In the Bible *Amen* demonstrated excitement and conviction about God's promises. Used at the beginning and/or end of solemn statements or praises (Rev. 7:12). Jesus' *amen (verily,* KJV) meant *truly* or *these words are God's words* or *may it happen* (Matt. 5:18,26; 6:2; John 1:51). Jesus was called "the Amen" (2 Cor. 1:20; Rev. 3:14) as the Person in whom we find the fulfillmet of God's promises.

● *To what truth about God would you most like to say amen?*

**AMOS** (AY muhs). 1. A shepherd from Tekoa of Judah whom God called to be a prophet. He was from the Southern Kingdom but preached to the Northern Kingdom. He was poor but preached to the rich. Amos' name means *burden bearer.* Read his message in the Book of Amos. 2. Ancestor of Joseph, husband of Mary (Luke 3:25).

**AMOS, BOOK OF.** This OT book was written by Amos, a shepherd whom God called to be a prophet. His main message was that God loves mercy more than formal sacrifices. He taught that greatness did not come through power but through justice and judgment (Amos 5:21-24). Amos reprimanded the wealthy for gaining their wealth at the expense of the poor, for their dishonesty and bribery, and for seeing God as a convenience. The Book of Amos encourages readers to repent and let God be Lord and Master.

**ANANIAS** (an uh NIGH uhs). 1. Believer who lied to Peter about the amount of money he had received for a possession and then died as an act of God's judgment (Acts 5:1-5). See **SAPPHIRA**. 2. A disciple at Damascus through whom God restored Paul's sight (Acts 9:10-18; 22:12-16). 3. A high priest who wanted Paul silenced (Acts 23:2; 24:1).

**ANATHEMA.** Accursed (1 Cor. 16:22). This Greek word appears only the one time in the KJV. It is as if Paul had said, "If a person does not love the Lord, let the person be turned over to the Lord for His judgment." "Our Lord is coming." (Maranatha is a Hebrew word meaning *come*; 1 Cor. 16:22).

▼ *The Hebrew and Greek words related to* anathema *basically mean to declare a thing or person turned over to God: as an act of devotion for a good thing, or for God's judgment if it is a bad thing.*

**ANCIENT OF DAYS.** Name for God Daniel used. Pictures a white haired God on a throne of judgment. Similar to "Most High" (Dan. 7:9,13,22). See **Names of God Chart** page 103.

● *The Bible uses many other names for God. Why do you think this image seems one of the most popular?*

**ANDREW** (AN droo). Disciple of Jesus (Matt. 4:18-19). One of the twelve apostles. He asked Jesus many questions (Mark 13:3-4), and he noticed the boy with the five loaves and two fishes (John 6:8-9). Andrew brought Simon Peter to Jesus (John 1:40-42).

▼ *He was a follower of John the Baptist before he met Jesus (John 1:35,37).*

■ **ANGEL**. Messenger, heavenly being created by God. Angels often serve as messengers for Him (Matt. 2:13-15; Gen. 18:2-10; 19:1ff.; Luke 1:26-38; Matt. 1:20-21. Luke 2:8-15). Angels serve in heaven (Rev. 8-9) and on earth (Luke 2:8-14); take care of and protect us (Matt. 18:10; Ps. 91:11-12); rejoice when someone becomes a Christian (Luke 15:10); and will help execute judgment (Matt. 13:41-43,49-50). They sometimes appear as humans (Gen 18:2-10); at other times they don't (Luke 2:13-14). Angels are not to be worshiped (Col. 2:18). Angels are not humans who have died and gone to heaven (Heb. 2:7).

▼ *Satan has evil angels who chose to disobey God and follow Satan (Jude 6; 2 Pet. 2:4; Rev. 12:9). We call these demons or evil spirits.*

● *How does God send His messages to you?*

**ANGER**. Fury (Ex. 32:19; Matt. 5:22), sadness turned outward. Feeling of hostility toward a person or event that has wronged or injured you. Ranges from simple frustration to lasting resentment or catastrophic violence. Emotions or actions closely related to anger include jealousy, cursing, revenge, violence, rebellion.

Several Hebrew and Greek words depict types of anger. In summary the words for angers carry these meanings: (1) kindling or burning anger. (2) rage or fury that overflows. (3) stormy anger. (4) passionate anger, and (5) anger about a moral wrong.

Anger appears in both humans and God. In the Bible, human anger is presented as an emotion that has to be dealt with in a Christlike way (Eph. 4:26; Prov. 14:17; Ps. 37:8). Divine anger is different from human anger in that its goal is righteousness and justice (Jas. 1:20; Rom. 12:19). It is always provoked by sin, and God's reaction is consistent. Often God's anger is distinguished from human anger by using two or more anger words in succession (Isa. 13:9).

● *What steps could you take to deal with your anger without sinning? (See Eph. 4:26.) When could anger lead to good?*

**ANNA** (AN uh). Prophetess who recognized the infant Jesus as the awaited Messiah (Luke 2:36-38).

**ANNAS** (AN uhs). A high priest who took part in Jesus' trial before the crucifixion (Luke 3:2; John 18:13,24; Acts 4:6).

**ANNIHILATE**. Utterly destroy, wipe out, slaughter, extinguish, abolish (NIV: Deut. 9:3; Esther 3:13).

**ANNUNCIATION**. The announcement to Mary that she would become the mother of Jesus. Read about it in Luke 1:26-38.

▼ *The angel's message explained that Jesus would be both human (Luke 1:32) and divine (1:34-35), the eternal ruler (1:33).*

**ANOINT**. To pour oil on. Usually a ceremony that indicates a person's appointment to a special task. Done for kings and priests (Ex. 28:41; 1 Sam. 15:1,17). Jesus was God's Anointed, Messiah representing the Hebrew word and Christ the Greek word for anointed one (Luke 4:18; Acts 10:38). Sometimes part of a healing process (Mark 6:13) or performed as a daily task (Ruth 3:3; Matt. 6:17).
▼ *A recipe for anointing oil is found in Exodus 30:22-25.*

*Anointing a king.*

**ANTICHRIST**. Opponent of Christ. 1. The evil figure to come during the last days who will oppose everything of God (1 John 2:18). 2. Anyone who denies through words or actions that Jesus is the Christ (1 John 2:19,22; 4:3; 2 John 1:7).

▼ *Many Christians understand 2 Thessalonians 2:1-12 as describing the antichrist.*

**ANTIOCH** (AN tih ahk). 1. *Antioch in Pisidia* was a Galatian city where Paul preached, started a church, and was persecuted. To this and nearby churches, he wrote the Book of Galatians (Acts 13; 2 Tim. 3:11). 2. *Antioch in Syria* was a major city and early center of Christianity. Jesus' followers were first called Christians there, and from there the first foreign missionaries were sent (Acts 11:26; 13:1-4).

**ANXIETY**. Worries, cares (1 Pet. 5:7, RSV), intense thoughts. To be anxious is to be afraid, worried, troubled, or distressed (Phil. 4:6; Dan. 7:15). The opposite of being anxious is trusting God and enjoying the peace He gives (Matt. 6:25-34, RSV).
● *What worries you? How can God help you with this anxiety?*

**APOCRYPHA AND PSEUDEPIGRAPHA**. Religious writings written between 300 B.C. and 150 A.D., but not commonly accepted as part of the Bible. Noncanonical writings. Roman Catholics accept the Apocrypha as a part of their Bible. *Pseudepigrapha* means false writings. These are not a part of the Apocrypha. See chart on next page.

**APOLLOS** (uh PAHL uhs). Teacher with deep scriptural knowledge whose public teaching won many people to Jesus Christ (Acts 18:24-28; 1 Cor. 3:6). He took coaching by Priscilla and Aquila that helped him better understand the Word of God (Acts 18:26).
● *How do you take coaching (better known as constructive criticism)?*

■ **APOSTLE**. One sent on a mission. An apostle has a message and is authorized to

# THE APOCRYPHA

| TITLES (listed alphabetically) | APPROX-IMATE DATES | LITERARY TYPES | THEMES | IN SEPTUAGINT? | IN ROMAN CATHOLIC CANON? |
|---|---|---|---|---|---|
| Baruch | 150 B.C. | Wisdom & narrative (composite) | Praise of wisdom, law, promise of hope, opposition to idolatry | Yes | Yes |
| Bel and the Dragon | 100 B.C. | Detective narrative at end of Daniel | Opposition to idolatry | Yes | Yes |
| Ecclesiasticus (Wisdom of Jesus Sirach) | 180 B.C. in Hebrew; 132 B.C. Greek Translation | Wisdom, patriotism; temple worship; retribution; free will | Obedience to law, praise of patriarchs, value of wisdom | Yes | Yes |
| I Esdras | 150 | History (621–458) | Proper worship; power of truth | Yes | No |
| 2 Esdras | A.D. 100 | Apocalypse with Christian preface and epilog | Pre-existent, dying Messiah: punishment for sin; salvation in future; inspiration; divine justice; evil | No | No |
| Additions to Esther (103 verses) | 114 B.C. | Religious amplification | Prayer; worship; revelation; God's activity; providence | Yes | Yes |
| Letter of Jeremiah | 317 B.C. | Homily added to Baruch based on Jer 29 | Condemns idolatry | Yes | Yes |
| Judith | 200 B.C. | Historical novel | Obedience to law; prayer; fasting; true worship patriotism | Yes | Yes |
| 1 Maccabees | 90 B.C. | History (180–161 B.C.) | God works in normal human events; legitimates Hasmonean kings | Yes | Yes |
| 2 Maccabees | 90 B.C. | History (180–161 B.C.) | Resurrection; creation from nothing; miracles; punishment for sin; martyrdom; temple angels | Yes | Yes |
| 3 Maccabees | 75 B.C. | Festival legend | Deliverance of faithful; angels | Some mss. | No |
| 4 Maccabees | 10 B.C. | Philosophical treatise based on 2 Macc 6–7 | Power of reason over emotions; faithfulness to law; martyrdom | Some mss. | No |
| Prayer of Azariah and Song of Three Young Men | 100 B.C. | Liturgy; hymn & additions to Dan 3:23 | Praise; God's response to prayer | Yes | Yes |
| Prayer of Manasseh | 120 B.C. | Prayer of penitence based on 2 Kgs 21:10-17 2 Chr 33:11-19 | Prayer of repentance | Yes | No |
| Psalm 151 | ? | Victory hymn | Praise to God who uses young & inexperienced | Yes | No |
| Susanna | 100 B.C. | Detective story at end of Daniel | Daniel's wisdom; God's vindication of faithfulness | Yes | Yes |
| Tobit | 200 B.C. | Folktale | Temple attendance; tithing; charity; prayer; obedience to Jewish law; guardian angel; divine justice and retribution; personal devotion | Yes | Yes |
| Wisdom of Solomon | 10 B.C. in Egypt | Wisdom personified; Jewish apologetic | Value of wisdom and faithfulness, immortality | Yes | Yes |

act on behalf of the sender. Jesus' disciples were first learners and then became apostles, taking the message of salvation (Luke 6:13; 9:10). Jesus, Himself an Apostle sent by God (Heb. 3:1), chose twelve disciples to send out as apostles. Barnabas, Paul, and a few others were also called apostles (Acts 1:26, 4:36; 1 Cor. 1:1; Acts 13:3). See **DISCIPLE**.

● *What does being a disciple (learner) have to do with being an apostle (one sent on a mission)?*

**APPALLED**. Repelled, morally offended, shocked, dismayed, turned off, strongly disappointed (NIV: 1 Kings 9:8; Job 17:8; Isa. 52:14, 59:16; Dan. 8:27).

**APPAREL**. Clothing, robe, dress. Apparel can show royalty, mourning, wealth, that one is God's messenger, and more (Esther 6:8; 2 Sam. 14:2; Ezek. 27:24; Acts 1:10; 1 Tim. 2:9).

● *What does your apparel say about you?*

*Much modern Middle Eastern apparel is very similar to apparel worn in Bible times.*

**APPEARING**. Refers to the return of Jesus Christ (1 Tim. 6:14; Titus 2:13; 1 Pet. 1:7).

**APT**. Prepared, ready, capable, inclined toward, leaning toward, likely. (2 Kings 24:16; Prov. 15:23, NIV; 1 Tim. 3:2).

**AQUILA** (uh KWIL uh). Husband of Priscilla. Together with Paul they worked on tents and ministered (Acts 18:2-3, 18; Rom. 16:3). They helped a believer named Apollos understand the way of God more perfectly. A church met in their house (Acts 18:24-26; 1 Cor. 16:19). See **PRISCILLA**.

**ARCHANGEL**. Chief messenger. Head angel named Michael (1 Thess. 4:16; Jude 9). See **ANGEL**.

**AREOPAGUS** (er ih AHP uh guhs). 1. A rocky hill in Athens called Mars' Hill (Acts 17:22). 2. The name of a council that met on Mars' Hill and primarily dealt with morals and education (Acts 17:18-19). Paul explained who the Unknown God was to that council on that hill (Acts 17:23).

**ARIMATHEA, JOSEPH OF** (ahr ih muh THEE uh). A Pharisee who became a disciple of Jesus. With Nicodemus, he prepared Jesus' body for burial and buried Him in his own tomb (Matt. 27:57-60; Mark 15:43).

**ARK.** 1. Large boat Noah built according to God's specifications. Only the people and animals on the ark survived the flood (Gen. 7:1-9:1). 2. The basket in which baby Moses was placed (Ex. 2:1- 5). 3. A beautiful chest that held varied items and also symbolized the presence of God to the Israelites (Deut. 31:26). See **ARK OF THE COVENANT**.

*Reconstruction of the Ark of the Covenant drawn in the Egyptian style, reflecting 400 years of captive influence in Egyptian bondage.*

**ARK OF THE COVENANT**. A beautiful chest that held the Ten Commandments. It later also held the book of the Law, manna bread, and Aaron's rod (Deut. 31:26; Ex. 16:33; Num. 17:10). For Israel, the ark was a symbol of God's promise. It was part of their tabernacle, a movable reminder of their exodus and of God's leadership (also called "ark of the covenant of the Lord," Deut. 10:8). Some scholars think the ark was lost in the 587 B.C. destruction of Jerusalem.

**ARMAGEDDON** (ahr muh GED uhn). The final battleground between good and evil. Mentioned by name only in Revelation 16:16. Comes from Hebrew for Valley of Megiddo.

**ART**. Old English verb form for *are* (Matt. 6:9).

*Return of the Ark of the Covenant*

■ **ASCENSION**. Going up. Refers to the return of the resurrected Jesus to the Father. Jesus appeared to His followers on earth before He ascended (Luke 24:51; Acts 1:6-11; Mark 16:19; 1 Cor. 15:6).

▼ *Jesus ascended to (1) prepare a place for His disciples (John 14:2-3), (2) sit at the right hand of the Father and intercede for his own (Rom. 8:34; Heb. 7:25), and (3) wait for His return to earth (1 Cor. 15:24-26).*

**ASHER** (ASH ur). 1. One of the twelve son of Jacob (Gen. 35:26). 2. The tribe composed of Asher's descendants (Num. 1:41).

**ASHERAH** (ASH uh ruh). Canaanite goddess who was worshiped in obscene ways. Wooden images of her were used for worship and were called a grove (Judg. 3:7) or

Asherah poles (NIV: Jdg. 6:25-32; Ex. 34:13).

**ASHTAROTH, ASHTORETH** (ASH tuh rahth). Pagan goddess who was the female counterpart to Baal. Worship of her was obscene (Judg. 2:13; 1 Kings 11:5).

**ASLEEP**. Gentle word early Christians used for *dead* (Acts 7:60; 1 Cor. 15:6; 1 Thess. 4:13). Also, physical sleep (Jonah 1:5; Matt. 8:24).

**ASP**. Snake, serpent (Isa. 11:8).

**ASS**. Donkey (Matt. 21:2; Num. 22:21).

**ASSAY**. Begin (1 Sam. 17:39) or try (Job 4:2; Acts 16:7).

**ASSEMBLY**. People who have come together for a common purpose (Joel 1:14). Used in NT for church or gathering of believers (Acts 19:39; Jas. 2:2). See **CHURCH, CONGREGATION**.

**ASSURANCE.** Confidence, trust, full conviction, certainty, firmness of mind. The basis of our assurance is Jesus Christ Himself (Isa. 32:17; Acts 17:31; Col. 2:2; Heb. 10:22; 1 Thess. 1:5).

**ASSYRIA.** Powerful kingdom of the ancient Middle East (2 Kings 15:29). Its armies conquered Israel (the Northern Kingdom) and other nations. It was a cruel nation that alternated between success and defeat until its capital, Nineveh, was conquered in 612 B.C. by the Medes and Babylonians. It then came to an end (2 Kings 17:6; 18:9-12).

*Shown below is a creature known to the Assyrians as lamassu. These and other similar creatures stood at the entrance to the palace of Sargon II at Korsabad.*

**ASTRAY.** Off course (Ex. 23:4), against God's ways, on a path to unhappiness and destruction (Ps. 58:3; Isa. 53:6; Prov. 28:10; Matt. 18:13).
● *What people or events lead you astray? What have you done or said that might have led someone astray? How do you get back on course?*

**ASTROLOGERS.** Persons who seek answers in the stars and try to predict the future by them. Astrologers feel that the position and movement of stars and planets influence people and events. Though astrologers were sometimes called wise, the Bible cautioned against them (Isa. 47:13). God's wisdom was demonstrated as ten times better than the astrologers' wisdom (Dan. 1:20; 2:2,10,27-28).

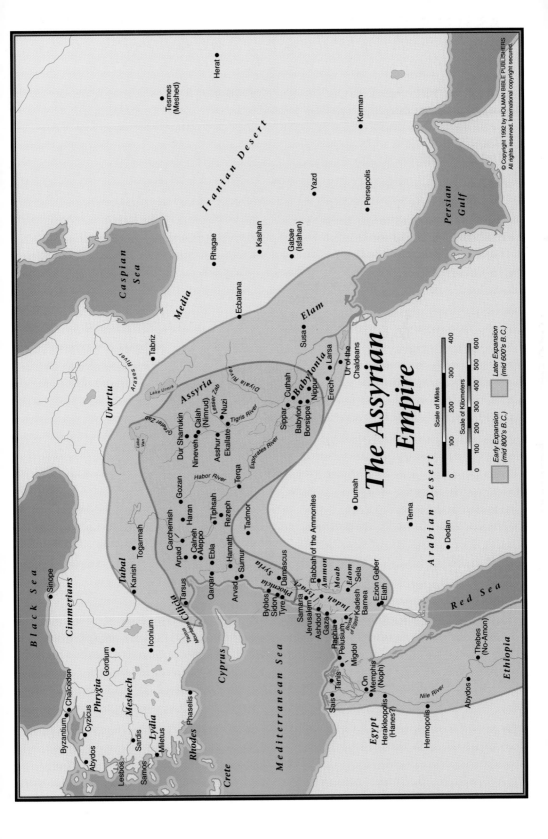

# The Assyrian Empire

**Scale of Miles**

0   100   200   300   400

**Scale of Kilometers**

0   100   200   300   400   500   600

Early Expansion (mid 800's B.C.)

Later Expansion (mid 600's B.C.)

Black Sea

Caspian Sea

Mediterranean Sea

Red Sea

Persian Gulf

Iranian Desert

Arabian Desert

Cimmerians

Tubal

Phrygia

Meshech

Lydia

Rhodes

Crete

Cyprus

Cilicia

Urartu

Media

Assyria

Babylonia

Elam

Syria

Phoenicia

Israel

Judah

Ammon

Moab

Edom

Egypt

Ethiopia

Herat

Tesmes (Meshed)

Kerman

Yazd

Persepolis

Rhagae

Kashan

Gabae (Isfahan)

Tabriz

Ecbatana

Susa

Larsa

Ur of the Chaldeans

Erech

Nippur

Cuthah

Babylon

Borsippa

Sippar

Nuzi

Ekallate

Asshur

Calah (Nimrud)

Nineveh

Dur Sharrukin

Gozan

Haran

Carchemish

Arpad

Calneh

Aleppo

Ebla

Tiphsah

Rezeph

Terqa

Tadmor

Hamath

Sumur

Arvad

Qarqar

Byblos

Sidon

Tyre

Damascus

Rabbah of the Ammonites

Sela

Ezion Geber

Elath

Kadesh Barnea

Samaria

Jerusalem

Ashdod

Gaza

Raphia

Pelusium

Migdol

Brook of Egypt

Tanis

On

Memphis (Noph)

Sais

Herakleopolis (Hanes?)

Hermopolis

Thebes (No-Amon)

Abydos

Dumah

Tema

Dedan

Sinope

Kanish

Togarmah

Tarsus

Iconium

Gordium

Byzantium

Chalcedon

Cyzicus

Abydos

Lesbos

Samos

Sardis

Miletus

Phaselis

Lake Urmia

Lake Van

Greater Zab

Lesser Zab

Tigris River

Diyala River

Euphrates River

Habor River

Araxes River

Nile River

Taurus Mountains

**ASUNDER.** Apart (2 Kings 2:11), divided, separated. Something put asunder usually involves pain (Acts 15:39). *Asunder* is used in the Bible to describe the divided Red Sea, broken emotions, split nations, the division of divorce, and divided friendships (Lev. 1:17; Ps. 136:13, NIV; Job 16:12; Hab. 3:6; Matt. 19:6).

**ATONEMENT, TO MAKE.** To cover or cancel one's sins (Ex. 30:5-16). Making two into one (Rom. 5:11). Atonement is motivated by the love of God. It occurs through the shedding of blood. The OT shedding of animal blood pictured repentance, turning to God, and God's forgiveness. It had to be repeated annually.

In the NT Jesus shed His blood on the cross, and no other blood sacrifice will ever be needed. Jesus made atonement so persons might become one with God. Its meaning can be remembered by "At-one-ment with God" (Ex. 29:36; Lev. 17:11; Neh. 10:33; Rom. 5:11).

**ATONEMENT, DAY OF.** A Jewish holy day with sacrifices and ceremonies related to God's forgiveness of sin (Lev. 16). At a certain point the high priest entered the holy of holies—the most holy place of the tabernacle (later the Temple)—to confess the sin of the nation and ask forgiveness. Jews now observe the Day of Atonement in early October and call it Yom Kippur, its Hebrew name (Ex. 29:36; Lev. 16:30; 23:27-28; 25:9). See **AZAZEL, SCAPEGOAT.** See the **Calendar Chart** pages 228 & 229 and the **Feast Chart** page 92.

**AUGUSTUS** (aw GUHS tuhs). Caesar Augustus, Roman emperor when Jesus was born (Luke 2:1). Also the title for several Roman emperors (Acts 25:21,25).

**AUTHORITIES.** Unseen powers in the heavenly realm (NIV: Eph. 3:10; 6:12; Col. 1:16). Also, people in positions of authority (Luke 12:11, RSV).

**AUTHORITY.** Power, right to exercise power over someone else (Matt. 21:23). When used rightly, authority brings happiness (Prov. 29:2). Jesus is the ultimate authority in any Christian's life (Matt. 7:29; Jude 25, RSV).

● *Name someone in authority over you who makes your life more enjoyable.*

**AVENGE.** Pay someone back for wrong done. Do full justice. Vengeance is to be directed by God or reserved for Him (Num. 31:2-3; Jer. 46:10; 1 Thess. 4:6). When tempted to avenge, substitute love (Lev. 19:18; Rom. 12:19).

**AWAKE.** Come to life after death (Isa. 26:19; Dan. 12:2). Give attention to (Ps. 35:23; 1 Cor. 15:34). Wake up physically (Mark 4:38).

**AWE.** Amazement, worship, respect. Admiration of God in response to something He has done (Ps. 4:4, 33:8; Hab. 3:2, NIV; Luke 5:26, RSV).

**AZARIAH** (as uh RIGH uh). Friend of Daniel who was renamed Abednego. Ate healthy food and entered fiery furnace with Daniel (Dan. 1:5-6, 15; 3:16-30).

**AZAZEL** (AZ uh zel). A Hebrew word with uncertain meaning (Lev. 16:8,10, NRSV). Could mean *removal*. Translated *scapegoat* in KJV. *Azazel* is left untranslated in the *Revised Standard Version* and some other versions. Probably represented symbolic removal of sins from the people. In Leviticus 16, one goat was killed as a sacrifice; the sins were symbolically transferred to a goat that was sent into the wilderness—the world of evil. All of this was part of the Day of Atonement ceremony. See **ATONEMENT, DAY OF, SCAPEGOAT.**

# BABYLON, BABYLONIA

**BABYLON** (BAB ih lahn), **BABYLONIA** (bab ih LOH nih uh). Capital city and its kingdom (Ezra 2:1; Gen. 10:10; 2 Kings 17:24). Babel is also the Greek spelling of Babylon. The kingdom location was also known as Shinar and Chaldea. The Babylonians captured Assyria in 612 and ruled Judah (the Southern Kingdom). They destroyed Jerusalem in 586 B.C. but were defeated by Cyrus of Persia in 538 B.C.

*Statuette of Baal, the Canaanite weather god, from Minet-el-Beida (15th– 14th century B.C.).*

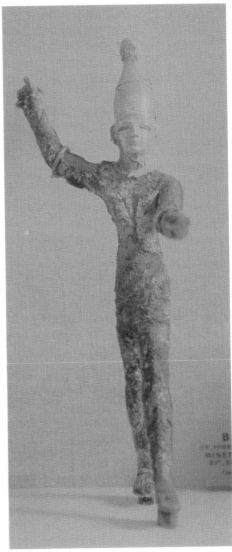

**BAAL** (BAY uhl). A false god (Num. 22:41). *Baalim* is the plural (Judg. 2:11). The *Canaanite* word for *husband*, *Lord*, and *master*. The male god worshiped by the people of Canaan and Phoenicia and sometimes by Israelites. The god was supposed to cause people and things to be fertile. The worship involved self-torture, child sacrifice, and sinful sexual practices outside of marriage.

**BABEL** (BAY buhl). Gate to God. Once people all spoke the same language. In pride and self-trust they tried to build a great city and brick tower—a gate to God—on the Plain of Shinar (Gen. 10:10; 11:1-9). In judgment, the Lord humbled them by confusing their language and scattering the people. So the Tower of Babel has come to stand for the Tower of Confusion.

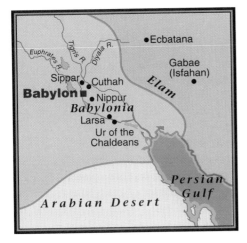

Babylon was so wicked that it came to stand for evil and opposition to God. The similar condition of Rome in NT times seemingly caused it to be referred to as Babylon in 1 Peter 5:13 and Revelation 17:5.

**BACKBITE.** Slander (Ps. 15:3; Prov. 25:23; Rom. 1:30; 2 Cor. 12:20). The basic idea is say something bad about someone behind his or her back.

● *How can you avoid backbiting? When others backbite, what can you do? What would Christ want you to do?*

**BACKSLIDE.** To turn back or away from God (Jer. 2:19). Selfishness and stubbornness are at the heart of backsliding (Prov. 14:14; Hos. 4:16). The answer to backsliding is to return to God (Jer. 3:14,22).

● *When anyone has decided to follow Jesus but turns back, that person backslides. Which direction are you going in your commitment to Jesus?*

**BALAAM** (BAY luhm). An evil prophet for hire. He found himself blessing instead of cursing Israel because God controlled his tongue (Num. 22-24). The Israelites he tried to lead away from God killed him (Num. 31). In the NT Balaam is cited as a bad example (2 Pet. 2:15; Jude 11; Rev. 2:14).

● *What does Balaam's life say to you about choosing a vocation? What are the results of trying to serve God without being committed to Him?*

**BALM.** Soothing ointment for medicine from a plant (Jer. 51:8).

**BAPTISM.** Immersion, submersion (Rom. 6:1-4). Water baptism for new Christians calls for special attention (Matt. 28:18-20). Baptism doesn't save a person, but is a picture of personal salvation and a sign of obedience to Christ.

Going under the water is like a dead person being buried under the ground; it pictures that a person has died to the old way of life. Rising up from the water is like a dead person coming up from a grave in the earth; it pictures new life that is eternal and future resurrection from the grave (Rom. 6:1-6).

This picture is not salvation any more than a picture of you is the real you, but the picture indicates what happens when a person accepts Christ as Lord and Savior. Baptism is never the salvation event but a picture of it.

Baptism is not a requirement of salvation, but it is a requirement of obedience. Baptism is the first step of discipleship.

Scriptural baptism occurs only once. It is a matter between God and the individual when that time occurs. Wise and mature Christians may give helpful counsel to those who know Christ as Lord and Savior but are uncertain about their baptism.

Baptism sometimes refers to the suffering and death of Christ (Mark 10:38-39; Luke 12:50). Christian baptism is in a sense a sharing of this death and resurrection and all that brought Christ to those events (Rom. 6:1-7; Col. 2:12). The baptism also gives witness to the death and resurrection of Christ; those who participate are identified with Him (Rom. 6:3-6; Gal. 3:27).

▼ *Before Christian baptism, other uses of baptism existed. The OT Mosaic laws included a baptism of washing (Ex. 30:17-21). Naaman baptized himself in the Jordan River as an act of obedience related to his healing (2 Kings 5:14). When non-Jews became Jewish, they immersed themselves.*

*John the Baptist's baptism was like death to the believer's old way of living and birth to a new kind of living (John 1:19-34). It had the same elements of later Christian baptism: repentance, confession, evidence of changed lives, coming judgment, and a focus on Jesus and His Spirit.*

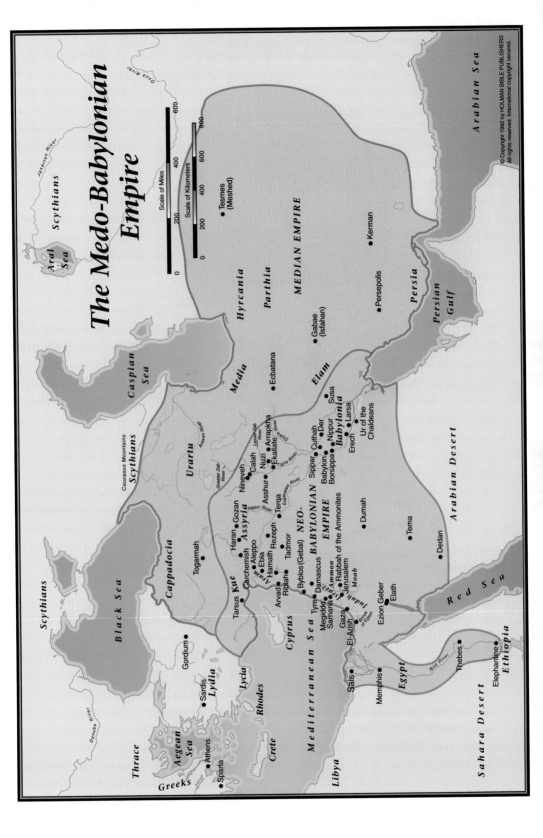

# The Medo-Babylonian Empire

*Ancient Byzantine baptistry at Avdat, Israel, showing the importance given baptism by the early church.*

*Water baptism is for believers (Acts 2:38; Eph.4:5). That rules out the need for infant baptism. Many parents wisely dedicate their children to God, but water is not needed.*

**BAPTISM OF JESUS**. John baptized Jesus, who never sinned (John 1:13-16; Mark 1:9-11). Thus His baptism was not one of repentance. Jesus said that His baptism was to fulfill all righteousness, which may simply mean that it was the right thing for Him to do (Matt. 3:13-17). In this way, He identified with people and was a model for us to follow. Jesus affirmed John and his message. Perhaps Jesus also implied He would bear the sin of the whole world in carrying out the commission of God (see Mark 10:38-40).

**BAPTISM WITH THE HOLY SPIRIT**. When Jesus comes into a life, the person is "baptized with the Spirit." That means the new believer is filled with the presence and power of the Holy Spirit. The usual sequence of events is this: The Spirit comes into a person's life at conversion, and then the believer is baptized in water (John 1:33; Acts 11:15-16). So all Christians have been baptized with the Holy Spirit at conversion.

A thorough study of the Holy Spirit is helpful in understanding what "baptism with the Holy Spirit" means (Acts 8:12-17). The unfolding drama of God's revelation through Pentecost and its sequence of events make the relationship between water baptism and the Holy Spirit clearer. The Holy Spirit is the gift who comes with salvation (Acts 2:38) and as its seal (Eph. 4:30).

**BAPTIST** (BAP tist). Biblical references identify John as the Baptizer because he preached and practiced baptizing (Mark 1:4-5). Today *Baptist* refers to a number of Christian denominations who baptize believers by immersion.

**BARABBAS** (buh RAB uhs). A treasonous murderer (Mark 15:7) and a robber (John 18:40). The angry crowd had Pilate release him instead of the innocent Jesus (Mark 15:6-15).
● *Every Christian is like Barabbas in at least one way: guilty of sin but freed from punishment by Christ. We don't know whether Barabbas ever accepted Christ as Lord and Savior. If not, it is sad that he accepted only the freedom of physical life and not the spiritual life Jesus came to bring.*

**BARBARIAN.** In the Bible, *barbarian* refers to anyone who did not speak Greek (Rom. 1:14) or anyone who was not a part of the Greek-Roman culture (Col. 3:11).
▼ *The idea of being a foreigner and being unable to understand each other's speech seems to apply to the word* barbarian *in 1 Corinthians 14:10-11.*

**BAR-JESUS** (bahr-JEE zuhs). A Jewish sorcerer and false prophet who was also known as Elymas (Acts 13:6-11). Not to be confused in any way with Jesus Christ. *Bar* means son in Aramaic, and *Jesus* was one of the spellings for Joshua, a popular Hebrew name.

**BARNABAS** (BAHR nuh buhs). Nickname that meant *son of encouragement* and was given to Joseph (or Joses), the son of Levi (Acts 4:36, RSV). The Greek word for *encouragement* implies the comforting, interceding, helping ministry that comes from the Holy Spirit (see John 14:16-17,26). Barnabas was a generous person who gave others a second chance (Acts 9:26-27; 15:37-39).
● *Although Barnabas wasn't perfect (Gal. 2:13), his life is a model of someone who didn't mind being in second place as long as Christ was in first place. Even if you have a nickname, why not try to earn another one: Son or Daughter of Encouragement?*

**BARREN.** Not bearing fruit (2 Kings 2:19); unable to bear children (Luke 1:7).

**BARTHOLOMEW** (bar THAHL uh myoo). An apostle (Matt. 10:3; Mark 3:18; Luke 6:14; Acts 1:13). We don't know anything else about him unless his other name was Nathanael Bartholomew (see John 1:43-51; 21:2). John doesn't mention Bartholomew, and the other Gospels don't mention Nathanael. In each list of the apostles, Bartholomew and Philip are listed together. It was Philip who brought Nathanael to Jesus (John 1:45-49). For these reasons, some scholars believe Bartholomew and Nathanael refer to the same person.

**BASE.** As an adjective in the KJV, *base* means humble or lowly (Dan. 4:17; Ezek. 29:15; 2 Cor. 10:1). This is true even in Acts 17:5 (compare contemporary translations). The noun form refers to a pedestal or thing to set something on (Ezra 3:3).
▼ *In today's English, we usually think of* base *as meaning bad, but that meaning does not apply in the KJV.*

**BASHAN.** Area east and northeast of the Sea of Galilee (Deut. 32:14). Fertile land famous for oaks and cattle (Amos 4:1).

**BATH.** A liquid measure of about 5.8 gallons (1 Kings 7:38).

**BATHSHEBA** (bath SHEE buh). The married woman David committed adultery with after he saw her bathing (2 Sam. 11). Bathsheba became pregnant by David. It obviously was not by her husband Uriah, for he had been away at war. So David caused Uriah to be thrust into the heat of battle to be killed. Then David took Bathsheba to be his wife. After their first son died, Bathsheba bore David four more sons (2 Sam. 5:14; 1 Chron. 3:5).

**B.C.** Before Christ. Jews use B.C.E., before the common era. See **A.D.**

**BEATITUDES.** These statements tell who's happy (or blessed) and why. The term *beatitude* is not found in the English Bible but is used widely by Christians to refer to Jesus' sayings in Matthew 5:3-12.

**BEELZEBUB** (bee EL zee buhb). Chief demon. A name for Satan, the prince of the demons (Matt. 12:24). Also spelled Beelzebul or Beelzeboul. Literally means *lord of flies* and was originally a Philistine god. All biblical uses of Beelzebub are in the NT.

**BEERSHEBA** (BEE ehr SHE buh). A historic site at the southern end of Canaan (Gen. 21:31-32; Judg. 20:1).

**BEFALL.** Something that happens to a person—usually with the idea that the something is bad (Deut. 31:17,21).

■ **BEGET.** To father or bring forth. Used to list Jesus' ancestry (Matt. 1:2-16). Usually refers to physical fatherhood, but can refer to one who influences another and becomes a spiritual father (1 Cor. 4:15). May be used of a woman to mean bearing children (see "gendereth," Gal. 4:24). *Begat* is the past tense and the form most often used.

**BEGOTTEN.** Past perfect form of beget. KJV translation of Greek word meaning *unique*, one and only (John 3:16,18, NIV). Only or unique, meaning one of a kind. John's writings use the word to refer only to Jesus (John 1:14,18; 3:16,18; 1 John

4:9). Some scholars translate the word with *only-begotten* or *begotten of the Only One.*

**BEHOLD.** Look! (John 1:29), consider (Luke 21:29). Often used for an introductory word as we use *now* or *then* (Matt. 1:20; Mark 1:2).

**BELIAL** (BEE lih uhl). A wicked or worthless person (1 Sam. 25:25). A synonym for Satan (2 Cor. 6:15).

■ **BELIEVE.** Trust, have confidence in, have faith in, make a commitment to. May mean simply to *know* (Jas. 2:19), but in the Bible *believe* usually means to trust in God with commitment, obedience, and faith (John 14:1; Rom. 10:9-11; Jas. 2:18-20). One who believes is willing to obey God, to put one's life in His hands. This belief is essential for eternal life and Christian living (John 20:31).

*Believe* and *faith* are the verb and noun forms of the same root word. See **FAITH.**

**BELTESHAZZAR** (bel teh SHAZ ur). Name given to Daniel in Babylon (Dan. 1:7; 5:12). Means *may he protect his life.* Bel was a Babylonian God (Dan. 4:8). Daniel's life was protected, but by God, not Bel (Dan. 3:19-28; 6:22).

**BENJAMIN** (BEN juh min). Means *son of the right hand* (Gen. 35:18). The youngest of Jacob's twelve sons; the smallest of Israel's twelve tribes (Num. 1:37). King Saul and the apostle Paul were Benjamites (1 Sam. 9:1-2; Phil. 3:5).

**BEREA, BEROEA** (buh REE uh). A city of southern Macedonia (Acts 17:10-14).
▼ *The Bereans set a good example: They willingly listened to preaching, but they checked the preaching against the Scriptures (Acts 17:11).*

**BERYL.** A hard stone that was usually

green or bluish-green but sometimes yellow, pink, or white (Ex. 28:20; Rev. 21:20). Used in Ezekiel's description of the wheels in his vision (Ezek. 1:16; 10:9).

**BESEECH.** Appeal to, ask, beg (Luke 9:38; Rom. 12:1). *Besought* is the past tense (Luke 8:38).

**BESET.** Surround, encircle (Ps. 22:12; Heb. 12:1).

▼ *The rope of sin that surrounds us will tighten, trip us up, and drag us down as we try to race toward God (Heb. 12:1). So we are to lay sin aside.*

**BESIEGE.** Surround a city with armed forces to starve it into surrender (Deut. 20:19; 28:52). Press or hem in (2 Sam. 20:15).

**BESTOW.** Put, place, or stow (Luke 12:17-18).

**BETHANY** (BETH uh nih). Means *house of figs*. A village about two miles southeast of Jerusalem, near the Mount of Olives. Home of Mary, Martha, and Lazarus (John 11:1).

**BETHEL** (BETH uhl). Means *house of God*. A town twelve miles north of

Jerusalem (Gen. 28:19; 35:15). In the OT only Jerusalem is mentioned more often. It was a sacred place to the Israelites but became the symbol of sin when Jereboam built a temple there for the northern kingdom rather than go to Jerusalem to worship.

▼ *Jacob had a life-changing, name-changing experience as God dealt with him at Bethel (Gen. 28:10-19; 35:1-15). Jacob experienced God there, and he later came back there to another experience with God.*

● *Have you had a Bethel experience in your life when you met God and received the new name* Christian? *If so, recall that experience and consider your present spiritual needs. If not, why not meet God now for a new life and a new name?*

**BETHLEHEM** (BETH lih hem). Town six miles southwest of Jerusalem. David and Jesus were born there. (See Micah 5:2 and Luke 2:1-7 for the prophecy and fulfillment of Jesus' birth in Bethlehem.) David was anointed there, and it was known as the City of David (1 Sam. 16:4,13; Luke 2:4,11).

▼ *Another Bethlehem lay seven miles northwest of Nazareth (Josh. 19:15). Jesus' birthplace was known as Bethlehem Judah, which distinguished it from the other Bethlehem. Bethlehem means* house of bread.

**BETHSAIDA** (beth SAY ih duh). City on the north shore of the Sea of Galilee—near the Jordan River. Home of Peter, Andrew, and Philip (John 1:44; 12:21). *House of fishing.*

**BETROTHED.** Engage to be married (Matt. 1:18 RSV; Deut. 20:7). "Espoused" in KJV. Much more binding than today's engagement. To end a betrothal required a divorce. Betrothal usually included exchange of gifts and a public announcement. Loyalty was required, and the cou-

*The city of Bethlehem in Israel*

ple sometimes called each other husband and wife. Sex was postponed until marriage (Gen. 29:20-23).

**BEWRAY**. Reveal or disclose (Matt. 26:73). Much like *betray* except that it didn't carry the idea of disloyalty usually involved in betrayal.

**BIBLE**. The Bible is the inspired Word of God. The sixty-six books that make up Holy Scripture (thiry-nine OT and twenty-seven NT books). *Biblia* is the Greek word for books; it is plural. But the books came to be known as one Book: the Bible. The Old Testament was written in Hebrew (except for a little Aramaic in Ezra, Jeremiah, and Daniel). The New Testament was written in Greek. So most of the people in the world have to read a translation of the Bible from these original languages.

**BIBLE TRANSLATIONS.** The Bible was first written in Hebrew and Greek, so translations are necessary for most of us. There are different kinds of translations. Word-for-word translations match the Hebrew and Greek as closely as possible in English (such as the *King James Version* and the *New American Standard Bible*). Other translations focus on thought-for-thought translation more than word-for-word translation (such as the *New International Version*).

Paraphrases are efforts to get the Bible into very readable English, but they take a lot of liberty with the original Hebrew and Greek languages (such as *The Living Bible, Paraphrased*).

● *Why not ask your pastor to list his favorite (1) word-for-word translation, (2) thought-for-thought translation, and (3) paraphrased edition? Then compare several chapters (such as John 5:39-40; Eph. 4:11-12; 1 John 3:6-9).*

**BILDAD** (BIL dad). Known as one of Job's comforters even though he brought no comfort (Job 8; 18; 25).

**BIRTHRIGHT.** Special rights based on order of birth and inheritance. For example, the firstborn Hebrew son received a double portion of the inheritance (Gen. 25:31-34; Deut. 21:15-17).

**BISHOP.** Spiritual "supervisor" (Acts 20:17,28; 1 Pet. 5:2). Used interchangeably with *elder* and *presbyter* (see Titus 1:5,7; 1 Tim. 3:1; 4:14).

**BISHOPRICK.** Supervision (Acts 1:20). The office or responsibility of a bishop.

**BITTER HERBS.** Herbs eaten with a lamb during the Passover feast that symbolize the bitter experiences of the Hebrews in Egypt before the Exodus (Ex. 12:8). The exact herbs are unknown, but horseradish is used today.

**BLASPHEME, BLASPHEMY.** Slander, insult the honor of, injure the reputation of, attack, say untruths about. Usually refers to cursing God or using abusive and cutting language about Him, His name, or His Word (Lev. 24:16; Rom. 2:24; Titus 2:5). Because the Pharisees did not believe Jesus was God's Son, they thought He was blaspheming God by admitting to be the Christ (Matt. 26:63-65).

**BLESS.** To give good, wish good, be thankful, praise God. When God blesses, He helps, favors, makes happy (Gen. 1:28; 12:2-3; 14:19-20; Acts 3:26; Matt. 5:3-12). When persons bless God, they praise, worship, and thank Him (Ps. 103). Persons can bless other persons (Gen. 27:4). To bless food is to be prayerfully grateful for it (Matt. 14:19). Peace, not material prosperity, is the main goal of blessings.

■ **BLESSED.** Made happy by God, fortunate (Matt. 5:2-12; Ps. 1:1). Used in OT to praise God (Ps. 18:46).

**BLOOD.** The fluid vital to animal and human existence often used as a synonym for life (Gen. 9:4). Most of the references in the OT use *blood* to refer to death or violence (Gen. 4:10; 9:6; Prov. 1:16). Blood was a key element in the OT sacrificial system (Lev. 1:5; 3:2; 4:18). In the NT the shedding of Christ's blood in His death provided our way to salvation (Rom. 5:9-10; Heb. 9:12-14).

**BLOODGUILTINESS.** Guilt resulting from killing someone (Ps. 51:14).

**BLOT.** To rub off or wipe away (Ex. 32:32-33). The OT speaks of blotting out

# THE BIBLE IN ENGLISH

(Some translations are omitted due to space constraints)

## OLD ENGLISH TRANSLATION (A.D. 300–1100)

A.D. 300s—First Christians arrived in Britain
A.D. 400s—Angles, Saxons, and Jutes arrive in Britain
A.D. 500–700—Evangelization of Angles, Saxons, and Jutes
A.D. 700–100—Only parts of the Bible translated into "Old English"

## MIDDLE ENGLISH TRANSLATION (1100–1500)

1066—Norman Invasion brings French influence into language development and creates "Middle English"
Important persons:

John Wycliffe—died 1384. Wanted to take gospel to the commoners. Began translating from Latin into English in 1380. Was assisted by:

Nicholas of Hereford—whose translation followed the Latin Vulgate very closely

AND

John Purvey—whose revision of Nicholas's translation used more idiomatic expressions.

Important events at the end of this period:

The Renaissance—a revival of learning occurred which prompted a renewed interest in the original Hebrew and Greek. A new challenge to authority also emerged.

The invention of the printing press (1453)—made printed material accessible to the masses rather than to a few.

The Protestant Reformation (beginning in 1517)—Martin Luther and those who followed had a tremendous desire to get the Bible into the hands of the common people.

## MODERN ENGLISH TRANSLATION (1500–1900)

1525/6    William Tyndale translated New Testament into English from Greek. Was translating Old Testament at the time of his death as a martyr in 1536.

1535    Miles Coverdale completed and published first complete Bible in English from Tyndale's work, Greek and Hebrew, and other sources.

1537    **Matthew's Bible.** A complete English Bible from Tyndale's and Coverdale's work by John Rogers. Received royal sanction of King Henry VIII.

1539    **The Great Bible.** A revision by Coverdale of Matthew's Bible. Was placed in every church in England at the order of King Henry.

1560    **The Geneva Bible.** Produced by Protestant scholars in Geneva from the original languages and from Tyndale's work. (Sometimes called "Breeches Bible" because in Gen 3:7 Adam and Eve made "breeches" for themselves from fig leaves.)

1568    **The Bishop's Bible.** A revision of the Great Bible. Was authorized by the Church of England as their official translation.

1582 and    **Rheims/Douai Translation.** Roman Catholic translation from the Latin Vulgate of the Old and New Testaments so named because of where they were
1609-10    translated: the Old Testament at Douai in 1609-10 preceded by the translation of the New Testament at Rheims in 1582.

1611    **The King James Version (or Authorized Version).** Commissioned by King James I of England and translated by a number of Bible scholars. A revision of the 1602 edition of the Bishops' Bible with the aid of the Hebrew and Greek texts and a dependence upon the work of William Tyndale.

1885    **The Revised Version.** A revision of the Authorized Version incorporating more recently discovered manuscripts and more modern language usage. By a group of British scholars and some American scholars

# TWENTIETH-CENTURY ENGLISH TRANSLATIONS (1900–    )

|  |  |
|------|-------------|
| 1901 | **The American Standard Version**. An American revision of the Authorized Version growing out of American scholars' participation in the Revised Version. |
| 1903 | **The New Testament in Modern Speech**. R. T. Weymouth's attempt to render Greek grammatical constructions carefully. |
| 1924 | **A New Translation of the Bible**. An idiomatic, colloquial, and sometimes Scottish translation by James Moffatt. |
| 1927 | **Centenary Translation of the New Testament**. Helen B. Montgomery's missionary heart produced a translation in the language of everyday life. |
| 1937 | **Williams New Testament**. By Charles B. Williams. A Baptist professor's attempt to translate into English the nuances of the Greek verbs. |
| 1938 | **The Bible: An American Translation**. E. J. Goodspeed and J. M. Powis Smith produced the first modern American translation with the Apocrypha. |
| 1952 | **The Revised Standard Version**. Revision of the American Standard Version and the King James Version by an international translation committee seeking to maintain literary awesomeness for worship. |
| 1955 | **The Holy Bible**. Translated by Ronald Knox, a Roman Catholic, from the Latin Vulgate. |
| 1958 | **The New Testament in Modern English**. A free translation by J. B. Phillips originally done for his youth club. |
| 1965 | **The Amplified Bible**. A version by the Lockman Foundation suggesting various wordings throughout the text. |
| 1966 | **The Jerusalem Bible**. Originally translated into French by Roman Catholic scholars from the original languages. |
| 1969 | **The New Berkeley (Modern Language) Bible**. A revision of the Berkeley Version of 1959 by Gerrit Verkuyl with attached notes. |
| 1970 | **The New English Bible**. A translation with literary quality but some idiosyncratic language. Translated by representatives of Britain's major churches and Bible societies and based on the most recent textual evidence. |
| 1970 | **The New American Bible**. A new translation by Roman Catholic scholars (the Bishops' Committee of the Confraternity of Christian Doctrine) from the original languages. |
| 1971 | **The New American Standard Bible**. A revision by the Lockman Foundation of the American Standard Version of 1901 with the goal of maintaining literal translation. |
| 1971 | **The Living Bible**. A conservative American paraphrase by Kenneth N. Taylor originally for his children (begun in 1962). |
| 1976 | **The Good News Bible (Today's English Version)**. A translation by the American Bible Society into "vernacular" English. |
| 1979 | **The New International Version**. A readable translation by evangelical scholars incorporating the most recent textual evidence. |
| 1982 | **The New King James Version**. A modernization of the King James Version of 1611. Based on the original language texts available to the King James Version translators. |
| 1987 | **The New Century Version**. A translation committee's update of the International Children's Bible. |
| 1989 | **The New Revised Standard Version**. A translation committee's update of the Revised Standard Version. |
| 1989 | **The Revised English Bible**. A British committee's update of the New English Bible maintaining literary quality but avoiding idiosyncratic language. |
| 1991 | **The Contemporary English Version (New Testament)**. A simplified text originally conceived for children and produced by the American Bible Society. |

# THE BOOKS OF THE BIBLE

## 39 Old Testament Books

Law  Poetry/Wisdom  Minor Prophets

History  Major Prophets

**Law**
Genesis
Exodus
Leviticus
Numbers
Deuteronomy

**History**
Joshua
Judges
Ruth
1 Samuel
2 Samuel
1 Kings
2 Kings
1 Chronicles
2 Chronicles
Ezra
Nehemiah
Esther

**Poetry/Wisdom**
Job
Psalms
Proverbs
Ecclesiastes
Song of Solomon

**Major Prophets**
Isaiah
Jeremiah
Lamentations
Ezekiel
Daniel

**Minor Prophets**
Hosea
Joel
Amos
Obadiah
Jonah
Micah
Nahum
Habakkuk
Zephaniah
Haggai
Zechariah
Malachi

## 27 New Testament Books

Gospels  Letters of Paul  Prophecy

History  General Letters

**Gospels**
Matthew
Mark
Luke
John

**History**
Acts

**Letters of Paul**
Romans
1 Corinthians
2 Corinthians
Galatians
Ephesians
Philippians
Colossians
1 Thessalonians
2 Thessalonians
1 Timothy
2 Timothy
Titus
Philemon

**General Letters**
Hebrews
James
1 Peter
2 Peter
1 John
2 John
3 John
Jude

**Prophecy**
Revelation

the enemy (Deut. 9:14). Both the OT and NT record requests asking God to blot out sin (Ps. 51:9; Acts 3:19).

● *Think of an action or attitude in your life that the Bible says is wrong. Have you asked Jesus to blot out that sin? Why or why not?*

**BOAST**. In a good sense, used to praise or speak about God, someone, or something (Ps. 44:8). In a bad sense, bragging about wrong actions or taking pride in oneself (Ps. 52:1; Eph. 2:9).

● *How have you used boasting in a good way? How have you used it in a bad way?*

**BOAZ**. Ruth's husband (Ruth 4:13). A wealthy relative of Naomi (Ruth's mother-in-law) who allowed Ruth to gather grain in his fields to support her and her mother-in-law. Boaz later married Ruth and became an ancestor of David (Ruth 1—4).

**BODY**. Often used as a symbol of the unity of the church or Christians (Rom. 12:4-5; 1 Cor. 12:12-14; Col. 1:18).

**BONDAGE**. Slavery (Ex. 13:3; Rom. 8:15). Also refers to life before knowledge of Christ (Gal. 4:7-9).

● *What unchristian habit enslaves you or puts you in bondage? How can Christ help you to be free?*

**BONDS**. Something that binds or restrains. The apostle Paul spoke of his imprisonment as bonds (Phil. 1:16; Col. 4:3).

**BONES**. In the Book of Ezekiel the valley of dry bones was a symbol of the people of Israel in their hopeless condition (Ezek. 37:11). God promised the bones would rise, thus offering Israel hope.

**BOOK**. In Bible times books were rolled up parchments or skins called scrolls (Jer. 36:2).

*A Torah (Genesis–Deuteronomy) scroll being held in its wooden case at a celebration in Jerusalem.*

**BOOK OF LIFE**. A book (or scroll) with the names of those who will have eternal life instead of judgment and punishment (Ex. 32:32-33; Rev. 20:12,15).

**BOOTHS, FEAST OF**. Also referred to as Feast of Tabernacles. Popular and joyful fall feast lasting for seven days and ending with a solemn assembly on the eighth day (Lev. 23:34-36). The feast celebrated the final harvest of olives and fruits and also the start of the civil new year. It was one of the three great feasts celebrated by the Hebrew people and would be similar to our Thanksgiving. See the **Feast Chart** page 92.

**BOOTY**. Property or people captured in war (Jer. 49:32). Sometimes the conqueror kept the booty for his own use, and sometimes he destroyed it. Booty is also referred to as prey or spoil (Num. 31:32).

**BORN AGAIN**. A second birth that is spiritual (John 3:3). In the Christian realm, to accept Christ as Lord and Savior and to commit your life to Him (1 Pet.

*Family observing Feast of Booths. See* **Feast Chart** *page 92.*

1:23). Jesus told Nicodemus that it was necessary to be born again to have a right relationship with God (John 3:5).

● *List actions people do to try to have a right relationship with God. What does John 3:16 say about the matter?*

**BORNE.** Carried, as a load (Matt. 23:4).

**BOSOM.** Chest or breast, center of emotions, heart (Ex. 4:6; Eccl. 7:9; Luke 16:23).

**BOUGHS.** Branches of a tree (Dan. 4:11-12).

**BOUNTY.** Blessing or benevolence (2 Cor. 9:5).

**BOW.** Rainbow (Gen. 9:13). Also, an important weapon in Old Testament times (1 Chron. 5:18). The bow was usually made of seasoned wood with the string made from ox-gut. The metal-tipped arrows were made of reed or light wood.

**BOWELS.** The inner part of the body (Job 30:27) or deep feelings (1 John 3:17).

◄ *Boaz inquiring about Ruth*

**BRANCH.** Sometimes refers to the Messiah (Isa. 11:1). Tree branches were used to make booths in the Feast of Tabernacles (also called the Feast of Booths; Lev. 23:40). People paved Jesus' path with branches when He made His triumphal entry into Jerusalem (Mark 11:8).

**BREACH.** An opening or broken place (2 Kings 22:5).

**BREAD.** Usually made from barley or wheat; extremely important in biblical life (Gen. 3:19). Not only was bread a part of the diet, but the grain to make bread was used for trade and commerce. Unleavened bread (made without yeast) played a key role in the Exodus from Egypt and in the Passover Feast (Ex. 12:15-17).

Satan tempted Jesus to turn a stone into bread (Matt. 4:3). Jesus claimed to be the Bread of Life (John 6:48) and used bread as a symbol for His broken body (Luke 24:30).

**BREASTPLATE.** A religious decorative garment worn by the high priest (Ex. 28:15-30). Also a protective garment of metal or leather worn by soldiers on the upper part of the body to protect the vital organs (Eph. 6:14).

**BREECHES.** Undergarments worn by men (Ex. 28:42).

**BRETHREN.** Brothers. Used of family members (Gen. 47:1), people of the same nationality (Ex. 2:11), and those who have a spiritual kinship (Acts 20:32).

**BRIDE.** Besides its usual sense, bride can also mean the church. In John's vision he referred to the church as the bride of Christ (Rev. 21:9). Along with the Spirit, the bride invites all to partake of salvation (Rev. 22:17).

**BRIDEGROOM.** Term from wedding language Christ used to refer to Himself in relation to his Church (Mark 2:19-20).

**BRIMSTONE.** The English word means *a burning stone*. Sometimes referred to as sulphur (Luke 17:29, RSV). Used in connection with God's judgment (Ps. 11:6; Rev. 19:20).

**BROOD.** Literally *nest*. Used to refer to young birds cared for by their mother (Luke 13:34).

**BUCKLER.** Round or oblong shield used for defense and protection (1 Chron. 5:18). Also used to refer to God's protective care (Ps. 18:2).

**BULL.** Animal used as a sacrifice (Heb. 10:4). See **BULLOCK.**

**BULLOCK.** Steer, young neutered bull. Used extensively in the Jewish sacrificial system (Ex. 29:11).

**BULRUSH.** A plant that grows by water; reed; papyrus (Ex. 2:3).
▼ *Papyrus was often used to make scrolls on which Scripture was written.*

**BULWARK.** Fortress (Eccl. 9:14).

*Bulrushes.*

**BURDEN.** A heavy load (2 Kings 5:17; Luke 11:46). Used with a prophecy of doom (Isa. 15:1).
● *What kind of heavy burdens are you carrying in life? What help can you find in Matthew 11:28-30?*

**BURIED.** Put in a grave or tomb (Num. 20:1). In biblical times people were buried in an open grave and covered with stones or a hillside cave or in a burial chamber. Paul compared baptism to death and burial (Rom. 6:4).

**BURN.** To consume or be consumed by fire (Ex. 3:2; Luke 3:17). Sometimes used to speak of emotions (Ps. 79:5; Luke 24:32; 1 Cor. 7:9). The burning of offerings was part of the Jewish sacrificial system (Ex. 29:25).

**BURNING BUSH.** Probably a thorny bush found in the Sinai area (Ex. 3:2). God caused this plant to burn so He could catch Moses' attention.
● *What are some ways God uses to get people's attention today? your attention?*

**BYWORD.** A proverb, a term of scorn or derision (1 Kings 9:7; Job 30:9). Usually used in connection with God's judgment on Israel.

**CAESAR** (SEE zur). Name of a Roman family. Title of all Roman emperors after Julius Caesar (Matt. 22:17).

**CAESAREA** (sess uh REE uh). City that Herod the Great built and named in honor of Caesar Augustus. Located twenty-three miles south of Mount Carmel on the coast of the Mediterranean Sea. Paul was imprisoned there for two years (Acts 23:33). Roman capital of Palestine.

**CAESAREA PHILIPPI** (FILL ih pigh). Different from Caesarea; located about twenty-five miles north of the Sea of Galilee in the mountains of Lebanon. Philip, son of Herod the Great, enlarged the city and named it in honor of the Roman Emperor. Peter made his confession that Jesus is the Christ the Son of the living God there (Matt. 16:13-17).

**CAIAPHAS** (KIGH uh fuhs). High priest who prophesied Jesus' death, plotted against Him, tried Him, and condemned Him (John 11:47-53; Matt. 26:3-68). Later took part in a trial of Peter and John (Acts 4:6-7).

▼ *Jewish priests did not have the power to put someone to death, so they came up with a charge that would anger the Roman authorities. The priests accused Jesus of claiming to be king of the Jews. The Romans saw this as a threat to Caesar's position.*

*Reconstruction of Caesarea Maritima where Paul was imprisoned for two years (Acts 23:31—26:32).*

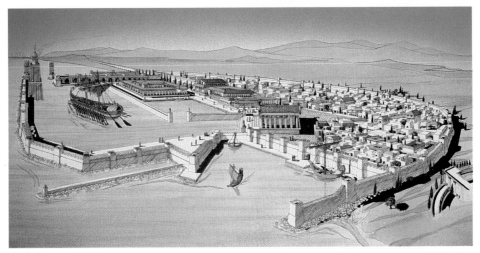

| EARLY CAESARS OF ROME | | |
|---|---|---|
| **Caesar** | **Dates** | **Biblical Reference** |
| Julius Caesar | 49–44 B.C. | |
| Second Triumvirate | 44–31 B.C. | |
| Augustus (Octavion) | 31 B.C.–A.D. 14 | Luke 2:1 |
| Tiberius | A.D. 14–37 | Luke 3:1 |
| Caligula (Gaius) | A.D. 37–41 | |
| Claudius | A.D. 41–54 | Acts 11:28; 17:7; 18:2 |
| Nero | A.D. 54–68 | Acts 25:11; Phil 4:22 |
| Galba, Otho, and Vitellius | A.D. 68/69 | |
| Vespasian | A.D. 69–79 | |
| Titus | A.D. 79–81 | |
| Domitian | A.D. 81–96 | |
| Nerva | A.D. 96–98 | |
| Trajan | A.D. 98–117 | |
| Hadrian | A.D. 117–138 | |

**CAIN** (KAYN). First son of Adam and Eve (Gen. 4:1). Cain and his offering were unacceptable to God. Cain murdered his brother Abel, who-along with his offering-was acceptable to God.

Cain committed the first murder. His act is an example of the progression of sin. Failing to please God led to jealousy, which led to anger, which led to murder, which led to lying to God, which led to abandoning God (Gen. 4:1-24; Heb. 11:4; 1 John 3:12; Jude 11).

▼ *From Cain came the expression "rais-ing Cain," which means making trouble.*

*What makes persons and their worship acceptable to God? For help in answering this question, see **BELIEVE, CONFESS, CONVICT OF SIN, REPENT.***

**CALDRON**. Large cooking pot (1 Sam. 2:14).

**CALEB** (KAY luhb). 1. Son of Jephunneh who was appointed one of twelve spies sent to scout the land of Canaan (Num. 13-14; 1 Chron. 4:15). Of the spies only

Caleb and Joshua believed the Israelites could conquer the Canaanites. The rest of the spies protested that the Cannanites were too big and strong for the Israelites to fight. Their doubts spread to the rest of the Israelites. Caleb and Joshua were rewarded by being the only adults of their generation to enter the Promised Land. See **CANAAN**. 2. A less well known Caleb, also of the tribe (family) of Judah, was the son of Hezron (1 Chron. 2:18-19,42).

▼ *Often we think of the Promised Land as empty and waiting for the Israelites. Instead, people already lived there. The Israelites had to decide whether to obey God and take the land.*

● *What do you think gave Caleb courage to stand against the majority? How might these same factors help you?*

**CALENDAR.** See **Feasts Chart** page 92 and **Calendar Chart** pages 228 & 229.

*Gordon's Calvary is one of two possible sites considered to be the location of Jesus' crucifixion.*

**CALL.** Noun: Summons or appointment from God to serve Him in a specific way for a specific purpose (1 Sam. 3:4; Isa. 6; 49:1).

Verb: Invite to become a follower of Christ—a Christian (Matt. 9:13; Phil. 3:14). Depend on God; Invite His attention in prayer (Gen. 4:26; Jer. 33:3). Name, describe; often includes beginning a relationship with a person or thing (Gen. 1:5, 2:19; Matt. 1:21; Mark 10:18).

▼ *Many Christians are called to be ministers. The call to be a schoolteacher or a machinist is just as important as more obvious ministerial calls (1 Cor. 7:20-24).*

● *What do you think God is calling you to do? to be?*

**CALVARY.** Literally *the skull*. Place near Jerusalem where Jesus was crucified (Luke 23:33). Greek equivalent for Hebrew "Gologotha" (Matt. 27:33; Mark 15:22; John 19:17).

▼ *Scholars are uncertain about the location of Calvary.*

**CANA** (KAY nuh). Village in Galilee north of Nazareth where Jesus attended a wedding and turned water into wine (John 2:1,11). He also healed a nobleman's son there (John 4:46-50). Nathanael's home (John 21:2).

● *How would turning water into wine invite people to believe in Jesus (John 2:11)?*

**CANAAN** (KAY nuhn). 1. The Promised Land God gave to the Israelites (Gen. 17:9). A land between the Jordan River and the Mediterranean Sea and north of Philistia. Old name for Palestine. 2. Son of

Ham, a son of Noah. Noah put a curse on Canaan because of Ham's improper behavior (Gen. 9:18,22-25).

**CANAANITES.** A Semitic tribe that lived in Canaan before the Israelites conquered it (Ex. 13:5). They worshiped false gods—such as Baal—in wild and evil ways. The Canaanites were the descendants of Ham, the son of Noah (Gen. 9:18-19).

▼ *A few Canaanites stayed and were a bad influence on the Israelites. This was even true after the Israelites were warned to have nothing to do with them (Gen. 28:6). The Canaanites were huge people. Ten of the twelve spies said they felt like grasshoppers in comparison (Num. 13:33).*

**CANON.** Means *rule* or *standard*. The canon is the list of books believers accept as the Bible. (The word itself is not in the Bible.) If a book is in the canon, it is recognized as inspired by God and is called canonical. These books are the rule for the Christian's faith and life.

▼ *Both Jewish and Christian believers decided with God's help which books were the Word of God. They thought the books showed themselves to be God's Word by their nature, content, usage, and authorship.*

*Jesus and His disciples had only the OT. The OT had come out of God's revelation of Himself to the Hebrew nation. God further inspired the NT through Jesus' teachings, the apostles' writings, and some other Christians' writings. Most Christians agree that the Bible was complete by about A.D. 100. All Scripture is to be tested against the life and teachings of Christ. See **BIBLE, BIBLE TRANSLATIONS.***

● *Why do you think some cults claim to have new writings from God? How can we tell these are false?*

**CANOPY** (NIV). 1. Used literally for a cover made of cloth, wood, or other material (2 Kings 16:18). The heavens are like a canopy to God (Isa. 40:22). 2. Used figuratively to signify God's protection (Isa. 4:5-6; 2 Sam. 22:12). 3. Nebuchadnezzar spread a royal canopy as a sign of God's sovereignty (Jer. 43:10).

**CAPERNAUM** (kuh PURR nay uhm). City on northwest shore of the Sea of Galilee. Jesus moved to Capernaum at the beginning of His ministry, and Capernaum became His home base (Matt. 4:13-15; 9:1). Though Jesus did much teaching and performed many miracles there, few people from Capernaum followed Jesus. So Jesus grieved over Capernaum for its lack of faith (Matt. 11:20-24). Miracles Jesus performed in Capernaum included healing a centurion's servant, a paralyzed man, and a nobleman's son (Matt. 8:5-13; Mark 2:1-12; John 4:46-53). Its present location is uncertain.

▼ *Literally means* Village of Nahum.

*Some of the intricately carved column pieces discovered in the excavations at Capernaum.*

**CAPTIVE, CAPTIVITY.** Being held as prisoner (Amos 1:15; Lam. 1:5). Usually refers to the time in which the Hebrews were removed from their homeland.

Ten tribes of Israel, the Northern Kingdom, were held captive by Assyria (2 Kings 17:6, RSV; 18:11). The captivity began in stages from about 740 B.C. to 722 B.C. (when Samaria fell).

The tribes of Judah and Benjamin made up the Southern Kingdom. These tribes were held captive in Babylon from about 587 B.C. to 537 B.C. Like the Northern Kingdom's captivity, the Southern Kingdom's captivity occurred in stages, with portions of the Israelites taken captive over a period of several years. This captivity is known as the Babylonian Captivity.

The Southern Kingdom's captivity began under Nebuchadnezzar and ended under Cyrus of Persia, who conquered Babylon the year before the release. It's uncertain what happened to the Northern Kingdom exiles.

In 538 B.C. the remnant of Hebrews returned to their home under the decree of Cyrus, king of Persia, who had conquered Babylon the year before. See **BABYLON, EXILE.**

▼ *Read about the invasions of the Northern Kingdom and the captivity in 2 Kings 15:29; 1 Chronicles 5:26; 2 Kings 17:3-7; Ezra 4:1-10. Read about the Southern Kingdom's similar fate in 2 Chronicles 36:2-7; Jeremiah 29:1,5-7; 45:1; Daniel 1:1-6; 2:48; 9:2; 2 Kings 24:14-16; 25:2-21; Ezra 1:1-4; 2:64-65; Nehemiah 1:11; Ezekiel 1:1; Zechariah 6:10.*

**CAREFUL.** Worried, anxious, afraid (Jer. 17:8; Dan. 3:16; Luke 10:41; Phil. 4:6). Also used as we use *careful* today: caring, concerned, cautious, attentive to detail (2 Kings 4:13; Phil. 4:10; Titus 3:8).

**CARMEL** (KAHR m'l). 1. Village in the country of Judah, south of Bethlehem and west of the Dead Sea where Nabal sheared sheep (1 Sam. 25). 2. Mount Carmel is a mountain at the head of a

*The western summit of Mount Carmel overlooking the modern Israeli port city of Haifa.*

range of mountains with the same name. It extends into the Mediterranean Sea. At Mount Carmel, Elijah challenged the prophets of Baal, and from Mount Carmel, Elisha came to heal the Shunammite woman's son (1 Kings 18:20-40; 2 Kings 4:25-57).

▼ *Literally means* garden-land *or* fruitful land. *Beautiful and plentiful plants covered Mount Carmel.*

**CARNAL.** Flesh, fleshly (Rom. 8:7; 1 Cor. 3:3). Controlled by human nature rather than by God. A carnal act is anything opposed to or in contrast to God and His purposes. Carnal attitudes and actions cannot please God (Rom. 8:5-9). Occasionally *carnal* means simply material (Rom. 15:27).

**CENSER.** Shovel-like holder used for carrying hot coals and for burning incense (Lev. 16:12; 2 Chron. 26:19; Heb. 9:4; Rev. 8:3,5). The coals and incense were used during worship and purification ceremonies, though not always together. Often incense was placed on top of the

hot coals to burn (Num. 16:46). Incense often represented prayers going up to God (Ps. 141:2; Rev. 5:8). See **INCENSE**.

▼ *Censers used in the Temple were made of gold. Sometimes they were called firepans.*

**CENTURION.** Leader of one hundred soldiers in a Roman army (Matt. 8:5-10; Acts 10). The highest rank an ordinary soldier could reach. Mentioned frequently in the NT.

**CEPHAS** (SEE fuhs). Literally means *rock.* A name Jesus gave Simon Peter (John 1:42). Used in New Testament to refer to Simon Peter (1 Cor. 1:12; 3:22; 9:5; 15:5; Gal. 2:9). The rock may signify Peter's strength as a leader in the early church.

**CEREAL OFFERING** (NRSV; meat offering, KJV; grain offering, NASB and NIV). 1. An offering presented to God in response to His command (Lev. 2). Consisted of flour, baked cakes, or raw grain combined with oil and frankincense. Can accompany burnt offerings and peace offerings (Num. 15:1-9).

2. Also used without the frankincense as a substitute for an animal sacrifice by those who could not afford an animal (Lev. 5:11-13). Giving one's best grain during worship was part of a ceremony that represented removal of past sins.

**CHAFF.** The bits of husk and other inedible parts of wheat plants which are blown away during threshing (Job 21:18). The edible grain falls to the ground and is kept. Chaff is also used as a figure of speech in the Bible to describe ungodly people (Ps. 1:4; Matt. 3:12). See **WINNOW.**
▼ *To picture what chaff is like, buy two ears of popcorn. Rub them together over a pan until all the kernels come off. Pour the kernels from one pan to the other in a breeze. Watch the white specks of popcorn chaff blow away.*

*The winnowing fork was a tool to aid the farmer in separating chaff from the grains of wheat.*

**CHARITY.** Used in the KJV for *love* (1 Cor. 13; Col. 3:14). God-inspired self-giving love for others. Translates the Greek word *agape* twenty-six times. In the Bible *charity* does not specifically refer to giving to the poor but to any expression of love.

**CHASTE.** Virtuous, morally pure, like God in thought and act (1 Pet. 3:2).

**CHASTEN.** Punish to make better (1 Cor. 11:32). Convict of sin, instruct, discipline (Deut. 8:5; Rev. 3:19).

**CHASTISE.** Instruct, discipline, punish to

make better (Ps. 94:10; 1 Kings 12:11-14; Luke 23:16; Heb. 12:8).

**CHEBAR** (KEE bahr). River or canal in Babylonia where the Jewish exiles settled and Ezekiel had visions (Ezek. 1:1,3; 3:15,23; 10:15,20,22; 43:3).

**CHERUB, CHERUBIM, CHERUBIMS.**
1. Type of angel with both human-like and animal-like characteristics. Some have human faces, and others have animal faces. They have two or four wings. Cherubim were assigned to guard the tree of life in the garden of Eden (Gen. 3:24). Models of cherubim perched on the mercy seat, adorned other articles of OT worship, and decorated Solomon's Temple (Ex. 25:18-22, 26:31; 1 Kings 6:23-28). (Note: Both *cherubim* and *cherubims* are plural forms.)
Cherubim were closely associated with God. At times He is pictured as dwelling between them or riding on them (Isa. 37:16; 2 Sam. 6:2).
2. A place in Babylon from which some Israelites came (Ezra 2:59).

**CHINNERETH** or **CHINNEROTH.** (KIN ih reth; KIN ih rahth). Old Testament names for the Sea of Galilee (Josh. 12:3; 13:27; Num. 34:11). Also a city (Deut. 3:17; Josh. 19:35).

**CHOOSE, CHOSEN.** Appoint, select, call out (1 Sam. 17:8; Matt. 20:16). It was God's choice to establish a unique and exclusive relationship by calling a people to be His own (Deut. 7:6-11).

**CHOSEN PEOPLE.** The Israelites, also called Hebrews or Jews (Gen. 17:7; Ps. 89:3). God chose to reveal Himself to and establish a covenant with this Chosen People. He then wanted them to share with everyone their knowledge of God and how to be close to Him.

Jesus was born a Jew and began a new

chosen people made up of everyone, Jew or non-Jew, who decides to follow Jesus (1 Pet. 2:9-10).

▼ *The Jewish race began with Abraham (Gen. 12:2; Rom. 4:16).*

■ **CHRIST**. Anointed One. One specially chosen for an important purpose. The title *Christ* identifies Jesus as the anointed Son of God, the true Messiah, the Savior of the world (Mark 14:61-62; Matt. 16:16; 27:43; Acts 10:38). Christ was Jesus' title but also became a personal name for Jesus (John 17:3). *Jesus* was used most often as His earthly name, and *Christ* as His eternal name. *Christ* is the Greek word for the Hebrew word *Messiah*. See **ANOINT** and the **Titles of Jesus Chart** page 130.

Because of the OT, Jews expected Christ. Because their expectations did not match the person and methods of Jesus, they rejected Him as the true Messiah.

● *Christians know that Jesus is the one anointed by God to give salvation. How do Christians know this is true?*

■ **CHRISTIAN**. Follower of Jesus Christ (Acts 11:26; 26:28; 1 Pet. 4:16). One who belongs to Christ. Christians commit themselves to Christ and become increasingly like Him. They trust Jesus Christ to guide their decisions, actions, and attitudes. The name apparently was first used by pagans to ridicule Jesus' followers, but it became a label Christians wear proudly.

*When others look at your life, do they see you as a follower of Christ? How? If not, why not? Do you wear Christ's name with pride?*

**CHRONICLES, 1, 2 BOOKS OF**. These OT books are a record of Israel's family history. The books retell, from a different perspective, events recorded in the Books of Samuel and Kings. The books emphasize the faithfulness and greatness of God as He uses events of history to work out His purpose. The books also emphasize the importance of demonstrating one's identity as a person of God. The purposes of these books are to show that God still keeps promises to His people in spite of disasters and to show the origin of the worship of God in the Temple at Jerusalem. Originally the two books were one.

To accomplish the first purpose, the books present evidence of God working, such as the achievements of David and Solomon, the reforms of Jehoshaphat, Hezekiah, and Josiah, and the actions of faithful people. To explain the worship, the books overview the organization of the priests and Levites, David's dream of the Temple, and Solomon's building of the Temple.

▼ *First and Second Chronicles are included in the books called Writings. The word* Chronicles *means the affairs of the days.*

▼ *First Chronicles begins by tracing Israel's genealogy back to Adam. Why is this useful?*

**CHRYSOLYTE**. A golden yellow stone used in the description of the new heaven and new earth (Rev. 21:20).

■ **CHURCH**. Summoned assembly; congregation. Believers who join together in a certain location (Matt. 18:17; 1 Cor. 4:17). May also mean all Christians everywhere, of all ages, of all times (1 Cor. 10:32; Eph. 1:22-23). In the Bible, *church* is not a building. Church is the Christians who inhabit it (Rom. 16:5).

New Testament pictures of the church include the bride of Christ (Eph. 5:25-27), the people of God (1 Pet. 2:9-10), and the body of Jesus Christ (Rom. 12:5; 1 Cor. 12:12; Eph. 4:16).

▼ *In the NT, church members accepted Jesus Christ as Lord and Savior, pictured this commitment in baptism, agreed to believe in and behave like Christ, and committed to share Christ and a ministry like His with others (Matt. 28:19-20; Acts 1:8).*

● *How does a person become a church member today? What do you think should be the requirements of church membership?*

■ **CIRCUMCISION**. Literally, *cutting around*. Physically, cutting around and off a small piece of excess skin that covers the tip of the penis. It was usually performed on the eighth day of life (Gen. 17:10-14; Rom. 4:11-12).

Spiritually, circumcision was a physical reminder of the covenant between God and His people. A pure heart and a right relationship show one to be circumcised in a spiritual sense that is more important than the physical surgery (Jer. 4:4; Rom. 2:25-29).

The Christian church refused to force non-Jewish Christians to be circumcised since the surgery is not required for salvation (Acts 15:5-11; Gal. 5:2).

▼ *Today, circumcision is a relatively painless operation that usually occurs shortly after birth if the parents so choose. Doctors suggest that circumcision may help guard against irritation and infection of the penis while also noting that cleanliness in the uncircumcised may accomplish the same purposes. Circumcision may occur as a medical consideration, a religious one, or both.*

**CISTERN**. Well, pit, artificial reservoir dug in rock or earth for collecting and storing water (Prov. 5:15). Cisterns were a necessity for Palestine's long and rainless summers.

▼ *Empty cisterns were sometimes used as prisons (Gen. 37:22, NIV).*

**CITY OF DAVID**. In the NT the reference is to Bethlehem as David's home (Luke 2:4,11). In the OT the reference is to Jerusalem, especially the part David built on Mount Zion (2 Sam. 5:7,9).

**CITY OF REFUGE**. City where a person who had accidentally killed another per-

*A cistern with a stone mortar in the foreground at Beersheba.*

son was safe from the vengeance of the dead person's loved ones (Ex. 21:13; Num. 35:9-34) There were six cities of refuge, three on each side of the Jordan River (Num. 35:14; Josh. 20).

**CLEAVE**. Hold fast to. Become inseparable with one's mate (Gen. 2:24-25) and with God (Deut. 11:22).

**CLOVEN**. Split, divided, especially referring to the hooves of an animal (Deut. 14:7; Lev. 11:3,7,26). When the Holy Spirit came at Pentecost, the believers saw cloven tongues that separated and rested on each one (Acts 2:3).

**COLOSSE** (koh LAHS ee). City in Asia where a Christian church was founded and to which Paul wrote a letter called Colossians (Col. 1:2).

**COLOSSIANS** (kuh LAHS uhns), **BOOK OF**. New Testament book which was a letter from Paul to the believers at Colosse. Paul wrote to counter false teachings in Colosse. Paul explained the true Christian message: unity with Jesus Christ brings salvation, and all the false teachings detract from Jesus. In the closing chapters, Paul gave examples of how to live in unity in Christ. He urged action based on Christ's love, not on legalism. Paul probably wrote the letter while under arrest in Rome.

**COMELINESS.** Attractiveness, pleasing appearance, beauty (Isa. 53:2).

**COMMANDMENT.** Law, ordinance, charge (Deut. 4:13). The most famous of God's commandments are recorded in Exodus 20:3-17 and Deuteronomy 5:7-21. These Ten Commandments, or Ten Words, were given to Moses on Mount Sinai and were intended to guide people to please God (first four commandments) and get along with each other (final six commandments).

True Christian love is the highest commandment and fulfills all the commandments of God (Matt. 22:36-40).

**COMMEND.** Praise (Luke 16:8), demonstrate (Rom. 5:8), entrust (Luke 23:46).

■ **COMMISSION.** Authorization, command, charge (Ezra 8:36; Acts 26:12). Matthew 28:19-20 is called "The Great Commission" because it is a command to share the good news of Christ with all the world.

■ **COMMIT.** Entrust to (Ps. 31:5; 2 Tim. 1:12; Titus 1:3). Or merely act or do (Lev. 5:17). To commit to Christ is to let Him take charge of life as Lord. To be committed to Him is discipleship expressed in Christlikeness.

■ **COMMITMENT.** Sense of devotion, obligation, and faithfulness to someone or something. A promise to do something in the future. Those who have made a commitment to Christ try to obey Him in everyday living and decision making. This commitment is the kind Paul wrote of in 2 Timothy 1:12.

**COMMUNE.** Communicate, discuss, think about, confer(Gen. 18:33; Ps. 4:4; Zech. 1:14). The results of communing can be negative as well as positive (Luke 6:11; 22:4).

**COMMUNION.** Sharing, participation with, fellowship, communication, having something in common, (2 Cor. 6:14; 13:14). Includes both someone and something. Used as a one word description for the Lord's Supper because partakers commune with Jesus Christ and one another (1 Cor. 10:16).

▼ *You may have heard the word* koinonia *described as fellowship and belonging.* Koinonia *is the Greek word translated* communion.

**COMPASSION.** To bear with, to suffer with, to love, to have mercy (Lam. 3:22; Matt. 9:36). "Sympathetic consciousness of others' distress together with a desire to alleviate it" (Webster, 9th Collegiate).

A human quality as well as a divine one. Anyone who has experienced God's compassion is responsible for having compassion on others. These others include fellow believers, outsiders, orphans, and widows (Deut. 10:18; 16:11; 24:19; Mic. 6:8; 1 John 3:17).

■ **CONCUBINE.** In the OT legal but secondary wife acquired by purchase, gift, or war victory. Often servants of wives. Bore children for the husband, especially when a wife could not conceive (Gen. 30:3; 1 Chron. 1:32).

Concubines were popular in the OT when believers failed to recognize God's ideal of creation: one wife for one husband. Those who had concubines included Abraham (Gen. 25:6), Gideon (Judg. 8:30-31), David (2 Sam. 5:13), and Solomon (1 Kings 11:3).

■ **CONDEMN, CONDEMNATION.** Declare guilty or wrong (Ex. 22:9). Refers to God's final judgment at the end of His time but also to other judgments. Condemnation by humans in a court is sometimes necessary (Deut. 25:1), but human judgment may be uncalled for (Matt. 7:1) or wrong (Matt. 12:7; Ps. 94:21). God's condemnation comes because of sin and is always accurate (Rom. 2:1-2). Because of Christ's redemption, believers who walk in the Spirit can be confident that God will not condemn them (Rom. 8:1; Ps. 34:22, NIV). God will take their side against all adversaries (Isa. 50:9). See **JUDGMENT**.

**CONFESS.** Openly admit personal wrongdoing (Lev. 5:5; Matt. 3:6). Confess to God (1 John 1:9) and to each other (Jas. 5:16). Declare or acknowledge Jesus as Lord (Phil. 2:11).

▼ *You can share any wrongdoing with God and know that He understands and still loves you.*

● *What good is confession without repentance?*

**CONFOUND.** Confuse or put to shame (Gen. 11:7,9). God's ways confound the world's ways; God's ways are not unreasonable but are beyond reason. Christians can find clarity and effectiveness in Jesus and no longer are ashamed or confused (1 Cor. 1:27).

**CONGREGATION.** Group of people gathered for a common purpose, especially a religious purpose (Ex. 12:3; Acts 13:43). In the OT *congregation* often referred to the entire Hebrew people, also called the People of Israel. Just as we have local congregations of believers today, *congregation* sometimes meant a specific group of believers in a specific place (Ex. 12:47; Num. 16:3; 1 Kings 8:65).

▼ Congregation *came to mean both the meeting place (synagogue) and the gathering.* Assembly *and* church *are other terms used for a congregation.* See **ASSEMBLY**.

**CONSCIENCE.** Self-knowledge that leads us to feel an obligation to do right or be good (John 8:9; Rom. 2:14-15; 1 Cor. 8:10). Awareness or sense that an action or attitude is right or wrong.

● *What happens when your conscience dies? What can you do to bring it back to life? What would make your conscience dull? When would it be possible to do wrong and not sense it?*

■ **CONSECRATE.** Devote, separate, set aside for worship or service to God. A person or thing can be consecrated (2 Chron. 29:31-33; Ex. 13:2, RSV).

In the OT *consecrate* may also refer to the installation of a priest and to offerings (Lev. 7:37; 8:22). In both the OT and NT the concept is most often translated *sanctify* or *make holy* (John 17:17). *Consecrate* may also carry the idea of make perfect (Heb. 7:28) or make new (Heb. 10:20).

*How does your life demonstrate that you are consecrated to God? What areas of your life need renewing?*

**CONTRITE.** Sorry for sin, humble (Ps. 34:18; 51:17; Isa. 57:15; 66:2).

**CONVERSATION.** Behavior, conduct, manner of life. In the KJV, *conversation* never meant merely talk; it meant way of life. (Ps. 50:23; Gal. 1:13; Heb. 13:5; Jas. 3:13).

■ **CONVERSION, CONVERT.** Turn, turn from sin to God, turn about (Ps. 51:13). Includes turning from wrong actions and attitudes to right ones (Jas. 5:19-20). Converted persons trust and learn from God as children (Matt. 18:3). Closely associated with repentance (Acts 3:19). *Conversion* has come to mean the experience of turning to God with a change of mind and heart to receive the gift of salvation (Acts 9:1-22).

● *Each person chooses whether to turn to or from God. What have you decided?*
*How has your life changed since you became a Christian? Or how would it change if you became one?*

■ **CONVICT OF SIN.** Convince one of one's sin. Firm feeling that God wants one to choose to stop an action (John 8:9; RSV: John 8:46; Jude 15). When a person becomes convinced that he or she is guilty of sin, then that person is in a position to turn from sin and turn to God (see Ps. 51).

**CORBAN.** A Hebrew word that stood for money or possessions set aside for God or religious use (Mark 7:11). During Jesus' earthly ministry *corban* seemingly was understood to be the dedication of something as a trust (like an inheritance) to be used later. People could will money or possessions to God or the Temple but keep usage while they lived. The Pharisees abused this practice by telling their needy parents they could not give them their "corban money." In this way, they avoided taking care of their parents.

Read Jesus' evaluation of this in Mark 7:9-13.

● *What religious sounding practices might you be using to keep from doing what God wants you to do?*

**CORINTHIANS, 1, 2, BOOKS OF.** These NT books are letters from Paul to a spiritually struggling church. The city of Corinth was famous for its wickedness, including such sins such as greed, drunkenness, prostitution, pride, and a variety of false religions. The church had let some of these sins creep into their lifestyles and cause problems in their church. Paul wrote 1 and 2 Corinthians to correct these problems and give advice on how to live the Christian life. The problems prompted powerful teachings. These include the Holy Spirit (1 Cor. 12), love (1 Cor. 13), the resurrection (1 Cor. 15), and close relationships (2 Cor. 6:14-18).

▼ *Read the classic description of true love in 1 Corinthians 13 and the triumph over troubles that God will give in 2 Corinthians 4:8-10.*

*Corinth was the capital of the Roman province of Achaia and was known for its prosperous commerce, multiple religions, and extensive immorality. The city was full of people like gamblers, prostitutes, and drug dealers. What sort of problems would a church have that was established in a place like this?*

**CORRUPTIBLE.** Perishable (Rom. 1:23).

**COUNCIL.** Gathering of people for deliberation or decision making (Ps. 68:27; Matt. 12:14; Acts 25:12). In the NT, usually the Jewish leaders in a body called the Sanhedrin (Matt. 26:59; Acts 24:20).

**COUNSEL.** Noun: Advice (Dan. 4:27; Luke 7:30). Verb: Advise, give advice (Luke 23:50; John 18:14). Examples of counselors include prophets, members of the Jewish Sanhedrin, and God (2 Sam. 17:11; Mark 15:43; Rev. 3:18).

**COUNTENANCE**. Noun: Facial expression (Ps. 10:4; Prov. 15:13), appearance (1 Sam. 16:7). Verb: Honor (Ex. 23:3).

■ **COVENANT**. Mutual agreement between two persons or parties. The covenant between God and people is unique because God alone sets the conditions. In a covenant between two persons, the two negotiate the terms and promise with words or a written contract to keep the covenant (Gen. 31:49-53), or a powerful ruler dictates the terms to a compliant subject. In a covenant between God and humans, God sets the requirements, and each person decides whether to agree to them and enter the covenant.

The covenant God offers requires obedience and loyalty to Him alone. For those who agree to this, God gives His protective care, His assurance, His guidance, and His presence. Of course Christians believe these benefits far outweigh the costs.

God has made covenants with people from Adam and Eve to the present. One of the most far-reaching covenants God initiated was with Abraham (Gen. 15). The covenant offered Abraham included the Hebrew nation as God's instrument to reach the world. The covenant was based on grace, law, and obedience. Sometimes this covenant is called the Old Covenant. God sent a new covenant of grace through His Son, Jesus Christ (Jer. 30:22; Heb. 7:22; 8:6; 2 Cor. 3:6). The New Covenant is often called the New Testament. See **TESTAMENT**.

● *As a Christian, you have a covenant with God. What does He expect from you? What do you expect from Him? If you're not a Christian, you can become one by entering the wonderful covenant God provides in Jesus Christ (see John 3:16; Rom. 10:9-10).*

**COVERING OF THE HEAD**. An example used in 1 Corinthians 11:5,15 to teach that ignoring social customs could hurt one's Christian testimony. In Bible times it was customary for women to cover their heads. Because immoral women appeared in public with their heads uncovered, observers might draw the wrong conclusions about Christian women who did not cover their heads.

● *What social customs do you tend to ignore that may hurt your Christian testimony? What will happen if you take notice of the custom and change your habits?*

**COVET**. Greedily want what belongs to someone else (Ex. 20:17). A person can covet things, money, people, or relationships (Acts 20:33; 1 Tim. 6:10; Rom. 7:7).

**CREATE, CREATION**. Make, produce, form, fashion, bring into being (Gen. 1:1; Ps. 51:10; Col. 1:16). The Bible clearly teaches that all matter had a beginning and that the beginning was initiated by God Himself. The Bible does not explain how much time occurred between "the earth was without form and void" and the creation of earth's structure, plants, and inhabitants. We do know that these things occurred by God's direction, not from natural causes. God determined that each plant and animal would produce after its kind (Gen 1:12,21,24-25). It is worth noting that scientists have discovered the same order of creation as in the Bible ("without form," light, plants, creatures from water, birds, creeping creatures, beasts, humans).

Only God is a true creator in that He can create from nothing. Others take materials already at hand and alter them to be used in a new way.

● *How does the fact that all people are created by God affect the way you treat them? (Mal. 2:10)*

• *Read Genesis 1:1-31. Make your own chart of the order in which things, animals, and people were created.*

**CRIMSON**. Bright red (Isa. 1:18). Crimson was used in the Temple (2 Chron. 2:7,14), in royal clothes (Jer. 4:30), and to symbolize the seriousness of sin (Isa. 1:18).

*The crucifixion of Jesus.*

**CROSS**. Structure made by crossing two beams of wood (John 19:17). Some condemned persons were nailed or tied to an upright cross for crucifixion. Some crosses looked like **X**'s, others like a capital **T**, others like the Christian symbol for a cross, resemble a lowercase **†**.

Jesus' cross is sometimes called a tree; being hung on a tree was an OT symbol of humiliation (Deut. 21:22-23; 1 Pet 2:24). The cross is used figuratively as a symbol for the gospel, the good news of Jesus Christ (Gal. 6:14). Taking up one's cross means being willing to obey Jesus Christ unconditionally, even if it means death (Luke 9:23).

**CRUCIFY**. To put someone to death by fastening him or her to a cross (Matt. 27:31). *Crucifixion* comes from the Latin *Cruci figo*, which means "I fasten to a cross." Christians refer specifically to Jesus' death on the cross when they say "the crucifixion." Roman crucifixion was a most shameful, painful, and lingering way to die. It was usually reserved for slaves and foreigners—not Roman citizens—and was carried on outside the city. Before crucifixion, most victims were beaten with a leather whip lined with bits of metal or bone tied to it (Matt. 20:19). The victim's hands and feet were then nailed or tied to a large wooden cross, and the cross was displayed upright. Death could come about from suffocation because each breath took extreme effort: the crucified one had to push up with the feet to fill the lungs with air. Exposure and starvation may have also contributed to death because most crucified persons hung on the cross for many days before death came.

Christians are said to be "crucified with Christ," which means they have let their old selves die so that Jesus can live in them (Rom. 6:6; Gal. 2:20).

● *If you are a Christian, how does your life show you are crucified with Christ?*

**CUBIT**. Linear unit of measure—from the elbow to the tip of the middle finger. Depending on the size of the person, a cubit was eighteen to twenty-one inches or about forty-six to fifty-two centimeters (Gen. 6:15).

**CUMMIN**. Plant whose seeds were used for seasoning foods (Isa. 28:25,27). Its name means *sharp smell*. It looks and tastes similar to caraway. Cummin was used especially during feasts and was believed to have medicinal properties. The scribes and Pharisees scrupulously paid tithes of their cummin, but Jesus charged them with neglecting more important matters (Matt. 23:23).

of the oldest cities in the world. It served as a natural communication center, linking the Mediterranean coast and Egypt on the west, Assyria and Babylonia on the east, Arabia to the south, and Aleppo to the north.

Paul, a Jew, became a Christian while traveling on the Damascus Road (Acts 9:1-31).

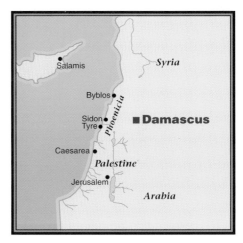

**DAGON** (DAY gahn). Pagan god the Philistines worshiped. He had the body of a fish and the head and hands of a human. He was probably a god of agriculture. Samson destroyed a temple of Dagon in Gaza (Judg. 16:23-30). When the Philistines stole the ark of God and brought it to Dagon's temple, they encountered disastrous results (1 Sam. 5:2-7). The Philistines later put Saul's head in a temple of Dagon (1 Chron. 10:10).

**DAMASCUS** (duh MASS cuss). Capital of Syria (Isa. 7:8; Acts 9:2-3). Damascus, more than four thousand years old, is one

*The city wall of biblical Damascus.*

**DAN**. 1. Son of Jacob and Bilhah (Gen. 30:5-6). Dan was also considered Rachel's son because Bilhah was her maid.

*Daniel in the lions' den.*

2. The tribe that descended from Dan and the territory where they lived (Num. 1:38-39; Ezek. 48:1). They originally lived between Judah and the Mediterranean Sea; but because they failed to conquer the Philistines who lived there, the Danites moved north (Josh. 19:40-48; Judg. 18:1- 29).

3. The northernmost city of Israel (Judg. 18:29). "From Dan to Beersheba" means the length of Israel from northernmost tip to southernmost tip (1 Kings 4:25).

**DANIEL** (DAN yuhl). 1. Governmental officer and prophet of God (Dan. 1:1-6; Matt. 24:15). As a young Jew he was taken captive and trained for service in the Babylonian royal court. He served in influential positions under four kings: Nebuchadnezzar, Belshazzar, Darius, and Cyrus. He firmly refused to do anything contrary to God's teachings, even when it meant risking his life (Dan. 1:8; 6:7-16). Daniel's gift of prophecy was evident early in life (Dan. 1:17; 2:16-19,28; 5:5,11-17;

7—12). He wrote the Book of Daniel. The name Daniel means *God is my judge*. Daniel was called Belteshazzar while in exile (Dan. 1:7). See **BELTESHAZZAR**.

2. The second son of David (1 Chron. 3:1).

3. A descendant of Ithamar who grew up with Ezra and helped seal the covenant (Ezra 8:2; Neh. 10:6).

● *Daniel was a refugee in a land far from home. Read Daniel 1—6 for ways he coped with this difficult situation. Which actions could help you get through your own rough situations?*

**DANIEL, BOOK OF.** This OT book depicts Daniel's loyalty to God in the face of imprisonment, pagan religion, and false teaching. It also includes Daniel's visions. Daniel and fellow Jews were captives in a foreign land during the Babylonian and Persian empires.

Daniel was frequently pushed to compromise his faith, but he didn't do it. The

*Daniel and his friends refusing the king's wine and meat.* ▶

Book of Daniel records Daniel's faithful decisions and their results. Well known choices include insisting on eating a healthy diet (Dan. 1), worshiping God rather than avoiding the fiery furnace (Dan. 3), interpreting the writing on the wall (Dan. 5), and praying to God rather than avoiding the lion's den (Dan. 6).

The last portion of the book (chapters 7—12) records visions God gave to Daniel that depict Israel's future. This portion of Daniel is apocalyptic literature; it tells about the future with symbols and signs. These passages gave hope that the cruelty would end and God's triumph would become obvious.

Daniel is a major prophet in the English Bible following the order of the earliest Greek translations. The Hebrews placed it in a section called Writings.

▼ *Because Daniel showed his faith, Kings Nebuchadnezzar and Darius honored God. How might your actions influence someone powerful to honor God?*

**DARIUS** (duh RIGH uhs). Common name

for rulers of the Medes and Persians. Three examples are: 1. Darius the Mede ruled Babylon briefly (Dan. 5:31). 2. Darius Hystaspes, the fourth and greatest of the Persian rulers, reorganized the government into provinces, extended boundaries of the empire, renewed the edict of Cyrus, and helped rebuild the Temple (Ezra 4:5, 6:1-12). 3. Darius the Persian, the last king of Persia, was defeated by Alexander the Great in 330 B.C. Many identify him with Darius Nothus (Neh. 12:22).

**DARKNESS.** 1. Absence of light, obscurity, gloom (Gen. 1:2; Amos 4:13). 2. Symbol of all that is evil, wrong, or opposed to God (1 John 1:5-7; 2:11). 3. A characteristic of death, especially for the unsaved (Job 10:22; 2 Pet. 2:4; Jude 6). See **LIGHT**.

**DAUGHTER.** 1. Female descendant (Gen. 26:34). 2. A woman (Mark 5:34). 3. Worshiper or group of worshipers of the true God (Zech. 2:10; Matt. 21:5).

*View of Jerusalem from the southwest during the time of David (1000–962 B.C.).*

**DAVID** (DAY vid). Youngest son of Jesse;

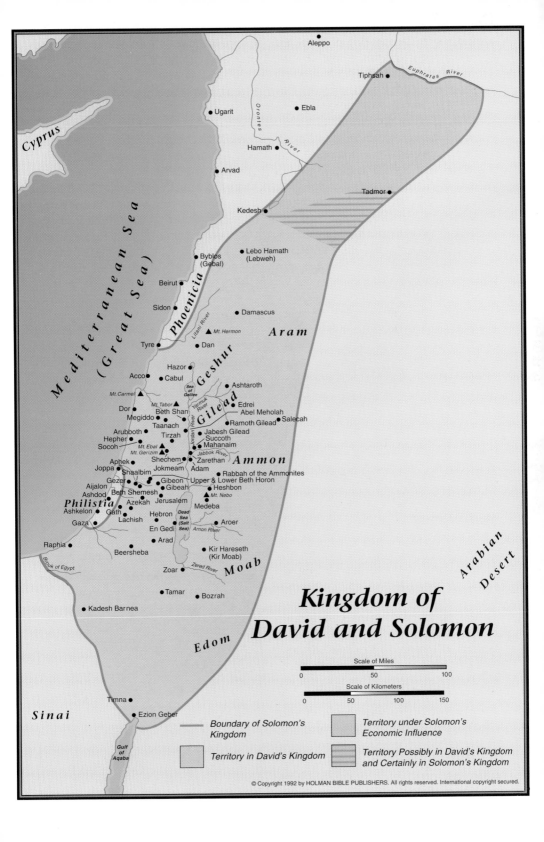

# Kingdom of David and Solomon

Aleppo

Euphrates River

Tiphsah

Ugarit

Ebla

*Orontes River*

Hamath

Arvad

Tadmor

Kedesh

Lebo Hamath
(Lebweh)

Byblos
(Gebal)

Beirut

*Phoenicia*

*Litani River*

Sidon

Damascus

Tyre

▲ Mt. Hermon

*Aram*

Dan

*Geshur*

Hazor

Acco

Cabul

*Sea of Galilee*

Ashtaroth

*Mt. Carmel* ▲

*Gilead*

Edrei

Dor

*Mt. Tabor* ▲

Beth Shan

*Yarmuk River*

Abel Meholah

Megiddo

Taanach

Ramoth Gilead

Salecah

Arubboth

Tirzah

Jabesh Gilead

Hepher

*Jordan River*

Succoth

Socoh

*Mt. Ebal* ▲

*Mt. Gerizim* ▲

Shechem

Mahanaim

*Jabbok River*

Aphek

Zarethan

*Ammon*

Joppa

Jokmeam

Adam

Shaalbim

Gibeon

Rabbah of the Ammonites

Gezer

Gibeah

Upper & Lower Beth Horon

Aijalon

Beth Shemesh

Heshbon

Ashdod

Azekah

Jerusalem

▲ Mt. Nebo

*Philistia*

Medeba

Ashkelon

Gath

Hebron

Gaza

Lachish

*Dead Sea (Salt Sea)*

Aroer

En Gedi

*Amon River*

Raphia

Arad

*Brook of Egypt*

Beersheba

Kir Hareseth
(Kir Moab)

Zoar

*Zered River*

*Moab*

Tamar

Bozrah

*Arabian Desert*

Kadesh Barnea

*Edom*

*Mediterranean Sea (Great Sea)*

*Cyprus*

*Sinai*

Timna

Ezion Geber

*Gulf of Aqaba*

Scale of Miles
0      50      100

Scale of Kilometers
0      50      100      150

—— Boundary of Solomon's Kingdom

Territory under Solomon's Economic Influence

Territory in David's Kingdom

Territory Possibly in David's Kingdom and Certainly in Solomon's Kingdom

he became the second king of Israel and was an ancestor of Jesus Christ (1 Sam. 16:7-13; Acts 13:22-23). While a young shepherd boy, David was anointed by Samuel to succeed Saul as future king.

At first Saul had great affection for David, his music, and his bravery. David's harp music soothed Saul when he felt troubled. Later Saul became jealous of David's military popularity and tried to kill him. After Saul died, David was crowned king and became the best-loved king of Israel.

David is remembered for many adventures: killing the giant Philistine with a slingshot, having a faithful friendship with Jonathan, and refusing to get revenge on king Saul (1 Sam. 17:32-54; 18:1; 26:9). He is also known for blatant disobedience against God: having sex with Bathsheba, Uriah's wife, and arranging Uriah's death so David could marry Bathsheba (2 Sam. 11:2-27). David wrote many psalms about both his disobedient actions and his obedient ones (compare Ps. 51 with Ps. 101).

▼ *Read about David's life and adventures in 1 Samuel 16-1 Kings 2:11.*

● *David's sin hurt both him and his family. His sin created family problems for generations and David was not permitted to build his beloved temple. How does your disobeying God hurt you? your family?*

■ **DAY OF THE LORD**. Scholars see this reference from different perspectives: 1. when the Lord will return, 2. when the world as we know it will end, or 3. when God will rid the world of evil once and for all (Joel 2:28-32; Phil. 1:6,10). The Day of the Lord will mean disaster and judgment for the enemies of the Lord, but salvation and deliverance for believers (Amos 5:18-20; Zeph. 1:14-18).

In the OT the Day of the Lord was something for the unfaithful to dread and for the faithful to anticipate (Amos 5:18; Dan. 7:22,27; 12:1-2). In the NT the Day of the Lord often refers to the day Jesus will return (Phil. 1:6,10). He will bring judgment and will deliver believers to eternal joy (John 5:27; 6:40; Rom. 2:5-11). The Day of the Lord will result in a new heaven and a new earth (2 Pet. 3:10-13).

**DEACON**. Servant, minister, helper (Phil. 1:1; 1 Tim. 3:8-13). A church leader who ministers to others.

Though *deacon* appears only five times in the KJV, the Greek word translated *deacon* appears over thirty times. It is usually translated *servant*, and many times describes how Christians meet material needs of fellow Christians (2 Cor. 8:4, NIV).

▼ *Phoebe is a woman in the NT referred to as a* diakonon, *translated servant (KJV) or deaconess (NIV, footnote; Rom. 16:1).*

**DEAD SEA**. Salt lake with no outlet into which the Jordan River flows. Usually called the Salt Sea in the Bible (Gen. 14:3; Num. 34:12). It is the lowest spot on earth with a surface about 1,300 feet below sea level and its deepest point 1,300 more feet below sea level. Because it has no outlet, the Dead Sea is several times saltier than an ocean. No plant or animal can live in its extra salty waters-so the name Dead Sea. The Dead Sea is located between Jordan and Israel with its northern half extending into Jordan.

Dead Sea Scroll fragment.

The Dead Sea's high salt content makes it virtually impossible for a person to sink in its waters.

Caves of the Qumran area in which the Dead Sea Scrolls were discovered.

**DEAD SEA SCROLLS.** Copies of OT text written on scrolls found near the Dead Sea beginning in 1947. These are 1,000 years older than the standard Hebrew Bible Manuscripts. They are important because they assure us of the accuracy of the Hebrew texts we have today and help us better know the precise wording of the OT. They also contain non-biblical texts that tell about the time just before, during, and after Jesus' earthly life. The Dead Sea Scrolls contain parts of every book of the OT except Esther. Some entire books are included. The scrolls are dated as early as the second century B.C.

▼ *Arabic Bedouins (nomadic desert dwellers) discovered the first scrolls in 1947 in caves about a mile west of the northwest corner of the Dead Sea at a place called Qumran. Near the caves are* *the remains of a monastery where Jews called the Essenes lived. Perhaps they hid the scrolls in the caves. These scrolls are also called manuscripts. See the **illustration** of scrolls following **BOOK.***

■ **DEATH.** Used at least four ways in the Bible: 1. End of physical life. After physical death, persons enter a new realm of life: believers to eternal joy and non-believers to eternal torment (Matt. 25:46; Rev. 20:15; 21:3-5). Jesus removes the sting of physical death (1 Cor. 15:55-57; Rom. 6:9-10).

2. Lack of spiritual life. Spiritual death means separation from God (1 John 3:14). All who do not accept Jesus are spiritually dead. They become alive only in Christ (Eph. 2:1-5).

3. End of an old way of life. Christians have died to their old lives without Jesus and have been raised to new life with Jesus (Rom. 6:4-8).

4. "Second death." A final and irreversible separation from God after judgment (Rev. 20:6).

● *How do you feel about death? How do you feel about eternal life? How does Jesus' promise of eternal life affect your feelings about death?*

■ **DEBAUCHERY.** Drunkenness, unbridled lust (NIV: Gal. 5:19; 1 Pet. 4:3).

**DEBORAH.** 1. A prophetess and judge of Israel (Judg. 4:4—5:15). Deborah's skilled leadership and presence gave courage to Barak and the people of Israel. She composed and sang a song of praise to God after He gave victory over Israel's enemies.

2. Rebekah's nurse (Gen 35:8). Rebekah was Isaac's wife, the mother of Jacob and Esau.

**DECAPOLIS** (dih KAP oh liss). Ten cities spoken of as a region (Matt. 4:25; Mark 5:20; 7:31). The name is Greek for *ten*

*cities.* These ten towns cooperated to protect their interests. They had their own coins, courts, and armies. Most of the original ten towns lay east of the Jordan River. More towns were added later.

Listings of the cities differ. One list of the original ten cities is: Damascus, Raphana, Kanatha, Hippos, Dion, Gadara, Scythopolis, Pella, Gerasa, and Philadelphia.

**DECEIT.** Subtle lie, fraud, treachery, making wrong look right or right look wrong (Prov. 12:20; Amos 8:5; Rom. 1:29). Deceit is not only destructive in itself but leads to other destroyers, such as using people, refusing to accept God's truth, and distancing friend from friend.

One of the devil's main tools is deceit. Temptation wouldn't be so appealing if it didn't look right, good, or fun (Rev. 20:10).

● *When have you been harmed by deceit? Recall a time you deceived someone or lied. How did someone suffer when you used deceit?*

**DECLARE.** Make known, tell good news, explain, tell fully (Acts 13:32).

**DECREE.** Official ruling, law, or order (Ezra 5:13; Esther 2:8; Dan. 2:13).

■ **DEDICATE.** Set apart or sanctify things or people for God's use (Eph. 5:26). Devote, make holy. Both things and people can be dedicated (Num. 7:10; 2 Sam. 8:11; Ex. 19:14).

● *What evidence is there that your life is dedicated to God? What skills do you have to dedicate to God's service?*

**DEDICATION, FEAST OF.** An eight-day Jewish festival that commemorated the cleansing and rededication of the Temple (John 10:22). Today known as Hanukkah (HA noo kah) or the Feast of Lights. See the **Feast Chart** page 92 and the **Calendar Chart** pages 228 & 229. See **HANUKKAH.**

**DEED**. Action, work (Jer. 25:14; Acts 7:22). Deeds can be good or evil (John 3:19-21).

**DEEP, THE**. 1. The ocean, the Red Sea, the deepest part of the sea, another deep body of water (Gen. 7:11; Ex. 15:5,8; Neh 9:11; Luke 8:31). 2. Very deep place or abyss. The abyss is a bottomless or unfathomably deep place understood as the underworld or place of the dead (Ps. 88:6; Rom. 10:7).

**DEFILE**. Make unclean, especially in the religious or ethical sense (Dan. 1:8; Mark 7:15).

**DEFRAUD**. Cheat, oppress, deprive of, gyp (Lev. 19:13). To misrepresent by claiming to have more than you have or less than you have; to take or keep away by willful deceit or trickery (Acts 5:1-11). The Bible strictly forbids defrauding (Mark 10:19; 1 Thess. 4:6).
● *How has someone cheated you? How did it make you feel? When are you most tempted to cheat? What helps you to refuse to cheat?*

**DEFY**. Rebel against, deliberately disobey, openly resist, challenge someone or something considered impossible, invite to combat (Num. 23:7-8; 2 Sam. 23:9-10).

■ **DEITY**. God or a god.

**DELIVER**. 1. Rescue, free, cause to escape from evil, give safety or salvation, redeem, transfer or allow another to take (2 Kings 18:30; Acts 7:25). Frequently used to describe God's deliverance of His people from the power of sin, death, and Satan through Jesus Christ. Deliverance goes hand in hand with salvation and redemption (Matt. 6:13; Luke 4:18). See **REDEEM**. 2. Simply give or bring to (2 Kings 18:23).

**DELIVERER**. God Himself or human deliverers sent by God (Ex. 3:7-8; 2 Sam. 22:2-3; Rom. 11:26; Judg. 3:9,15).
The next of kin (*go'el*) served as deliverer by rescuing relatives from distress, slavery, suffering, oppression, and danger (OT).

**DEMAS** (DEE muhs). A fellow disciple with Paul at Rome who later deserted Paul (Col. 4:14; 2 Tim. 4:10; Philem. 24).

**DEMETRIUS** (dih MEE trih uhs). A Christian commended for his witness (3 John 12). Also, a silversmith in Ephesus who stirred up a riot against Paul (Acts 19:24-41).

**DEMONIAC** (NRSV). Someone possessed by a demon or demons (Matt. 8:28-33; Mark 5:15-16).

**DEMONS** (NASB). Evil spirits who oppose God and work against people (Matt. 4:24, 8:16; Luke 10:17).
▼ *Demon and devil are represented by different words in the Greek language (demon, Luke 4:33; devil, 4:2—NRSV). KJV translates both with the English word devil.*
● *Can you be demon possessed? Not if you live in the Spirit of Christ, because no*

*A Roman denarius.*

*demon was able to face Christ and stay (Mark 1:34).*

**DENARIUS** (NIV, NRSV). Roman silver coin which amounted to one day's wage in Jesus' time (Matt. 20:1-16; footnote, Mark 12:15). Equivalent to a Greek drachma. Translated *penny* in the KJV. See previous page.

**DENY**. 1. Reject, pretend not to know, decide not to believe, disown (Matt. 10:33; Luke 20:27). 2. Decide to give other things priority (Matt. 16:24). 3. Lie, withhold, keep back (Gen. 18:15; 1 Kings 20:7).

**DEPRAVITY** (NIV). Moral pollution that biases a person toward evil action and away from God (Rom. 1:29; 2 Pet. 2:19). Depravity comes as a result of human choice. Not in KJV.

**DEPTH, DEPTHS**. Deep places, lowest parts, depths of the sea, uttermost reaches (Ps. 130:1; Ex. 15:5; Rom. 8:39).

**DERBE** (DUR bih). City in the province of Galatia where Paul preached while beginning churches in that area (Acts 14:6,20; 16:1; 20:4).

**DERIDE**. Make fun of, ridicule, laugh at, turn up nose at (Hab. 1:10; Luke 16:14; 23:35).

**DERISION**. Scorn, ridicule, mocking, criticism (Ps. 79:4; Jer. 20:7).

**DESCEND**. Go down or come down (Gen. 28:12; Matt. 7:25; Luke 3:22).

**DESCENDANT** (NIV). One who comes from a parent or ancestor; child of, grandchild of, great grandchild of, and so on (Lev. 21:21; Luke 1:27; Rom. 11:1). KJV often uses "seed of" or "house of" rather than "descendant of." Jesus was a descendant of David (Matt. 1:1, NEB).

**DESIRE**. Want, long for, request, delight in, urgently seek after (1 Pet. 2:2; Ps. 37:4).

**DESOLATE**. Lonely, deserted, gloomy, separated from people, not occupied (Isa. 49:21; Jer. 33:12).

**DESPAIR**. Loss of hope. Feel there is no possible way out (Eccl. 2:20; 2 Cor. 4:8).

**DESPISE**. Detest, loathe, reject, scorn, look down upon (Prov. 1:7; Matt. 6:24; Heb. 12:2; 1 Tim. 4:12).
● *What does God want you to despise?*

**DESTITUTE**. In great need, naked, exposed, deprived of, lacking (Ps. 141:8; 1 Tim. 6:5).

**DETESTABLE**. Abominable, disgusting, arousing intense dislike (Deut. 7:26; Ezek. 5:11).

**DEUTERONOMY, BOOK OF**. Fourth book of the OT; means *second law*. Deuteronomy reviews and explains God's work with His people and encourages renewed commitment to God. This commitment is prompted by God's love and blessings. It is to be expressed through loyalty and obedience. Deuteronomy explains repeatedly that God's way is the way to true life (Deut. 30:19-20).

Deuteronomy was delivered by Moses shortly before he died. He commissioned Joshua as the next leader of God's people (Deut. 34:5-12). The book contains Moses' addresses to the people of Israel in Moab on the edge of the Promised Land (Canaan). Deuteronomy reviews the Ten Commandments, emphasizing the First Commandment. Deuteronomy was probably the "book of the law" found by Josiah and prompting widespread religious reform (2 Kings 22:1-23:28).

● *Many call Deuteronomy 6:4-5 the key words of Deuteronomy. How have you lived or betrayed these words in your life?*

**DEVICE**. Thought, meditation (Prov. 19:21; Acts 17:29).

**DEVIL**. Satan. Opponent to God (1 Cor. 10:20). Supernatural being who tries to take away people's happiness by blocking God's purposes. He does this mainly through temptation and deception. He is also called Beelzebub, the evil one, and Lucifer. The devil has superhuman power but can be resisted with God's help. His powers are limited to what God permits.

▼ *The devil was not created evil. Many believe that the devil is a rebellious angel (see Isa. 14:12-20; Ezek. 28:12-19; Luke 10:18). Second Peter 2:4 indicates that other angels, now called demons, rebelled with him. The devil does not live only in hell but also on earth (Rev. 12:12). He will be cast in hell on judgment day (Rev. 20:10).*

● *Though the devil cannot possess a Christian, he can influence one. Do you see the devil working in your life? If so, how? (See 1 John 1:6.)*

● *James 4:7 encourages you to resist the devil and submit to God. Why?*

**DIDYMUS** (DID ih muhs). Means *twin*. It is the Greek name for the apostle Thomas (John 11:16; 20:24; 21:2). Thomas is Aramaic for *twin*.

■ **DISCERN**. Be able to separate the things from God and the things not from God (Job 6:30; Ezek. 44:23). Distinguish between good and evil (1 Kings 3:9; Heb. 5:14). "Discerning of spirits" is the ability to tell whether one is speaking by the Holy Spirit or a false spirit (1 Cor. 12:10).

■ **DISCIPLE**. Learner, student, follower, apprentice. Implies acceptance of the teacher's teachings and imitation of his practices (Luke 6:40; Isa. 8:16). Jesus' followers were called disciples (Luke 22:39) as are all Christians (Luke 14:26-27; Acts 9:36). See **APOSTLE**.

▼ *The word* disciple *is used only in the four Gospels and Acts. After the disciples learned from Jesus, they were sent out as apostles (disciples sent on a mission).*

■ **DISCIPLESHIP**. The commitment to live as a disciple of Jesus Christ. Discipleship is a process that includes learning Bible truth, applying that Bible truth to everyday life, becoming like Christ, sharing Christianity with others, serving the church, and fulfilling the goals God has personally designed for each person (Matt. 28:19-20, NASB).

■ **DISCIPLINE**. God's teachings in the lives of His people: both formative and corrective (Job 36:10). In KJV the word *discipline* occurs only in Job 36:10, but the concept weaves through many passages in words such as "correction," "instruction," "chastisement," "reproof," and "nurture" (for example 2 Tim. 2:25; Eph. 6:4).

Discipline includes training and knowledge balanced with correction and punishment. Based in love and concern for our well-being, its purpose is our maturity and happiness (Ps. 94:12-13; Prov. 3:11-12).

| DISCIPLES OF JESUS | | | |
|---|---|---|---|
| **Matthew 10:2-4** | **Mark 3:16-19** | **Luke 6:13-16** | **Acts 1:13-14** |
| Simon Peter | Simon Peter | Simon Peter | Peter |
| Andrew | James son of Zebedee | Andrew | John |
| James son of Zebedee | John | James | James |
| John | Andrew | John | Andrew |
| Philip | Philip | Philip | Philip |
| Bartholomew | Bartholomew | Bartholomew | Thomas |
| Thomas | Matthew | Matthew | Bartholomew |
| Matthew the tax collector | Thomas | Thomas | Matthew |
| James son of Alphaeus | James son of Alphaeus | James son of Alphaeus | James son of Alphaeus |
| Thaddaeus | Thaddaeus | Simon who was called the Zealot | Simon the Zealot |
| Simon the Zealot | Simon the Zealot | Judas son of James (compare John 14:22) | Judas son of James |
| Judas Iscariot | Judas Iscariot | Judas Iscariot | (Judas Iscariot) Matthias (v. 26) |

▼ *Discipline may be self-imposed to learn a skill or body of knowledge. Bible reading, prayer, and service are often called the Christian's daily disciplines.*

● *What discipline could you choose to serve God more effectively? How do you think God is disciplining you now?*

**DISPENSATION.** Law or arrangement. The NT uses it in two ways. When referring to one in authority, it means a plan, specifically God's plan of salvation in Ephesians 1:10. When referring to one under authority, it means managing for the one in authority (1 Cor. 9:17; Eph. 3:2; Col. 1:25). Some Bible students use "dispensation" to refer to different periods of history.

**DISPERSE.** Scatter, spread, burst forth (Prov. 15:7; Ezek. 12:15; 2 Cor. 9:9).

**DISPERSION.** Scattering (Jer. 25:34; Acts 5:37). When capitalized, usually refers to the scattering of the Jews to many non-Jewish lands. The scattered Jewish people themselves were called the Diaspora. See **CAPTIVE, CAPTIVITY.**

**DIVERS.** Different kinds (Deut. 22:9; Prov. 20:23; Mark 1:34).

**DIVES** (DI vez). The name traditionally given the rich man in Jesus' parable about Lazarus and the rich man (Luke 16:19-31). The Bible does not name him.

**DIVINATION.** Practice of foreseeing or foretelling the future through such unreliable efforts and methods as astrology, reading omens, consulting with the dead, and casting lots (Deut. 18:10; Ezek. 21:21; Acts 16:16). Condemned except when God is the source of information about the future (Num. 22:7; Mic. 3:6-7; Ezek. 13:6-7; Zech. 10:2).

**DIVINE**. Adjective: Godly, godlike (2 Pet. 1:3-4; Heb. 9:1). Verb: To seek what to do from a religious or magic source other than God—obviously not a wise practice (Gen. 44:5,15; 1 Sam. 28:8).

■ **DIVORCE**. End of marriage. Contrary to God's ideal (Mark 10:4-9) but seemingly permitted if one is sexually unfaithful (Matt. 5:31-32) or if one deserts the other (1 Cor. 7:15). Old Testament guidelines recognized that the hardness of people's hearts led to divorce; therefore requirements and limitations for divorce were set (Deut. 24:1-4; compare Matt. 19:8). Jesus commanded married couples to work toward lifelong love and unity (Matt. 19:5-6).

■ **DOCTRINE**. Instruction, teaching about God and how to live for Him (Prov. 4:2). Doctrine affects words and actions (Titus 2:1; 1 Tim. 1:10). Jesus Himself was the best teacher of doctrine (Matt. 7:28; John 7:16-17).

**DOMINION**. Rule, power to rule, own, or control (Gen. 1:26; 37:8). Exercise lordship over (Rom. 6:9).

**DOOM** (NIV). Calamity, judgment (Deut. 32:35; Rev. 18:10).

**DOOR**. Entrance, opening (Gen. 6:16; Matt. 6:6). Often used in the NT as a name for Christ (John 10:1) or as an opportunity (Matt. 25:10; Acts 14:27; Col. 4:3).

**DOORKEEPER**. One who stays at the door to guard it or wait for someone (Mark 13:34, RSV). Doorkeepers served buildings, temples, and walled cities. Sometimes called a porter (2 Kings 7:10). This humble

task would be a joy for a believer in the house of the Lord (Ps. 84:10).

**DOORPOSTS**. Lintels, pieces that support the structure around a door and that the door fits into (Ezek. 41:6).

*Doorposts.*

**DORCAS** (DAWR kuhs). Means *gazelle* and is the Greek translation of Tabitha. Dorcas was a female disciple who did many good works in Jesus' name. After she had died, Peter prayed for her and called her name. She was restored to life (Acts 9:36-42).

**DOUBLE-MINDED**. Literally, two-souled. Uncertain, wavering, divided (Jas. 1:8; 4:8). The word implies instability, unsettledness, maybe deceitfulness.

**DOUBLE-TONGUED**. Literally, double-worded (1 Tim. 3:8). The word suggests insincerity, hypocrisy, or lack of integrity.

**DOUBT**. Lack of faith or belief (Matt. 14:31). Literally, to be without resource, to judge differently, or to stand divided (Acts 10:17; Mark 11:23; Matt. 28:17). In addition to doubting God, one may also doubt a person's actions or motives (Acts 25:20).

▼ *Doubt needs to be resolved. When Thomas doubted, he admitted it; Jesus gave evidence that satisfied his doubt (John 20:24-28).*

**DOVE.** Bird similar to a pigeon (Gen 8:8; Matt. 10:16). At Jesus' baptism, God's Spirit descended like a dove (Matt. 3:16; Mark 1:10; Luke 3:22; John 1:32). In Song of Solomon, *dove* was a term of affection, possibly because doves are loyal to their mates and gentle (2:14; 4:1). Doves were sold as items for a sacrificial offering (John 2:14).

**DOWRY.** Marriage present; the property, money, or servant that came with a bride for her husband in marriage (Gen. 30:20). Sometimes a dowry was a price paid by the suitor to parents of the bride (1 Sam. 18:25).

**DRACHMA.** Silver coin equivalent to a day's pay (Luke 15:8-9; see footnote). Equivalent to a Roman denarius. Translated "piece of silver" in KJV and "silver coin" in several other translations. *Drachma* is referenced in Bible footnotes but does not appear in KJV.

**DREAD.** Verb: Fear, be afraid (1 Chron. 22:13). Source of reverence (Isa. 8:13).

**DREAM.** Thought or experience while asleep (Gen. 20:3; Acts 2:17). God can communicate with His people through dreams (1 Kings 3:5; Ezek. 2:1; Matt. 1:20), but not all dreams are from God (Deut. 13:1-3). God gave some the ability to interpret dreams. Examples include Joseph (Gen. 40:5-23) and Daniel (Dan. 4:19-27). Most dreams simply derive from the experiences of the day (Eccl. 5:3).

**DRUNK, DRUNKENNESS.** Stupor caused by consumption of an alcoholic beverage (Gen. 9:21). Drunkenness was a major vice of Bible times, especially among the wealthy. Drunkenness is condemned in the Bible (Lev. 10:9; Eccl. 10:17; Gal. 5:21). Being filled with the Spirit is advocated instead (Eph. 5:18).

● *Why do people drink alcohol? How does God provide for those needs or wants in a way that helps instead of harms?*

**DULCIMER.** Musical instrument, perhaps like a bagpipe (Dan. 3:5,10,15).

**DULL.** Slow to understand, not paying attention, lazy, mentally sluggish (Heb. 5:11).

**DUMB.** Silent, voiceless, mute, cannot talk (Mark 7:37). In the KJV *dumb* does not mean stupid or unable to learn.

**DUNG.** Manure, excrement of humans and animals (Ezek. 4:15). There were rules about sanitary disposal of dung (Lev. 16:27). Dried dung was used for fuel, fertilizer, or sacrifice (Ezek 4:12,15; Luke 13:8; Ex. 29:14; Lev. 8:17). Also simply dirt or rubbish (Neh. 2:13; Phil. 3:8).

**DUNGHILL.** Place where manure was piled up to use as fertilizer (Isa. 25:10).

**DURST.** Past tense of *dare* (Esther 7:5; Luke 20:40).

**DUST.** Clay, earth, small bits of matter (Isa. 40:15; Mark 6:11). God formed people from dust, and their bodies will return to dust (Gen. 2:7; 3:19).

**DWELL.** Live, stay, make your home, settle among (Ps. 4:8; 2 Pet. 3:13). Christ dwells in Christians (Eph. 3:17).

● *How does Christ's dwelling in you affect your words? your actions? your attitudes?*

**EARNEST**. A down payment or pledge (Eph. 1:14).

**EARTH, EARTHLY**. Place people live, as opposed to heaven (John 3:12,31). Can include the people who live on the earth and their characteristics (2 Cor. 5:1). *Earthly* describes actions, attitudes, and ideas that are opposed to God or pertain to this life only (Jas. 3:15; Phil. 3:19). Including, but not limited to, physical things (such as revenge, jealousy, greed).

**EAST, MEN OF**. People of lands east of Palestine (Job 1:3). East was the place of the sunrise and a significant direction for the Hebrews (Num. 3:38).

**EAST WIND**. Refers to a hot, dry, dusty, destructive wind from the desert (Gen. 41:27; Isa. 27:8).

**EBEDMELECH** (EE bed-MEE lek). Ethiopian eunuch who served King Zedekiah and who helped Jeremiah escape from prison and death (Jer. 38:7-13; 39:16-18).

**EBENEZER** (EB uhn-EE zur). 1. A stone Samuel set up as a memorial of God's help in defeating the Philistines (1 Sam. 7:12). The word means *stone of help*. 2. Town of Ephraim where the Philistines were defeated by the Israelites (1 Sam. 5:1).

**ECCLESIASTES, BOOK OF**. Book in the OT emphasizing that life not centered in God is meaningless. The book reflects on the shortness, contradictions, and mysteries of human life.

Traditionally, the writer of Ecclesiastes is known as The Preacher. He repeatedly concludes that life is empty (Eccl. 1:2). However, he advises people to work hard, enjoy the gifts of God as much and as long as they can, and let nothing turn them away from faith in and obedience to God.

Though the book appears negative, it gives assurance that God is the source of hope that gets us through tough times. Perhaps the most popular passage from Ecclesiastes is "To every thing there is a season and a time to every purpose under the heaven . . . " (3:1-8).

**EDEN** (EE d'n). Place God created people and the place they first lived (Gen. 2:8ff.). Means *delight*.

**EDICT** (NIV). Official order (Esther 1:20; Heb. 11:23).

■ **EDIFY, EDIFICATION**. Build up, encourage, strengthen, unify (Eph. 4:12,29). Edification can come from other Christians, from the Holy Spirit, or from activities (Rom. 14:19; Acts 9:31; 1 Cor. 10:23). Its goal is wholeness in Jesus and harmony with other Christians.

● *How do your words and actions edify those you see daily?*

**EDOM** (EE duhm), **EDOMITES** (EE duhm ights). Isaac's older son, who was named Esau (Gen. 25:30). He was later renamed Edom, meaning red. As a young man, he sold his birthright to his twin brother Jacob for a pot of porridge. His descendants, the Edomites, became enemies of Israel (Deut. 23:7; 2 Kings 8:21-22; Isa. 34:5-8). See **ESAU**.

**EGYPT** (EE jipt). Land northeast of Africa, watered by the Nile River (Gen. 12:10). One of the oldest nations. Jacob's sons came to buy food in Egypt when their land was barren. Jacob's descendants later became slaves in Egypt, but God used Moses to lead them to freedom (Gen. 42:2; Ex. 3:9-10). Jesus' parents fled with Jesus to Egypt for safety (Matt. 2:13).

**ELAM** (EE luhm). At least six Bible per-

*View of Giza, Egypt, showing two of the three pyramids located near the sphinx.*

sons were named Elam. The most prominent was a son of Shem and grandson of Noah. This Elam gave his name to a land south of Assyria and east of Persia, which his descendants inhabited (Gen. 10:22). Also one of the earliest civilizations (Isa. 11:11; Acts 2:9).

**ELDER.** Older member of a family, tribe, or religious group (Gen. 27:42). Elders were respected because of wisdom and experience (Ex. 3:16; 1 Tim. 5:17). Some elders led well (Acts 20:17,32); others caused problems (Mark 7:3).

**ELEAZAR** (EL ih AY zur). Aaron's third son, who became a high priest (Ex. 6:23; Num. 3:32). The name means *God has helped*. Others were also called by this name, such as Abinadab's son who kept the ark of the Lord (1 Sam. 7:1).

**ELECTION.** Choosing, selection. God's sovereign decision to choose people to be

His own. It occurs in relationship to Christ (2 Pet. 1:10; Eph. 1:4-5,11). Election does not remove each person's freedom and responsibility to choose God in Christ as Lord and Savior.

**ELI**. A judge and high priest for Israel. Eli taught young Samuel (1 Sam. 1-4). Samuel came to live and serve with Eli at Shiloh following a vow made by Samuel's mother. Eli failed to discipline his own sons, and both they and he bore the consequences.

**ELI, ELI, LAMA SABACHTHANI** (EE ligh EE ligh Lah mah-sah bahk thah NEE). "My God, my God, why has thou forsaken me?" This Aramaic expression is a quote from Psalm 22:1. Jesus spoke it as He died on the cross (Matt. 27:46). Same as "Eloi, eloi, lama sabachthani" (Mark 15:34).

**ELIEZER** (el ih EE zur). Abraham's chief servant (Gen. 15:2; 24). Also, Moses' second son, whose name is a tribute of grati-

tude to God (Ex. 18:4). The name means God is help. Several other persons bore this name (1 Chron. 7:8; 15:24; 27:16; 2 Chron. 20:37; Ezra 8:16; 10:18,23,31; Luke 3:29).

**ELIJAH** (ih LIGH juh). A well-loved prophet of Israel who took a stand for God against false religious leaders and kings (1 Kings 17:1; 18; 21:17-29). He is best known for discrediting Baal and Baal's prophets on Mount Carmel and for hearing a still small voice (1 Kings 18; 19:12-13). Rather than dying, Elijah was taken up into heaven in a whirlwind (2 Kings 2:11). John the Baptist was sometimes referred to as Elijah. Elijah appeared to Jesus on the mount of transfiguration (NIV: Matt. 11:14; 17:3; compare Mal. 4:5).

The name Elijah means *Yahweh is God*. Elijah was succeeded by Elisha.

**ELISABETH** (ih LIZ uh beth). Wife of Zacharias and mother of John the Baptist.

*Elijah being taken up into heaven.*

She came from a priestly family and was a relative of Mary, the mother of Jesus (Luke 1:5-57). Her name means *God is my oath*.

**ELISHA** (ih LIGH shuh). Shaphat's son who became a disciple of and successor to Elijah (1 Kings 19:16-21). Elisha ministered to Elijah when he was worn out after confronting the prophets of Baal. Elisha performed miracles and ministered during the reigns of the Israelite kings Jehoram, Jehu, Jehoahaz, and Joash (2 Kings 2:12-13:20). The name Elisha means *God is salvation*.

**EMMANUEL** (ih MAN yoo el). Name for Jesus that means *God with us* (Isa. 7:14; Matt. 1:23). Also spelled Immanuel.

**EMMAUS** (eh MAY uhs). Village about seven miles from Jerusalem. Jesus walked with some followers from Jerusalem to Emmaus (Luke 24:13-35).

**ENCHANTMENT**. Use of any form of magic or charm, strictly forbidden in the Bible (Lev. 19:26). Whisper or secret (Eccl. 10:11).

**ENDURE**. Stay, remain, lodge, be firm, bear up under (Ps. 30:5; 2 Tim. 2:3).

**ENGEDI** (en GED ih). Town on the western shore of the Dead Sea (1 Sam. 23:29).

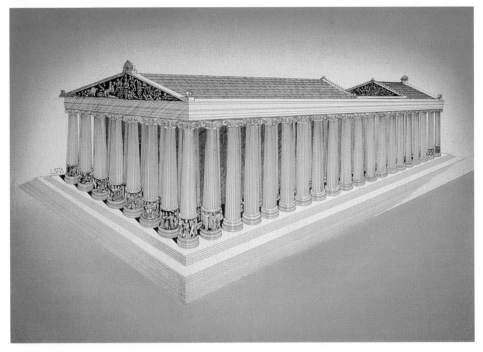

*Reconstruction of the Artemision, the great Temple of Artemis (Roman Diana) at Ephesus.*

**ENMITY**. Opposition, hatred (Gen. 3:15; Rom. 8:7; Eph. 2:15).

**ENOCH** (EE nuk). Eldest son of Cain (Gen. 4:17). He lived close to God and went to heaven without dying (Gen. 5:24; Heb. 11:5).

**ENSAMPLE**. Example, model (Phil. 3:17).

**ENTICE**. Bait, persuade (Jas. 1:14).

**ENTREAT, INTREAT**. Ask, desire (Ruth 1:16; Phil. 4:3). Treat (Jer. 15:11; Luke 20:11).

**ENVY**. Jealousy (Job 5:2; 1 Tim. 6:4).
● *You can't always stop envy from beginning, but you can stop it from continuing. How does God help you do this?*

**EPHAH**. Unit of dry measure equaling about fifteen cups or 3/5 bushel or twenty-two liters (Judg. 6:19).

**EPHESIANS, BOOK OF** (ih FEE zhuhns). This NT book is a letter from the apostle Paul to Christians in the city of Ephesus. Most scholars think it was a circular letter to Christians in other cities also. Paul was probably in prison in Rome while he wrote Ephesians, and the time may have been about A.D. 62.

Ephesians gives readers mountaintop views of Christ, His church, the Holy Spirit, salvation, and how to live the

*The Great Theater of Ephesus.*

Christian life. No wonder the book has been called the Alps of the NT. Ephesians explains that the church is composed of individual Christians, drawn from different backgrounds and nationalities, each redeemed by Jesus Christ. Jesus is the Head of this church and each member has a specific purpose.

▼ *Ephesians uses beautiful images of the church such as the body of Christ, the temple of God, and the bride of Christ.*

**EPHESUS** (EF uh suhs). Famous seaport city in Ionia. Ephesus was located at about the middle of the western coast of Asia Minor (Acts 18:19). Paul founded a church and preached for three years in Ephesus. Paul wrote the Bible book of Ephesians to the church at Ephesus (and to other churches in Asia Minor also).

▼ *The temple to the goddess Diana (also called Artemis) was in Ephesus. When people began converting to Christianity, those who profited from worship of the goddess became worried and started a riot (Acts 19:23-41).*

**EPHOD.** Short smock worn by priests and later by others (Lev. 8:7; 1 Sam. 2:18).

*The high priest's ephod.*

**EPHRAIM** (EE frah ihm). 1. Name of Joseph's second son (Gen. 42:50-52). 2. A tribe of Israel (Gen. 48; Josh. 16:5). 3. A name for Israel when its territory was almost all that was left of the Northern Kingdom (Hos. 5:3). 4. A forest (2 Sam. 18:6). 5. A gate of Jerusalem (2 Kings 14:13). 6. A town north of Jerusalem (John 11:54).

**EPICUREAN** (ep ih kyu REE uhn). Type of person usually thought of as believing "Eat, drink, and be merry; for tomorrow you may die" (see Acts 17:16-33). The name came from the Greek philosopher Epicurus (who lived 341-270 B.C.).

● *What is appealing about this philosophy? Besides being inaccurate, why is it dangerous?*

**EPISTLE**. Letter (2 Pet. 3:1). Bible books called epistles are letters that God inspired people to write to give instruction and encouragement to other Christians.

Examples: *Romans* is one of Paul's epistles and was written from Paul to the church at Rome. First, Second, and Third John are John's epistles and were written to individuals.
● *Read Colossians 3 from Paul's letter to the Christians at Colossae. Which instruction best fits your need?*

**EQUAL**. Upright (Ps. 17:2) or having the same value (Ps. 55:13; John 5:18). To be unequal is to be thin or weak (Prov. 26:7).

**ER** (UR). 1. Eldest son of Judah (Gen. 38:3). 2. A grandson of Judah (1 Chron. 4:21). 3. An ancestor of Jesus through Joseph (Luke 3:28).

**ESAU** (EE saw). Elder son of Isaac and Rebekah (Gen. 25:20-28). Isaac favored Esau, and Rebekah favored Esau's twin brother Jacob. Jacob talked Esau into selling his birthright (or blessing) to him for a pot of stew (Gen. 25:29-34). Rebekah later helped Jacob trick his father into giving Esau's birthright to Jacob (Gen. 27). Esau sought to kill Jacob for tricking him out of Isaac's blessing but was later reconciled to Jacob (Gen. 27; 32). Esau's descendants lived in the land of Edom (Gen. 36:8). See **EDOM**.

**ESCHATOLOGY**. The study of last things or the end time, particularly referring to the return of Christ (see Matt. 25; Mark 13; Rev. 22).

**ESPOUSE**. Engage to be married (Matt. 1:18). Much more binding than today's engagement. To end it required a divorce. To be espoused required faithfulness. Such couples sometimes called each other husband and wife. In keeping with God's good plan, sex was postponed until marriage (Gen. 29:20-23). See **BETROTHED**.

**ESTABLISH**. Strengthen, harden, confirm, make stable or strong, cause to dwell, make firm (Prov. 8:28; Ps. 78:69; Job 36:7; Heb. 13:9).

**ESTEEM**. Consider, value, judge, think of (Isa. 53:3-4; Phil. 2:3; Heb. 11:26).

**ESTHER** (ESS tur). Jewish cousin of Mordecai who became queen of Persia (Esth. 2:7). Using her position and great courage, she saved her Jewish people from destruction.

**ESTHER, BOOK OF**. Old Testament book about God's use of Queen Esther to save the Hebrew people. It explains the background and meaning of the Jewish festival of Purim, a feast that celebrates deliverance from a cruel and subtle anti-Jewish plot. The book of Esther does not mention the name of God but is obviously about the people committed to Him. See **PURIM, FEAST OF**.

**ESTRANGE, ESTRANGED**. Make unknown, become strange (Jer. 19:4; Ezek. 14:5).

■ **ETERNAL LIFE**. Life that begins the instant a person turns from sin in commitment and trust to Jesus Christ as Lord and Savior (John 3:16). It refers to supreme quality of life as well as unending life. Heaven is the ultimate home for Christians to enjoy eternal life in fellowship with God (Phil. 3:20).
● *How does eternal life affect your present decisions and actions?*

**ETHIOPIAN** (ee thih OH pih uhn). Descendant of Cush, a son of Ham. The people who occupied Ethiopia, a land in eastern Africa (Jer. 13:23). Ebedmelech and the man Philip told about Jesus were Ethiopians (Jer. 38:7; Acts 8:27).

■ **EUNUCH.** A male who is impotent because he lacks functioning sexual organs. The word refers to a male who is castrated or from birth lacks the ability to have sexual relations (2 Kings 9:32; Acts 8:27).

**EUPHRATES** (yoo FRAY teez). Great river whose name means *bursting* or *sweet*. Located in western Asia, it stretches from Armenia to the Persian Gulf. It is sometimes called the great river or simply, the river (Deut. 1:7; Isa. 7:20). Today called the Firat (in Turkey).

**EUTYCHUS** (YOO tih kuhs). Name that means *fortunate* (Acts 20:9). During one of Paul's long sermons, Eutychus fell asleep, fell off his window seat to the ground below, and died. Paul interrupted his preaching just long enough to revive Eutychus miraculously (Acts 20:7-12).
● *If you were Eutychus, would you have gone back to church? Why or why not?*

■ **EVANGELIST, EVANGELIZE.** A "good-newser." An evangelist announces the good news about Jesus Christ (2 Tim. 4:5). The verb form is usually translated as *preach the gospel* (Luke 1:19; Rom. 15:20-21; Gal. 3:8; Acts 21:8; Luke 9:6). Christians can evangelize in any place (Acts 8:4). Though all Christians can evangelize, the Holy Spirit especially endows some with the spiritual gift of evangelism (Eph. 4:11).
● *How and where do you share the good news about Jesus Christ?*

**EVE.** First woman (Gen. 1:27). Made by God from Adam's rib (Gen. 2:21-23). See **ADAM.**

**EVERLASTING LIFE.** Never ending life (Dan. 12:2; John 4:14). Life that lasts forever, continues, perpetuates. The opposite of dying. Also speaks of quality of life. See **ETERNAL LIFE.**
▼ *Everlasting also describes the covenant between people and God, the arms of God, God Himself, the kingdom of God, joy, and more (Gen. 9:16; Deut. 33:27; Ps. 41:13; 145:13; Isa. 51:11; Jer. 31:3).*

**EVIL.** Bad, wrong, worthless, vain (Ps. 23:4; Rom. 12:21). Any force, action, or attitude that works in opposition to God; anything not in harmony with God.
● *First Timothy 6:10 explains that the love of money is a root of all kinds of evil. Name several specific evils that grow from love of money.*

**EVIL ONE** (NIV). Satan, the devil (John 17:15; 1 John 3:12).

**EWE.** Female sheep (Lev. 14:10).

**EXALT.** Lift up, make high, raise high (Ex. 15:2; Matt. 23:12; Acts 5:31; 1 Pet. 5:6). To exalt God is to worship or praise Him.
● *Why is God worthy of exaltation?*

**EXAMPLE.** Sample, type, model, someone or something to be copied or learned from (1 Tim. 4:12). Can be positive or negative (1 Pet. 2:21; Jude 7). Jesus is our supreme positive example.

**EXCEEDING.** Beyond measure, abundant, more than usual, extreme, very strong (Gen. 13:13; Eph. 1:19).

**EXECRATION.** Oath, curse (Jer. 42:18; 44:12).

■ **EXHORT, EXHORTATION.** Encourage, comfort, or appeal to (Acts 27:22). Speak seriously to in order to prevent a

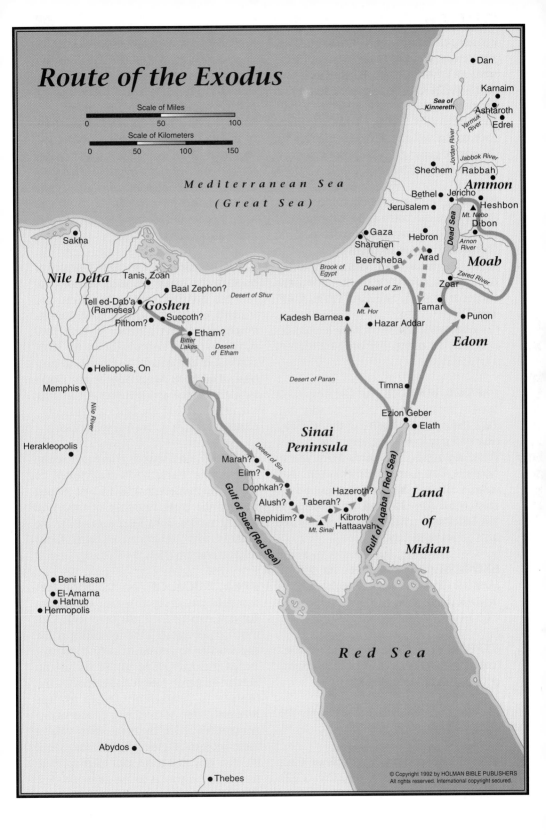

# Route of the Exodus

Scale of Miles

0   50   100

Scale of Kilometers

0   50   100   150

*M e d i t e r r a n e a n   S e a*
*( G r e a t   S e a )*

Sakha

**Nile Delta**

Tanis, Zoan

Baal Zephon?

Tell ed-Dab'a
(Rameses)

**Goshen**

Succoth?

Pithom?

Etham?

*Bitter*
*Lakes*

*Desert*
*of Etham*

Heliopolis, On

Memphis

*Nile River*

Herakleopolis

Marah?

Elim?

*Desert of Sin*

Dophkah?

Alush?

Taberah?

Rephidim?

*Mt. Sinai*

Kibroth
Hattaavah?

Hazeroth?

**Sinai
Peninsula**

*Gulf of Suez (Red Sea)*

*Gulf of Aqaba (Red Sea)*

Timna

Ezion Geber

Elath

**Land
of
Midian**

*Brook of
Egypt*

Kadesh Barnea

*Desert of Zin*

*Mt. Hor*

Hazar Addar

*Desert of Paran*

Gaza

Sharuhen

Beersheba

Arad

Hebron

Tamar

Zoar

Punon

**Moab**

**Edom**

*Zered River*

*Arnon
River*

Dibon

*Mt. Nebo*

Heshbon

**Dead Sea**

Jericho

Bethel

Jerusalem

Shechem

Rabbah

**Ammon**

*Jabbok River*

*Jordan River*

*Yarmuk
River*

Edrei

Ashtaroth

Karnaim

Dan

*Sea of
Kinnereth*

*Desert of Shur*

Beni Hasan

El-Amarna

Hatnub

Hermopolis

Abydos

Thebes

*R e d   S e a*

© Copyright 1992 by HOLMAN BIBLE PUBLISHERS
All rights reserved. International copyright secured.

dangerous action or to bring such an action to an end (1 Thess. 5:14). Bring the truth to light. Motivate to live God's way (Acts 14:22). Can be translated *admonish.* Remind of past knowledge or give new knowledge (Col 3:16). Warn, exert influence on the will and decision making with the goal of guiding a believer toward obeying God (Col. 1:28).

**EXILE.** The period when the Hebrews (Jews) were overcome and a large number of the people were taken from their homes and placed in captivity in foreign lands. The Exile often refers only to the Babylonian captivity of the Southern Kingdom (Judah). See **CAPTIVE, CAPTIVITY**.

Occasionally in the NT *exile* is used figuratively to mean life on earth (Heb. 11:13, RSV).

**EXODUS, BOOK OF.** An Old Testament book. Literally, a *going out* or *way out.* Tells about Moses' leading of the Israelites out of Egyptian captivity and to the Promised Land (over some forty years). Contains Ten Commandments (ch. 20), Israel's sin and Moses' intercession for them (chs. 32—33) and the building of the Tabernacle (chs. 35—40). See related map on previous page.

**EXORCIST.** One who drives out demons (Acts 19:13). Jesus has true authority over demons (Matt. 12:27-28; Mark 9:38; Acts 19:13-16).

**EXPEDIENT.** Beneficial, helpful, in one's interest, profitable. Literally *to bear together* (John 11:50; 1 Cor. 6:12).

**EXTOL.** Exalt, raise up, praise highly (Ps. 68:4).

**EYESERVICE.** Doing right to please those who are watching (Eph. 6:6; Col. 3:22). Service performed to attract attention, not service for its own sake or to please God or conscience.

**EZEKIEL** (ih ZEE kih uhl). Ezekiel was a priest who prophesied to the exiles as a fellow captive in Babylonia. He prophesied before the fall of Jerusalem that Jerusalem would be punished for its sin. After Jerusalem was destroyed in 587 B.C. Ezekiel spoke of hope and encouragement for the future restoration of Israel and more importantly of hope for the coming kingdom of God.

**EZEKIEL, BOOK OF.** Old Testament book in the major prophets section that records divinely inspired visions and insights of the prophet Ezekiel. Ezekiel emphasizes inner renewal of heart and spirit, personal responsibility for sins, renewal of the nation, and personal holiness. The book helps people see God's steady presence and involvement in daily events. Many find the Book of Ezekiel fascinating because of its vivid symbolism.

**EZRA** (EZ ruh). Jewish priest and scribe who came back from Babylonia to Jerusalem probably in 458 B.C. He helped restart the pure worship of God and taught God's laws (Ezra 7—10). He worked with Nehemiah to bring about religious reform (Neh. 8—10).

**EZRA, BOOK OF.** An OT book that describes the return of Jewish exiles from Babylon, where they had been held captive. Ezra documents the rebuilding of life and worship in Jerusalem. A first group of exiles, who returned under Cyrus the Persian emperor, rebuilt and dedicated the temple in Jerusalem. Other groups returned later, including a group under Artaxerxes II led by Ezra. Ezra helped them reorganize their religious and social life in a way that expressed their spiritual heritage. Ezra is a sequel to 1-2 Chronicles.

**FACE**. The front of a person; presence (Ps. 13:1). Often used in connection with emotions. Falling on one's face was a sign of reverence, respect, humility (Gen. 17:3; Rev. 7:11). Setting one's face was a sign of determination (Luke 9:53).

**FAINT**. Adjective: Weary, weak (Isa. 40:30). Verb: Give up (2 Cor. 4:16).

■ **FAITH**. Belief, trust (Hab. 2:4; Mark 11:22). Faith in Jesus Christ is essential for salvation (Eph. 2:8-10). Faith is always active: It is a commitment of both mind and heart.
● *List some ways faith in Jesus Christ helps you meet the pressures of every day.*

**FAITHFUL**. True (Prov. 20:6), steady (Acts 16:15).

**FAITHLESS**. Unbelieving (Matt. 17:17).

**FALL, FALLEN**. Stumble (Isa. 31:3; Rom. 11:11). The coming of sin into the world is sometimes referred to as the fall of humanity. Those who commit sin are sometimes called the fallen.

**FALLOW**. Type of deer (Deut. 14:5). Unplowed ground (Jer. 4:3).

**FALSE, FALSEHOOD**. Lie, untruth (Deut. 5:20; Mic. 2:11); emptiness (Lam. 2:14).

**FAMILY**. Household. In biblical times included parents and children and often in-laws and servants (Ex. 12:21). *Family* also referred to tribes or a nation (Jer. 2:4).

**FAMINE**. Lack of food brought on by drought, insects, war (Ruth 1:1; Luke 15:14). God sometimes used famine as a discipline for His unbelieving and disobedient people (Jer. 29:17). In Amos 8:11 lack of the Word of God—or of hearing the Word of God—is called a famine.

**FARE**. Noun: Peace, prosperity, completeness (1 Sam. 17:18). The Hebrew word used here is the greeting *Shalom*. Verb: To make merry (Luke 16:19).

**FAST**. Go without food or drink for a period of time (Jer. 36:9; Matt. 6:16). Fasting was done as a group or by individuals. Sometimes it was done for spiritual purposes, such as in connection with a religious observance (Joel 1:14) or to have a better relationship with God (Ezra 8:23). Fasting was also done as an expression of grief (2 Sam. 1:12). Jesus fasted for forty days and nights (Matt. 4:1-2).

**FATHER**. Male parent (Gen. 2:24). Founder (Gen. 17:4). God is our spiritual Father (Phil. 1:2).

**FATHOMS**. Length of outstretched arms, about six feet; used to measure the depth of water (Acts 27:28).

**FATLING**. An animal fattened for a special occasion such as an offering to God or a banquet (Ps. 66:15; Matt. 22:4).

**FAULT**. Error, sin, failure (Dan. 6:4; Gal. 6:1).

**FAVOR**. Grace, approval, kindness, good will (Esther 2:15; Luke 1:30; 2:52).

# JEWISH FEASTS AND FESTIVALS

| NAME | MONTH: DATE | REFERENCE | SIGNIFICANCE |
|---|---|---|---|
| Passover | Nisan (Mar./Apr.): 14-21 | Exod 12:2-20; Lev 23:5 | Commemorates God's deliverance of Israel out of Egypt. |
| Feast of Unleavened Bread | Nisan (Mar./Apr.): 15-21 | Lev 23:6-8 | Commemorates God's deliverance of Israel out of Egypt. Includes a Day of Firstfruits for the barley harvest. |
| Feast of Weeks, or Harvest (Pentecost) | Sivan (May/June): 6 (seven weeks after Passover) | Exod 23:16; 34:22; Lev 23:15-21 | Commemorates the giving of the law at Mount Sinai. Includes a Day of Firstfruits for the wheat harvest. |
| Feast of Trumpets (Rosh Hashanah) | Tishri (Sept./Oct.): 1 | Lev 23:23-25 Num 29:1-6 | Day of the blowing of the trumpets to signal the beginning of the civil new year. |
| Day of Atonement (Yom Kippur) | Tishri (Sept./Oct.): 10 | Lev 23:26-33; Exod 30:10 | On this day the high priest makes atonement for the nation's sin. Also a day of fasting. |
| Feast of Booths, or Tabernacles (Sukkot) | Tishri (Sept./Oct.): 15-21 | Lev 23:33-43; Num 29:12-39; Deut 16:13 | Commemorates the forty years of wilderness wandering. |
| Feast of Dedication, or Festival of Lights (Hanukkah) | Kislev (Nov./Dec.): 25-30, and Tebeth (Dec./Jan.): 1-2 | John 10:22 | Commemorates the purification of the temple by Judas Maccabaeus in 164 B.C. |
| Feast of Purim, or Esther | Adar (Feb./Mar.): 14 | Esth 9 | Commemorates the deliverance of the Jewish people in the days of Esther. |

**FEAR**. Reverence, respect, realization of holiness (Job 25:2; Luke 5:26; Acts 2:43). Not terror but honor and recognition of position. True religion includes fear of God (Prov. 1:7). See **AWE**.

**FEAST**. Festival, banquet, religious celebration (Dan. 5:1; John 12:20). The Hebrews established several feasts to celebrate God's intervention in history or His daily care. The Feast of Unleavened Bread or the Passover Feast celebrated God's deliverance from slavery in Egypt (Ex. 23:15). See **PASSOVER**. The Feast of Weeks was later called Pentecost (Deut. 16:16). See **WEEKS, FEAST OF**. The Feast of Tabernacles or Booths lasted seven days (Deut. 31:10). See **BOOTHS, FEAST OF**.

The Day of Blowing Trumpets was a memorial feast and a time of sacrificial offerings and rest from work (Num. 29:1). The Day of Atonement occurred once a year to make atonement for the peoples' sins (Lev. 16). See **ATONEMENT; ATONEMENT, DAY OF**. The sabbath was a time of solemn assembly, rest from work, and joy (Hos. 2:11). See **SABBATH**. The Feast of Purim was started during the time of Esther to celebrate God's deliverance of the Jews from their enemy (Esther 9). See **PURIM**.

**FELIX** (FEE liks). A cruel Roman governor of Judea who heard Paul's first trial in Caesarea and kept Paul in prison (Acts 23:24ff). Felix kept Paul jailed to please the Jews (Acts 24:27).

■ **FELLOWSHIP**. The family feeling and partnership between Christians (Gal. 2:9). Translates the Greek word *koinonia* (koy-know-KNEE-ah). Association, close relationship, participation with, sharing. You experience fellowship when you share life events, commitment, trust, and understanding with other Christians.

Fellowship expresses like-mindedness (Phil. 2:1), communicates acceptance (Gal. 2:9), helps believers grow (Acts 2:42), encourages the sharing of the work of the church (2 Cor. 8:4), and includes bad times as well as good (Phil. 3:10). The Bible points out the dangers of fellowshiping with wrongdoers (Ps. 94:20; Eph. 5:11), with unbelievers (2 Cor. 6:14), and with demons (1 Cor. 10:20). The person who lives in sin does not live in fellowship with God (1 John 1:6: NRSV).

● *What do you like best about being with other Christians?*

**FESTUS** (FESS tuhs). Governor of Judea following Felix. He conducted a trial of Paul and finally sent him to Rome (Acts 24:27—26:32).

**FETTERS**. Chains for the feet of prisoners (Ps. 149:8; Mark 5:4).

*Prisoner in fetters.*

**FIERY**. Burning, blazing (Dan. 3:6; Eph. 6:16). Shadrach, Meshach, and Abednego survived Nebuchadnezzar's fiery furnace with God's protection (Dan. 3).

**FIG, FIG TREE**. A fruit tree native to Asia Minor and Syria. A fig looks like a small pear but is brownish when ripe. Adam and Eve sewed fig leaves together to make clothing.

▼ *Jesus placed a curse on a fig tree that took up space and nourishment but bore no fruit (Mark 11:13).*

● *What lesson does the cursing of the fig tree imply for us?*

*A ripening fig.*

**FILLETS.** Fastenings, used for the hanging of curtains in the tabernacle (Ex. 27:10).

**FILTH.** Dirt, excrement (Isa. 4:4; 1 Pet. 3:21).

**FIRM.** Steadfast, sure (Heb. 3:6).

**FIRMAMENT.** Sky, expanse (Gen. 1:6).

**FIRSTBORN.** First child (Gen. 27:19; Matt. 1:25). In the Hebrew culture the firstborn son ranked in authority after the father. His inheritance was double that of any other sons.

**FIRSTFRUITS.** The first part of the harvest; used as a sacrifice offering to God (Neh. 10:35). Also used in the NT as a figure of speech to speak of Christ's resurrection as the first, with other Christians to follow in resurrection (1 Cor. 15:22-23). See the **Feast Chart** page 92 and the **Calendar Chart** pages 228 & 229.

**FIRSTLING.** Firstborn of an animal, used in the sacrificial system (Lev. 27:26).

**FISH GATE.** A gate on the east side of Jerusalem where Tyrians held a fish market (2 Chron. 33:14).

**FIT.** Ready (Lev. 16:21; Luke 9:62).

**FLAGON.** Large wine pitcher (Isa. 22:24); in some verses should be translated "a cake of raisins" (2 Sam. 6:19).

**FLATTER.** Compliment with a view to advantage or gain (Prov. 28:23). Make false statements to hide selfish aims (1 Thess. 2:5).
● *Do you ever use flattery to get your way with others? Why? Is there a better way?*

**FLEE.** To run away (Gen. 16:8; Matt. 2:13).

**FLESH, FLESHLY.** Besides the usual meaning of body tissue, the Bible often uses *flesh* to refer to anything worldly in contrast to anything spiritual or godly (Rom. 8:9). Also used to describe the sinful condition of humans (Rom. 8:3).

**FLINT.** Hard rock used for making tools and weapons (Deut. 8:15).

**FLOCK.** Herd or group of animals, usually sheep or goats (1 Sam. 30:20; Luke 2:8). Jesus used this term to describe His followers (Luke 12:32).

**FLOOD.** A deluge of water (Isa. 28:2; Matt. 7:25). God sent a great flood to destroy those who would not turn from sin. God spared the righteous Noah and his family who obeyed Him (Gen. 6—8).

**FOE.** Enemy (Ps. 27:2; Matt. 10:36).

**FOLD.** Fenced or hedged place for animals (Num. 32:16). Flock (John 10:16).

**FOLLOW.** To come after (Josh. 14:8; Mark 2:14). To be actively committed to a leader regardless of the cost (Luke 9:23).
● *Each person has the responsibility to choose whom or what he or she will follow: the ways of the world or the will of God. List the actions you carried out during your social activities this past week. How did these actions reflect the choice of followship?*

**FOLLY**. Foolishness, senselessness (Prov. 5:23; 2 Tim. 3:9).

**FOOL**. A person who is self-confident or thinks too highly of self, lacking in judgment, careless (Rom. 1:22; Prov. 12:23; Luke 12:20).

**FORBEAR**. To quit, neglect, or refrain (Deut. 23:22; Num. 9:13). To endure or put up with (Eph. 4:2).

▼ *Notice the almost opposite meaning of these words in the Old and New Testaments.*

**FORBEARANCE**. A holding back, delaying, pausing (Rom. 3:25).

**FORBID**. Restrain, hinder, prevent (Num. 11:28; Matt. 19:14).

**FORD**. A shallow area in a stream where people and animals can cross to the other side (Gen. 32:22).

**FOREFATHER(S)**. Ancestors (Jer. 11:10; 2 Tim. 1:3).

**FOREIGNERS**. Strangers, those from other nations (Deut. 15:3). The Israelites were warned not to marry those of other nations because those people worshiped other gods and would lead the Israelites away from God (Deut. 7:1-6). One who lives in a place that is not home and is away from relatives (Eph. 2:19).

**FOREKNOW, FOREKNOWLEDGE**. To know first or beforehand (Rom. 8:29). Also used to indicate that God knows everything: past, present, and future (1 Pet. 1:2).

**FORESKIN**. A fold of skin that covers the end of the penis (Gen 17:11). See **CIRCUMCISION**.

■ **FORGIVE, FORGIVENESS**. Pardon or excuse a wrong (Matt. 6:12,14-15). Cancel a debt. Give up claim for revenge or resentment. Reestablish a broken relationship. To forgive is to trust others as if the wrong is forgotten. It includes a new start in attitudes and actions (John 8:11).

● *How easy or difficult is it for you to forgive? To be forgiven? Forgiving others opens us to receive forgiveness from God. Jesus forgave sins (Mark 2:5) and encourages us to forgive each other the same way (Col. 3:13; Matt. 18:22-35).*

**FORM**. Verb: To bring forth, to give shape to (Gen. 2:7; Ps. 90:2). Noun: Appearance (2 Tim. 3:5).

■ **FORNICATION**. Sexual intercourse between two people who are not married to each other (1 Thess. 4:3-5). Sometimes translated *immorality*, the word can refer to sexual or sensual sins in general. Fornication is not a new sin. The OT records that many sinned this way, including King David (2 Sam. 11). Old Testament prostitutes practiced fornication in religious ceremonies. (Obviously this was condemned by God—Lev. 19:29.) In the NT fornication is included in several lists of sins (Rom. 1:29; Acts 15:29; Col. 3:5). Fornication hurts people (1 Cor. 6:18; 1 Thess. 4:6). The word is also used to picture unfaithfulness to God (Isa. 23:17; Jude 1:7; John 8:41).

▼ *Sex itself is not bad. Sexual expression of love within marriage is God's good plan. The Bible points to marriage as the way to enjoy sex and to avoid fornication (Prov. 5:18-19; 1 Cor. 7:2).*

● *Why is sex designed for marriage only? Why is sex outside of marriage so attractive even though it leads to pain?*

**FORSAKE**. Leave, let go, abandon (Deut. 31:6; Matt. 19:27).

**FORTH**. Forward, outside, out (Gen. 39:13; John 11:43).

**FORTRESS**. Fenced place, stronghold (Isa. 25:12). The psalmist spoke of God as his fortress (Ps. 18:2).

**FOUL**. Adjective: Unclean (Mark 9:25). Verb: To trample (Ezek. 34:18).

**FOUNDATION**. Base or support, anything laid down as beginning point on which to build (2 Chron. 23:5; Acts 16:26). In the NT often used in a spiritual sense (1 Cor. 3:11).

**FOWL**. Any type of bird or birds (Gen. 1:21; Matt. 6:26).

**FRAME**. Verb: Establish, form (Jer. 18:11; Heb. 11:3). Noun: A form (Ps. 103:14).

**FRANKINCENSE**. Substance made from tree resin. Used in OT religious ceremonies and presented as a gift from the wise men to Christ (Ex. 30:34; Matt. 2:11).

**FREE**. At liberty, not enslaved (Ex. 21:2; John 8:36; Rom. 6:18).

**FREEWILL OFFERING**. Voluntary offering (Lev. 22:18).

**FRO**. Back. Used with *to and* to mean back and forth (Gen. 8:7).

**FRONTLET**. Small box made of animal skin that contained Scripture passages (Deut. 6:8). Men strapped it to their foreheads during morning prayer except during sabbaths and festivals.
▼ *Scriptures contained were Exodus 13:1-16; Deuteronomy 6:4-9; 11:13-21.* See **PHYLACTERIES**.

**FROWARD**. Turned the wrong way, wicked, corrupt, perverse (Ps. 101:4; Prov. 2:15; 1 Pet. 2:18).

▼ *In the KJV, seventeen of the twenty-four uses of* froward *and* frowardness *are in Proverbs. As a preposition,* froward *is the opposite of* toward.

**FRUIT**. Besides the usual reference to food (Gen. 1:11), *fruit* is often used in a symbolic sense. It may refer to children as fruit of the womb (Ex. 21:22) or to good characteristics as fruit of the Spirit (Gal. 5:22).

**FRUSTRATE**. Cancel, put aside (Ezra 4:5; Gal. 2:21).

**FUGITIVE**. One who runs away (Gen. 4:14).

**FULFIL**. Complete the measure of, fill up, make full (1 Kings 2:27; Matt. 3:15).

**FULLNESS OF TIME**. The time when everything was just right (Gal. 4:4). Christ's birth occurred at the exact time God planned—when time was brim full. Rome ruled the world; there was a time of peace; Greek was the universal language; Roman-built roads allowed travel to all parts of the civilized world. People were in need of the Savior.

**FURNACE**. Different types of ovens used for baking bricks, pottery, bread, or smelting metals (Dan. 3:6). Sometimes used in connection with God's judgment (Matt. 13:42).
▼ *Daniel's three friends were thrown into a fiery furnace because they would not bow down to a pagan God (Dan. 3).*

**FURY**. Rage, violent anger (Nah. 1:6).

**FUTURE**. What lies ahead unseen. An opportunity to trust what God has done in the past to give us faith and hope in what He will do in the future (Jer. 31:17, NRSV).

# GALILEE, SEA OF

▼ *Galatians is often called "Little Romans" because Romans is a fuller development of the themes of Galatians.*

**GABRIEL** (GAY brih uhl). An angel of God who brought messages to people on earth (Dan. 9:21; Luke 1:19). Gabriel helped interpret Daniel's visions, announced the upcoming birth of John the Baptist to Zacharias, and foretold the birth of Jesus to Mary (Luke 1:5,11-38).

**GAD.** Seventh son of Jacob whose mother was Zilpah (Gen. 30:10-11). His descendants became the tribe of Gad, one of the twelve tribes of Israel. Also the name of a prophet during the time of King David (1 Sam. 22:5).

**GADARA, GADARENES** (GAD uh ruh; GAD uh reen). One of the ten cities of the Decapolis or its inhabitants, where Jesus healed a demon-possessed man (Mark 5:1-15).

**GALATIA** (guh LAY shuh). An ancient kingdom of Asia Minor that later became a Roman province (Acts 16:6). Paul established churches in the cities of this region on his first missionary journey. He later wrote a letter to the churches, which is the NT Book of Galatians.

**GALATIANS, BOOK OF** (guh LAY shuhns). This NT book is Paul's letter to the church at Galatia. He wrote the letter to combat the heresy of the Judaizers. The Judaizers believed that Gentiles had to be circumcised in addition to their commitment to Christ to be saved.

**GALILEE** (GAL ih lee). Small region in northern Palestine (Israel). In Galilee Jesus grew up, chose His disciples, and did much of His ministry (Matt. 3:13; 4:15,18,23,25; 21:11). Nazareth, Jesus' hometown, was part of Galilee. Galilee was rich agriculturally; its sea provided plentiful fish; and it was crossed by several major routes through the Roman empire. Though Galilee was mainly a Jewish region, Gentiles (non-Jews) and early Christians also lived there.

▼ *In the OT, Galilee was part of the land allocated to the twelve tribes of Israel and prophesied to be the home of the Messiah (Isa. 9:1-4; Matt. 4:14-15).*

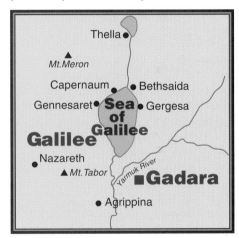

**GALILEE, SEA OF.** Heart-shaped freshwater body, more the size of a lake than a sea (Mark 1:16). Located about sixty miles north of Jerusalem, it was about thirteen miles long and eight miles at the widest point. Many of Jesus' ministries and miracles took place on or around this lake (Matt. 8:23-27; Mark 3:7-12; 6:35-56). On its shores were the towns of Capernaum, Bethsaida, Magdala, and Tiberias. The sea is prone to sudden dangerous storms because of the way the wind whips down nearby mountains (Mark 4:37).

*The Sea of Galilee as viewed from the northwest.*

▼ *Also called Tiberius, Gennesaret, and Chinnereth (Chinneroth, Cinneroth).*

**GALL.** A bitter thing (Job 20:14; Matt. 27:34). A bitter and poisonous plant. Bile, secretion of the gallbladder (Job 16:13).

**GAMALIEL** (guh MAY lih uhl). A leader in the OT tribe of Manasseh (Num. 7:54). Also, a NT Pharisee and teacher of the Law, who defended the apostles (Acts 5:34-40) and taught Paul (Acts 22:3).

**GARMENT.** Piece of clothing (2 Kings 5:22; Matt. 9:16).

**GARRISON.** A military station or stronghold (1 Sam. 14:1).

**GATE.** Door, entrance to houses, buildings, or cities (Gen. 19:1; Acts 3:10).

**GAZA** (GAY zuh). One of the five main Philistine cities, located southwest of Jerusalem on the seacoast (2 Kings 18:8; Acts 8:26).

**GEHENNA**—See **HADES, HELL**.

**GENEALOGY.** List of names of ancestors and descendants (2 Chron. 31:16; Titus 3:9). Jesus' ancestors are listed in Matthew 1:1-17 and Luke 3:23-38.

**GENERATION.** Descendants; people living at the same time (Gen. 6:9; Mark 8:12).

*Bedouin woman from the area of Gaza.*

**GENESIS, BOOK OF**. The first book in the Bible. Hebrew word meaning *beginning*. Genesis tells about the beginning of creation and the beginning of human disobedience to God. Genesis is the seedbed of doctrine for the NT. It tells familiar stories of flood, Tower of Babel, and patriarchs. See **GALILEE, SEA OF**.

▼ *The book of Genesis gets its name from the first words of the book, "In the beginning . . ." (Gen. 1:1).*

**GENNESARET, LAKE OF** (geh NESS uh ret). New Testament name for the Sea of Galilee (Luke 5:l). In OT, same as Sea of Chinnereth. See **GALILEE, SEA OF**.

**GENTILE** (JEN tighl). Literally, *nation*. The word refers to a person who is not a Jew (Rom. 9:24). Jewish Christians at first had trouble accepting Gentiles. However, they learned that Gentiles become a part of God's family just as Jews do: by accepting Jesus Christ as Savior and Lord (Gal. 3:14).

● *Are you a Jew or Gentile? How do you become a part of God's family?*

**GERGESENES** (GUR guh seens). Inhabitants of a district southeast of the Lake of Tiberias (Matt. 8:28).

**GETHSEMANE** (geth SEM uh nih). A place about a mile from Jerusalem at the Mount of Olives (Mark 14:32). Jesus prayed His prayer of agony here shortly before His crucifixion. See map on next page.

**GIANTS**. People who were strong, mighty, and of great stature (Deut. 2:20).

**GIDEON** (GID ih uhn). Son of Joash, called by God to free the Israelites from Midian (Judg. 6:13-14). God led him to accomplish this with only three hundred men. Gideon ruled the Israelites as a judge for forty years.

*Looking toward the Garden of Gethsemane with the Church of All Nations in the center of the photo.*

**GIFT**. Present, offering, favor (Dan. 2:6; 2 Cor. 9:15). In Romans 6:23 the gift of God is eternal life. The gift of the Holy Spirit comes with salvation (Acts 2:38).

▼ *Gifts are always free. Salvation is a gift from God that cannot be worked for; it comes only by trusting Jesus as Lord and Savior.*

■ **GIFTS, SPIRITUAL**. Abilities or powers given to an individual by God through the Holy Spirit (1 Cor. 7:7). Each person has at least one gift and the responsibility to use that gift (1 Pet. 4:11).

▼ *For listings of some spiritual gifts, see 1 Corinthians 12—13 and Romans 12.*
● *Write at least one spiritual gift you feel God has given you. How are you using this gift each week?*

**GILEAD** (GILL ih uhd). Wooded and hilly area east of the Jordan River (Gen. 37:25). Known for its medicinal balm and as a refuge for fugitives.

**GILGAL** (GILL gal). City located west of the Jordan River, not far from Jericho (Josh. 4:19). First camp of the Israelites after they crossed the Jordan River to claim the Promised Land.

**GIRD**. Put on an article of clothing such as a belt, or fasten with a belt (1 Sam. 17:39; Acts 12:8).

**GIRDLE**. Belt made of cloth or leather (2 Kings 1:8; Mark 1:6). Often same as loin-cloth or waistcloth.

**GLEAN**. Gather (Ruth 2:2). A Hebrew

*The rugged hill country of Gilead.*

law allowed the poor and strangers to gather grain or grapes left from a harvest (Lev. 19:9-10).

■ **GLORIFICATION**. Process of becoming pure or holy. Becoming all God

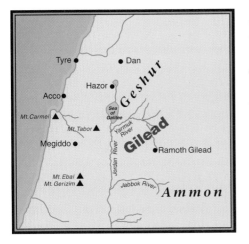

wants us to be. Completion of salvation when God exalts us after we die and go to heaven.

■ **GLORIFY**. Praise, worship (Ps. 86:9). Admire, point out the good in, recognize as glorious. A Christian's greatest calling is to glorify God through his or her actions, words, and character (Matt. 5:16). Christians glorify God by obeying Him and living His way. Specific examples include sexual purity (1 Cor. 6:20); choosing the right words (1 Pet. 4:11); living as a Christian (Rom. 15:6); imitating Jesus (John 17:10-11).

▼ *In the OT people glorified God (Lev. 10:3-4); God glorified His people (Isa. 60:7); and God glorified Himself (Ezek. 28:22; Isa. 44:23). In the NT Jesus' actions caused observers to glorify God (Matt. 9:8; 15:31), and God glorified Jesus (Heb. 5:5; Luke 4:15).*

● *With what actions and attitudes do you glorify God?*

■ **GLORY**. A divine quality (Acts 7:2; 1 Cor. 2:8; Jas. 2:1). Literaly, "heavy," "weighty." The brightness, splendor, and radiance of God's presence. God's visible revelation of Himself. Our word *doxology* comes from *doxa*, the Greek word for *glory*.

▼ *God has revealed Himself through His glory. God's glory was known by Moses, Ezekiel, and others in the OT, by the shepherds at the time of Jesus' birth in the NT, at the transfiguration, and will be seen by everyone when Jesus returns. Paul described God's glory as unapproachable light (1 Tim. 6:16). We will experience God's glory as part of our inheritance with Him (Eph. 1:18) and as a reward for present trials (1 Pet. 1:7; 5:4).*

*In the NT, Jesus demonstrated the personality, presence, and character of God. He made the glory of God forever visible (John 1:14; 2 Cor. 4:6). Jesus' presence in Christians enables them to reflect God's glory (Col. 1:27).*

● *How do you experience God's glory?*

**GLUTTON**. Excessive eater, hoggish person (Prov. 23:21; Matt. 11:19).

**GNASH**. Grinding of teeth together that expresses great emotional upheaval, such as rage or anguish (Lam. 2:16; Matt. 8:12).

**GNAT.** Tiny insect (Matt. 23:24).

▼ *Jesus chided religious leaders for strain-ing out gnats but swallowing camels.*

● *What does this say about your priorities and your values?*

**GNOSTICISM.** A know-it-all religion whose leader taught that salvation comes through a special or secret knowledge of God. Gnosticism taught that the body was either evil or did not matter. Gnostics expressed this belief in one of two ways: either by living a life of extreme self-denial or, in contrast, by self-indulgence. To the Gnostics, spirit was eternal and was what really mattered. (The word *gnosticism* is not in the Bible. Full-blown Gnosticism developed a hundred years later. Biblical writers argued against people holding ideas that later developed into Gnosticism.)

■ **GOD.** The Eternal One without begin-ning and without end (Ex. 3:14). The uncreated One who created everything and everyone (Gen. 1:1; John 1:1-3). He is One (Deut. 6:4-9); yet He reveals Himself to us as three in One: God the Father, God the Son, and God the Holy Spirit (Matt. 3:16-17). He is characterized by His creative work, the grace of His loving mercy, His intolerance of sin, His forgive-ness of people who turn from sin and trust Him, and His guidance for quality living (Gen. 1:31; Eph. 2:8-10; Rom. 6:22-25; 10:9-10; John 3:16; 10:10).

The way to come to know God the Father and God the Spirit is to come to know God the Son, who is Jesus Christ (John 14:15-20). God is all-powerful, all-knowing, all-present, and all-loving.

▼ *No definition of God is adequate, but perhaps a definition is helpful. See also* **FATHER, HOLY SPIRIT, JESUS, TRINI-TY.**

**NAMES FOR GOD** = The Bible uses many names for God and each one describes something about His character, abilities, or the way He relates to us. These first six are Hebrew words that are translated into English in your Bible. How does each one make a difference in your life?

**ELOHIM** = God, Majesty, Mightiness, Unchanging love (Gen. 1:1). The one who brought order out of chaos. This name describes the one True God. It stresses God's Almighty Mind and Creatorship. This name is used to describe God who wants a covenant rela-tionship with His people. Elohim is a plural form of a Hebrew word with a sin-gular meaning. It could also be used for idols and false gods.

**YHWH** = Often translated Lord; God's personal name (Ex. 3:14; Col. 1:15). God is both loving and righteous and must therefore judge evil. YHWH expresses God's moral and spiritual attributes of love, holiness, righteousness. (Notice YHWH has no vowels. The correct pro-nunciation is probably *Yahweh* rather than *Jehovah*.)

**EL SHADDAI** = God Almighty who is able to carry out His own will and pur-pose (Gen. 17:1; 2 Cor. 6:18). His strength is made perfect in our weak-ness. *El* is translated God and primarily means might or power. God gives or pours out Himself and His power for the sake of others.

**EL ELYON** = Most High God (Gen. 14:22; Rom. 3:29). El means *God* as in El Shaddai. Elyon refers to the special and distinct nature of God, that He is the highest God ruling all other heavenly beings and superior to all beings claiming to have divine power. Though God made us human beings like God in many ways, He and only He has the power to rule, possess, and be exalted above all other beings, powers, and elements of creation.

**ADONAI** = Lord (Gen. 15; Ps. 8:9; Acts 9:6). This term is distinct from YHWH (see above) and focuses on God's

| NAMES OF GOD | | | |
|---|---|---|---|
| **NAME** | **REFERENCE** | **MEANING** | **NIV EQUIVALENT** |
| HEBREW NAMES | | | |
| Adonai | Ps 2:4 | Lord, Master | Lord |
| El -Berith | Judg 9:46 | God of the Covenant | El -Berith |
| El Elyon | Gen 14:18-20 | Most High God/ Exalted One | God Most High |
| El Olam | Gen 21:33 | The Eternal God | The Eternal God |
| El Shaddai | Gen 17:1-2 | All Powerful God | God Almighty |
| Qedosh Yisra'el | Isa 1:4 | The Holy One of Israel | The Holy One of Israel |
| Shapat | Gen 18:25 | Judge/Ruler | Judge |
| Yahweh-jereh | Gen 22:14 | Yahweh Provides | The LORD Will Provide |
| Yahweh-seba'ot | 1 Sam 1:3 | Yahweh of Armies | LORD Almighty |
| Yahweh-shalom | Judg 6:24 | Yahweh Is Peace | The LORD Is Peace |
| Yahweh-tsidkenu | Jer 23:6 | Yahweh Our Righteousness | The LORD Our Righteousness |
| ARAMAIC NAMES | | | |
| Attiq yomin | Dan 7:9 | Ancient of Days | Ancient of Days |
| Illaya | Dan 7:25 | Most High | Most High |

personal relationship to us, He as Creator and us as created. It highlights the characteristics of both a master/slave (ownership) and a husband/wife (together forever) relationship. God takes care of our needs and is sufficient for us. When Israel came to believe the divine name YHWH was too holy to pronounce, they spoke the word *adonai* whenever they read YHWH. They inserted the vowels of *adonai* into the text to remind them to say Adonai. The combination of the consonants of YHWH and the vowels of Adonai produced the word *Jehovah*, a word the Jews never said.

**EL OLAM** = Everlasting God or God of the Age who reveals Himself to persons (Heb. 1:1). He works in time to help us understand Him, how to serve Him, how to act as His people.

● *The above Hebrew names are translated into God, Lord, or other English words. The following are English descriptions of God. What do you like about each?*
**I AM** = (Ex. 3:14).
**ABBA** = Daddy (Mark 14:36; Rom. 8:15).
**LOVE** (1 John 4:8).
**THE LIVING GOD** (Matt. 16:16).
**FATHER, SON, AND HOLY GHOST** (Matt. 28:19).

**GODS**. Any persons or things that are objects of worship (Ex. 20:23; Acts 19:26). People have always struggled with the pull toward worship of false gods (idolatry). There is only one true God.

● *Name some gods youth have today.*

■ **GOD'S WILL**. The design and desire of God for all of His creation (Matt. 6:10; Mark 3:35).

▼ Scholars view God's will from different perspectives: (1) God has a will that will be done because He is God and controls eternity and creation. (2) God has a will that He allows to be frustrated because He chooses to give freedom of choice to mankind. (3) When a person chooses against God's will, God does not give up on that person; He wills what is the best considering the circumstances.

**GOLGOTHA** (GAHL guh thuh). Hebrew word for **skull**. The spot near Jerusalem where Jesus was crucified (Matt. 27:33; Mark 15:22; John 19:17.) Same as Calvary (Luke 23:33).

▼ *No one today knows the precise location of Golgatha or whether it was a hill.*

**GOLIATH** (guh LIGH uhth). A Philistine warrior over nine feet tall, killed by David with a slingshot and stone (1 Sam. 17).

**GOMORRAH** (guh MAWR uh). One of the five cities of the plain in the vicinity of the Dead Sea. When God announced He was going to destroy the city because of the people's sin, Abraham begged God to change His mind. God agreed if a minimum number of righteous people could be found. When they could not, the unrepentant people were not spared. Only Lot's family escaped the destruction (Gen. 19).

▼ *Sodom and Gomorrah have become symbols for wickedness and destruction.*

**GOOD**. Pleasant, joyful, agreeable, admirable, worthy (Gen. 1:31; Matt. 7:11). God alone is morally perfect and is our example of goodness (Matt. 19:17). We please God when we try to follow His example of goodness.

▼ *Although living a good life and doing good works are pleasing to God, this does not bring salvation. Only repentance and trust in Jesus Christ can accomplish this.*

**GOPHER WOOD**. Wood, probably similar to cypress; used in the building of Noah's ark (Gen. 6:14).

**GOSHEN** (GO shuhn). An area in Egypt assigned to Joseph's family by Pharaoh (Gen. 47:6). The Hebrews lived there until the time of the Exodus.

**GOSPEL**. Good news (Mark 1:14). Christian message about the life and sacrificial death of Jesus Christ that brings salvation to all who believe. The first four books of the New Testament which tell about Jesus are referred to as the Gospels.

*The fertile land of Goshen in the delta country of northern Egypt.*

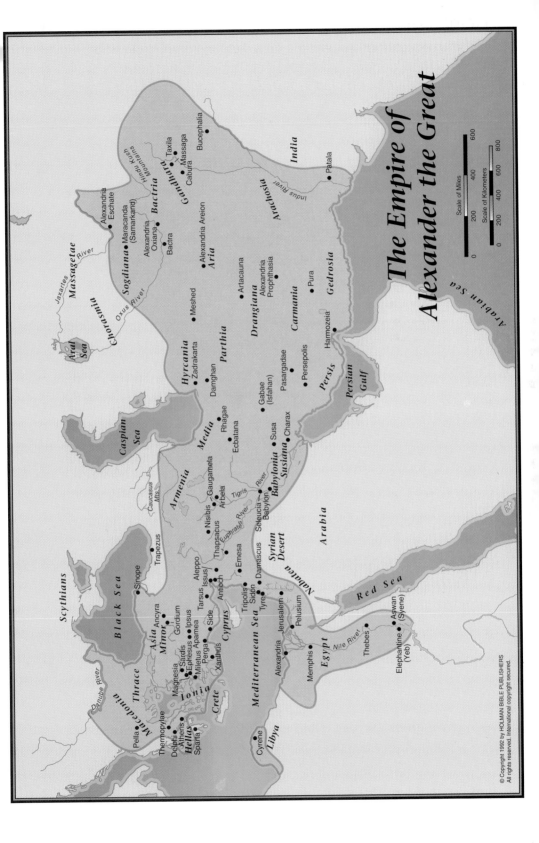

# The Empire of Alexander the Great

Scythians

Black Sea

Caspian Sea

Aral Sea

Massagetae

Jaxartes River

Chorasmia

Sogdiana

Alexandria Eschate

Maracanda (Samarkand)

Oxus River

Alexandria Oxiana

Bactria

Bactra

Hindu Kush Mountains

Gandhara

Taxila

Massaga

Cabura

Bucephalia

India

Patala

Indus River

Arachosia

Alexandria Areion

Aria

Artacauna

Alexandria Prophthasia

Drangiana

Carmania

Pura

Gedrosia

Harmozeia

Meshed

Hyrcania

Zadrakarta

Parthia

Damghan

Rhagae

Media

Ecbatana

Gabae (Isfahan)

Pasargadae

Persepolis

Persis

Persian Gulf

Arabian Sea

Caucasus Mts.

Armenia

Gaugamela

Arbela

Nisibis

Thapsacus

Tigris River

Euphrates River

Seleucia

Babylon

Babylonia

Susa

Susiana

Charax

Emesa

Damascus

Syrian Desert

Arabia

Nabatea

Red Sea

Trapezus

Sinope

Aleppo

Issus

Antioch

Tarsus

Tripolis

Sidon

Tyre

Jerusalem

Pelusium

Egypt

Nile River

Aswan (Syene)

Elephantine (Yeb)

Thebes

Memphis

Alexandria

Cyprus

Mediterranean Sea

Asia Minor

Ancyra

Gordium

Ipsus

Sardis

Magnesia

Ephesus

Apamea

Miletus

Perga

Side

Xanthus

Ionia

Crete

Libya

Cyrene

Hellas

Sparta

Athens

Delphi

Thermopylae

Macedonia

Pella

Thrace

Danube River

Scale of Miles

0   200   400   600

Scale of Kilometers

0   200   400   600   800

## THE GREEK ALPHABET

| | | | | | | | | |
|---|---|---|---|---|---|---|---|---|
| A | α | alpha | I | ι | iota | P | ρ | rho |
| B | β | beta | K | κ | kappa | Σ | σ,ς | sigma |
| Γ | γ | gamma | Λ | λ | lambda | T | τ | tau |
| Δ | δ | delta | M | μ | mu | Υ | υ | upsilon |
| E | ε | epsilon | N | ν | nu | Φ | φ | phi |
| Z | ζ | zeta | Ξ | ξ | xi | X | χ | chi |
| H | η | eta | O | ο | omicron | Ψ | ψ | psi |
| Θ | θ | theta | Π | π | pi | Ω | ω | omega |

**GOVERNMENT.** Rule, power (Isa. 9:6; 2 Pet. 2:10). The Old Testament world saw a variety of authority structures and figures: heads of families; theocracy (rule of God); kings. In New Testament times Rome ruled the known world.

**GOVERNOR.** A ruler of an area, who was under the authority of another ruler—such as a king (Gen. 42:6; Luke 2:2). Joseph served as governor under Pharaoh; Pontius Pilate and Felix were governors in the New Testament.

■ **GRACE.** Favor (Gen. 6:8). God's free and undeserved love that never quits (Eph. 2:8). Grace is the gift of God that comes as eternal life through Jesus Christ our Lord (Rom. 6:23).

**GRANT.** Give (Ps. 85:7; Rev. 3:21).

**GRAVE.** Burial place (Gen. 50:5; John 12:17). Burial practices were similar in the Old and New Testaments. Often the deceased were buried in a family tomb. Graves were in the ground, natural caves, or cut out caves. Sometimes graves were marked with stones or pillars.

**GRECIAN.** See **HELLENISTS.**

**GREEK.** Language spoken in Greece and made international, political, and cultural language by Alexander the Great. A complex language capable of expressing nuances of meaning. Language of philosophers, such as Plato and Aristotle and poets like Homer. The NT was written in Greek. Pilate had "Jesus of Nazareth the King of the Jews" inscribed on the cross in Hebrew, Greek, and Latin (John 19:19-20).

**GROPE.** To feel or search (Job 12:25).

**GROW.** Increase and mature-physically, mentally, and spiritually (Gen. 21:20; Luke 2:40). Christians are to grow in their spiritual lives (2 Pet. 3:18).

**GUILTY.** Responsible for a crime, delinquency, or sin (Lev. 6:4; 1 Cor. 11:27).
▼ *Guilt may be a condition or a feeling. True guilt occurs when we disobey God's will-a real condition whether we feel guilty or not. False guilt occurs when we're OK with God but feel guilty and shouldn't.*

**HABAKKUK** (huh BAK uhk). Prophet of Judah about 720 B.C. responsible for the Book of Habakkuk. His name apparently means *to embrace*. He lived and prophesied at the same time as Jeremiah. He spoke to people who had seen prosperous and free times change to disastrous and oppressive times.

**HABAKKUK, BOOK OF** (huh BAK uhk). Old Testament book containing dialogs with God, prophecies, and poetry from prophet. Habakkuk asked God why bad people seem to win and why good people suffer. God answered that evil eventually destroys people who do it, but the just shall live by faith (2:4). The rest of the book celebrates God's faithfulness in every circumstance.

**HABITATION**. Place to live, stopping or resting place, fixed place (Ps. 89:14; Eph. 2:22).

**HADES** (HAY deez). Place or state of the dead. The word *hades* does not appear in the KJV but in other translations (see Matt. 16:18, NIV).

▼ *The Greek word* hades *appears eleven times in the Greek NT and is translated ten times with the word* hell *in the KJV (Matt. 11:23; 16:18; Luke 10:15; 16:23; Acts 2:27,31; Rev. 1:18; 6:8; 20:13-14). In 1 Corinthians 15:55,* hades *is translated* grave *in the KJV. All other KJV usages of* hell *translate* sheol

*in the OT and* gehenna *in the NT. See* Hell.

**HAGAR** (HAY gahr). Sarah's maid who became the mother of Ishmael by Abraham (Gen. 16:1-16). Hagar's pregnancy was a source of animosity between Hagar and Sarah because Sarah hadn't been able to have children. Sarah later drove Hagar away, and God took care of Hagar and Ishmael (Gen. 21:1-21).

▼ *It was common OT practice to have children by a wife's maid. Abraham had a child by Hagar to replace the one God had promised but Sarah had not yet borne. The division caused by Ishmael's conception and birth continued for generations. This illustrates the danger of not waiting for God to fulfil His promises His way. See* **CONCUBINE.**

**HAGGAI** (HAG ay igh). Prophet in Jerusalem who encouraged returning Jewish exiles to rebuild God's Temple. He prophesied about 520 B.C. and was a contemporary of Zechariah. His name means *festive.*

**HAGGAI, BOOK OF**. An OT book written by the prophet of the same name. Contains God's messages through Haggai after the Israelite people returned from exile. They had rebuilt their community but not the Temple. Haggai asked God's question, "Why should you be living in well-built houses while my Temple lies in ruins?" (1:4, GNB). The people then rebuilt the Temple.

**HAIL**. 1. Rejoice, be of good cheer (Isa. 32:19; Matt. 28:9). 2. Balls of ice that fall like rain from the sky (Ex. 9:23).

**HALF TRIBE**. Term used in OT referring to parts of the tribe of Manasseh (Josh. 12:6). Manasseh's tribe was divided into two half tribes because after Moses defeated Sihon of Heshbon and Og of Bashan, half of the tribe requested permission to settle east of the Jordan (Num. 32). This group is usually called the half tribe. It settled along with the children of Reuben and Gad. The other half of the tribe settled in on the west side of the Jordan.

**HALLELUJAH** (NIV). Praise God! (Rev. 19:1-6). "Alleluia" in KJV. Hebrew combination of divine name Jah, short for Yahweh, and *hallel*, to praise.
● *What causes you to say or shout, "Hallelujah?*

**HALLOWED.** Set apart, separated from ordinary things (Ex. 20:11; Matt. 6:9).
● *Christians hallow God's name when they call positive attention to Him through their attitudes, actions, and words. How do you hallow God's name?*

**HAMAN** (HAY muhn). Prime minister of King Ahasuerus (Xerxes). Haman plotted to destroy all the Jews in the Persian empire because Mordecai, a Jew, would not bow to him (Esther 3:2.) Queen Esther, herself a Jew, foiled his plot. Haman was hanged on the gallows he had constructed for the Jews.

**HANANIAH** (han uh NIGH uh). Friend of Daniel. He was renamed Shadrach. He ate healthy food and entered the fiery furnace (Dan. 1:6,15; 3:16-29).

**HANDMAID.** Female slave or servant (Gen. 29:24; Luke 1:38).

**HANNAH** (HAN uh). Samuel's mother who prayed for his conception and birth and then dedicated him to God's work (1 Sam. 1:2-11). She was the wife of Elkanah.

**HANUKKAH.** Modern day transliteration of the Hebrew word for the eight day religious festival that commemorates the cleansing and rededication of the Temple following the victories of Judas Maccabeus in 167-165 BC. Same as the Feast of Dedication or Feast of Lights. John 10:22 mentions the feast of Dedication. See the **Feast Chart** page 92.

**HARAN** (HAY ran). The most prominent Haran was the third son of Terah and youngest brother of Abram (Abraham). Haran was the father of Lot and also had two daughters (Gen. 11:26-28). Haran is also the place to which Abram and his family moved from Ur of the Chaldees (Gen. 11:31). There were other persons and places by that name.

**HARD BY.** Close to (Lev. 3:9).

**HARDHEARTED.** To be hardhearted is to close oneself off from God (Ezek. 3:7).

**HARDEN.** Besides the usual meaning, to turn proudly away from God (2 Kings 17:14).

**HARLOT.** Prostitute; one who has sexual relations for pay or possibly as a pagan religious duty (Judg. 16:1). Also used figuratively to describe unfaithfulness to God (Hos. 4:15). Both are strictly forbidden by God.
● *Which harlotry do you think is more common-unfaithfulness to a spouse or unfaithfulness to God?*

**HAST.** Old form of *have* meaning "you (singular) have" (Job 33:32).

**HASTE.** Hurry, speed (Ex. 12:11; Luke 1:39).

**HAUGHTY.** Arrogant, proud (Ezek. 16:50).

**HEAL.** Repair, make thoroughly sound or whole (Ex. 15:26; Matt. 4:23).
● *What physical, emotional, or spiritual sickness do you want God to heal in you?*

**HEAP.** Pile upon, add, press together (Prov. 25:22; 2 Tim. 4:3).

**HEAR**. Besides physical hearing, also means to listen, pay attention, and respond obediently (Ps. 135:17; Isa. 41:17; Matt. 13:43).

**HEARKEN**. Listen carefully, be attentive, give ear, obey an authority (Isa. 28:23; Acts 27:21).

**HEART**. In addition to the usual meaning, the Hebrews believed the heart was the place of thought, will, and decision (Gen. 6:5; Acts 1:24). Hebrews referred to the heart when we would say *mind* or *brain* (1 Kings 3:9; Rom. 1:21). Without God, the heart is wicked and selfish (Jer. 17:9).
● *How would God describe your heart?*

**HEARTH**. Stove, firepan, burning (Jer. 36:22; Zech. 12:6; Ps. 102:3).

**HEATHEN**. A person who is not a Jew (Neh. 5:17; Ps. 47:8; Gal. 2:9). Also a person who does not know or obey the true God (2 Kings 17:15; Matt. 6:7).

■ **HEAVEN**. 1. Place of perfect happiness. A Christian's home after death. Though heaven is indescribable in human terms, we know these facts about heaven: (1) Christians will be with God. (2) There will be no more tears, death, sorrow, or pain (Rev. 21:4). (3) We will have new bodies and new experiences (1 Cor. 15:35-57; 2 Cor. 5:1-10). 2. The physical heaven in which God placed the sun, stars, and moon (Gen. 1:1; 22:17).
▼ *God is not limited to heaven; He exists on earth also (Deut. 4:39).*
● *What do you think heaven will be like?*

**HEBREW** (HEE broo). Abraham or a descendant of Abraham; same as an Israelite or Jew (Gen. 14:13). Also, the language in which the OT is written (except for some Aramaic). The language is written from right to left. Hebrew is a colorful language dominated by verbs. Its alphabet has twenty-two letters, four of which have alternate styles. In Bible times Hebrew writing indicated only consonants. Later, small vowel points were added above and/or below the letters to indicate vowels.

**HEBREWS, BOOK OF**. New Testament book written to Christians who were in danger of abandoning the Christian faith. They were tempted to give in to persecution or to return to the lure of old beliefs. The key word of the book is *better*. The writer knew that the Christian life was far better than any alternatives. We don't know who the divinely inspired writer was, but he showed

**HEBREW ALPHABET**

Khaph　Kaph　Yod　Teth　Heth　Zayin　Vav　He　Daleth　Gimel　Veth　Beth　Aleph

Tav　Sin　Shin　Resh　Koph　Tsadi　Feh　Peh　Ayin　Samekh　Nun　Mem　Lamed

Jesus as the true and final revelation of God: the eternal Son of God superior to all prophets and angels, an eternal Priest superior to all priests, and the only provider of true salvation. Hebrews encourages readers to face opposition with God's power by confidently standing on His truth. It emphasizes the uniqueness of Christianity.

**HEBRON** (HEE bruhn). 1. A city nineteen miles southwest of Jerusalem. Abraham lived there and was buried nearby (Gen. 13:18; 25:9). It was David's first capital city (2 Sam. 2:11). 2. A son of Kohath (Ex. 6:18); 3. A town in Asher; 4. A relative of Caleb (1 Chron. 2:42).

**HEED.** Give careful attention, observe, watch, be warned against (Jer. 18:19; Matt. 16:6; 1 Tim. 1:4).

**HEIFER.** Young cow (Gen. 15:9; Hos. 10:11).

**HEIR.** One who inherits another's possessions or position (Gen. 15:3; Rom. 8:17). Christians are heirs of the kingdom of God with its security and blessings, both present and future.

■ **HELL.** Place and condition of eternal punishment for those who reject Jesus Christ as Lord and Savior (Deut. 32:22; Matt. 5:22,29-30; 10:28; 16:18). Words related to *hell* include *gehenna*, *hades*, and *Sheol*.

**HELLENISTS** (hehl lih NIHST) (NRSV). People who spoke Greek and came under Grecian culture-especially Jewish people in the NT who spoke Greek. *Grecian* in KJV and *Grecian Jew* in NIV (Acts 6:1; 9:29).

**HELMET.** Head protection worn during battle (1 Sam. 17:5). Figurative for salvation (Eph. 6:17).

**HEMORRHAGE** (NASB). Uncontrolled bleeding (Mark 5:25).

**HENCE.** From this place (Gen. 37:17; Matt. 17:20); after this time (Acts 1:5).

**HENCEFORTH, HENCEFORWARD.** From this time on (Num. 15:23; John 15:15)

**HERALD.** One who shouts an important message (Dan. 3:4).

**HERB.** Tender grass, grain, or green plant; not necessarily limited to the plants we call herbs today (Isa. 66:14); also a cultivated garden plant (Luke 11:42).
▼ *Bitter herbs were eaten with a lamb during the Passover Feast to symbolize the bitter experiences of the Hebrews in Egypt before the Exodus (Ex. 12:8). The exact herbs are unknown, but Jews use horseradish today. See **PASSOVER***

**HEREAFTER.** After this, from now on (Isa. 41:23; Rev. 4:1). May refer to our life in heaven or simply the future (Mark 11:14).

**HERITAGE.** Inheritance, that received from parents or ancestors (Ex. 6:8; Ps. 16:5-6; 1 Pet. 5:3). May be spiritual or material.

**HEROD** (HAIR uhd). A line of Judaean kings who were evil. 1. Herod the Great was king of Judea when Jesus was born. Herod killed many baby boys in an attempt to locate and kill Jesus (Matt. 2:1-22). He lived from 47 B.C. to 2 A.D. 2. Herod Antipas had John the Baptist beheaded and led one of Jesus' trials (Mark 6:17-28). His two brothers ruled the other parts of the kingdom. 3. Herod Agrippa I had James killed and planned to execute Peter (Acts 12:1-3). He died in A.D. 44. 4. Paul appeared before Herod Agrippa II (Acts 26:28). See the **King Chart** page 141.

*Excavations of Herod's Palace at Jerusalem.*

**HERODIANS** (hih ROH dih uhn). A political Jewish party that opposed Jesus and supported the Herods. They wanted to be ruled by the Herods rather than by Rome (Mark 3:6).

*King Hezekiah's tunnel which brought water from the Spring of Gihon to the pool of Siloam.*

**HERODIAS** (hih ROH dih uhs). Granddaughter of Herod the Great and daughter of Aristobulus. She married her uncle Herod Philip but left him for his brother Herod Antipas. She told her daughter to demand the head of John the Baptist who had rightfully opposed Herodias' marriage to Herod (Mark 6:17-27).

**HESHBON** (HESH bahn). Levitical city twenty miles east of Jordan (Num. 21:25; Josh. 21:39). Originally belonging to Moab, Heshbon was conquered by Israel

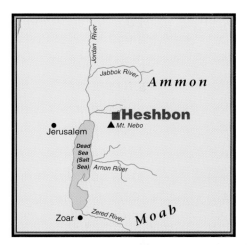

*The rock-cut altars of the high place at Petra in southern Jordan.*

who gave it to Reuben and then Gad. Heshbon means *stronghold*.

**HEW**. Cut, dig, cut out, cut down (Deut. 19:5; Mark 15:46).

**HEZEKIAH** (hez ih KIGH uh). Son and successor of Ahaz as the thirteenth king of Judah (2 Kings 16:20; 18—20). Hezekiah means *Yahweh has strengthened*. Hezekiah was a great religious reformer and a good king (2 Chron. 29-32; Isa. 36-39). See the **King Chart** page 141.

**HIGH PLACES**. Places of worship on high ground, which were often associated with immorality and human sacrifice (Num. 33:52). God commanded the Israelites to destroy all the high places, but they did not. Later they used the high places to worship Baal. Occasionally, God's people worshiped Him on high places (1 Kings 3:2). God judged the kings of Israel and Judah on the basis of whether or not they destroyed the high places.

**HIGH PRIEST**. The highest religious position among the Hebrews (2 Chron. 24:11; Matt. 26:3). The high priest supervised other priests and performed special ceremonies such as going into the most holy place in the temple to make a sacrifice for the sins of the people. This happened once a year. Only the high priest could enter this holy place (Lev. 16). Jesus is our true High Priest (Heb. 2:17). See **HOLY OF HOLIES, TEMPLE, AARON.**

**HILKIAH** (hil KIGH uh). Several Hilkiahs are mentioned in the Bible. The two most notable are: 1. A High priest during Josiah's reign as king of Judah who found the book of the Law and sent it to Josiah (2 Kings 22:4; 2 Chron. 34:14). 2. A priest who stood by Ezra while Ezra read the book of the Law to the people (Neh. 8:4).

**HIN**. Liquid unit of measure equaling about 3.66 liters or one gallon (Ex. 30:24). See **Weights and Measures Chart** pages 244 & 245.

**HINDER**. Adjective: Behind, last, rear (Zech 14:8). Verb: Delay, keep back, withhold, injure, interrupt (Gen. 24:56; Neh. 4:8; 1 Thess. 2:18).

**HINNOM** (HIN ahm). A valley where human sacrifices were burned, located on land owned by the son of Hinnom (2 Chron. 33:6). It was associated with the worship of Molech. After Josiah put an end to the sacrifices, the site was used to burn corpses and garbage and came to be used as a synonym for *hell* providing *gehenna* as a name for hell since the Hebrew *ge'hinnom* or Valley of Hinnom was translated into Greek as *Gehenna*. See **HADES, HELL.**

**HIRAM** (HIGH ruhm). 1. King of Tyre who was friendly with both King David and King Solomon. He sent logs of cedar and cypress for Solomon's building pro-

jects (1 Kings 5:8). 2. Brass worker and architect from Tyre who worked on Solomon's Temple (1 Kings 7:13). See **King Chart** page 142.

**HIRE.** Besides the usual sense, can mean *to bribe* (Ezek 16:33).

**HISS.** Scoff (1 Kings 9:8), to catch one's breath in amazement or derision.

**HITHER.** Here (Gen. 15:16; John 4:15).

**HITHERTO.** From then, from that time, until now (2 Sam. 15:34; John 16:24).

**HITTITE** (HIT tight). Descendant of Ham through Heth who was the second son of Canaan. The Hittites were a powerful people who inhabited the mountains of Judah. Some lived among the Israelites (Gen. 15:20; 2 Sam. 11:6). Original Hittites con-

*The Hinnom (or Gehenna) Valley in Jerusalem, just south of the ancient city.*

*The King's Gate at the Hittite city of Hattusas in Asia Minor (modern Turkey).*

trolled empire centered in Hattushah in Asia Minor from about 1780 until 1270 B.C.

■ **HOLY.** Persons, places, or things set apart for use by God (Deut. 7:6). All holiness originates with God, and all Christians are called to live a holy life-a life like God wants you to live (Lev. 21:8; Acts 3:12; 1 Thess. 3:13-4:1; 1 Pet. 2:9).
● *How are your life, your words, your personality holy?*

**HOLY GHOST.** Frequent KJV translation of *Holy Spirit* (Matt. 1:18).

**HOLY OF HOLIES.** The innermost part of the tabernacle or Temple (Ex. 26:34). Only the high priest could enter, and he could enter only once a year. There he made a sacrifice for the sins of the people. Inside the holy of holies was the ark of the covenant, a small wooden structure covered with gold; it contained the Ten Commandments, a pot of manna, and Aaron's rod

(Ex. 25). See **MOST HOLY PLACE** and the **ORACLE**.

■ **HOLY SPIRIT.** God's Spirit. Lives within all Christians to help them, communicate God's truth to them, convict them of sin, convince them that God's ways are right, and comfort them when they are sad (John 15:26; 16:7-8,13-15). Also called the Holy Ghost, the Comforter, the Counselor, the Helper.

God sent the Holy Spirit to guide us after Jesus left earth (John 14:16-17). The Holy Spirit gives gifts and godly characteristics called fruit of the Spirit (Rom. 12:4-13; 1 Cor. 12-13; Gal. 5:22-23) to each Christian.
▼ *God the Father, God the Son, and God the Holy Spirit complete God's expression of Himself (Matt. 28:19). See* **GOD, TRINITY.**
● *How is your life different because the Holy Spirit lives in you?*

**HOMER.** A dry measure equaling ten ephahs, about six bushels, or about 220 liters (Hos. 3:2). See **Weights and Measures** pages 244 & 245.

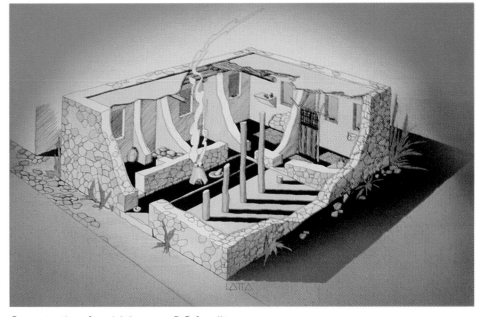

*Reconstruction of an eighth-century B.C. Israelite house, showing rooms for sleeping on straw mats and for storage. The outer courtyard was used for food preparation, cooking, and to house small animals. Construction of houses did not change much over the centuries until the New Testament period. So, this was a typical pattern for the average home of the Old Testament period.*

**HONOR**. Noun: Respect, reverence, greatness, value, dignity given or received (1 Chron. 16:27). God is most worthy of honor (1 Tim. 1:17). He has given honor to each person (Ps. 8:5). Persons lose their honor when they disobey God.
Verb: Value, show respect for, esteem, cherish. We are to honor God and persons to whom honor is due (Prov. 3:9; Rom 12:10).
● *God has commanded us to honor our father and mother (Ex. 20:12). Why would God ask this of you?*

**HOMOSEXUAL**. One whose sexual preference is with the same sex (1 Cor. 6:9, NIV). Homosexuality is against the will of God (see Rom. 1-2).

■ **HOPE**. Belief that God will accomplish what He has promised (Ps. 71:5; Eph.

2:12). Christian hope is based on the fact that God has always been faithful to do what He said He would do. In the NT, Christian hope is never wishful thinking; it is a divine certainty. It points to resurrection (1 Cor. 15).

**HOREB** (HOH reb). Hebrew name meaning "drought, desert"; alternate name for Sinai, "the mountain of God" (Ex. 3:1; 1 Kings 19:8).

**HOSANNA**. Help or save, I pray (Ps. 118:25; Matt. 21:9-15).

**HOSEA** (hoh ZAY uh). Old Testament prophet about 750 B.C. The name means *salvation*. Hosea's preaching produced the Book of Hosea. His personal experience with an unfaithful wife matched that of the nation of Israel in its unfaithfulness to God (Hos. 1-14).

**HOSEA, BOOK OF**. An OT book of the prophet Hosea's sermons from about 750 B.C. The sermons reflect the unfaithfulness of Israel to God and of Hosea's wife to Hosea. The book offers hope of restoration after repentance. It shows God's devoted love for his people (Hos. 11:1-9).

**HOST**. Army (Josh. 5:14; 1 Sam. 17:45); huge number (Gen. 2:1; Jer. 33:22); one who shows hospitality (Luke 10:35). The "host of heaven" in 1 Kings 22:19 is a group of heavenly beings who work with and for God. They are not to be worshiped (Deut. 4:19).

**HOUSE**. Family, family line, household (Josh. 24:15; Jer. 21:12; John 4:53); place to live (Ezra 1:2; Mark 1:29). People lived in caves, tents, or houses made of limestone, clay, straw, and other materials. Sometimes animals lived downstairs, and the people upstairs. The more wealthy built houses with open courtyards or other elaborate features. See the house **illustrations** that follow.

**HUMANS**. See **MAN**.

■ **HUMILITY**. Freedom from pride (Prov. 18:12; Matt. 11:29, NIV). A humble per-

son has the right view of God, self, and others (2 Chron. 7:14; Luke 18:14; Jas. 4:6). Humility is not weakness but a strong quality, praised in the Bible and commanded for all Christians (Prov. 15:33; Jas. 4:10). Humility shows trust in God (1 Pet. 5:6).

● *How does humility strengthen relationships? What fears do you have about being humble?*

**HYPOCRITE**. Pretender, a play actor (Matt. 6:2,5,16). One whose walk and talk do not match. A person who doesn't possess what he professes and doesn't do what he says.

● *Tell about someone who has rejected Jesus Christ because of the way a Christian has acted. What impressions of Jesus do people get from watching you?*

*What's the difference between a hypocrite and a Christian who makes a mistake?*

**HYSSOP**. A small, bushy plant used in religious ceremonies and in relieving pain (Ex. 12:22; John 19:29).

*Cut-away reconstrucion of a first-century A.D. Israelite house.*

**IDOL.** Image of a god (Ex. 20:3-4).

● *We often think of idols as statues. Anything that takes God's place can be an idol. What do youth idolize today?*

**IDOLATRY.** Putting anything in the place of God or putting anything ahead of God (Ex. 20:4-6). Idols are usually things, but they can be people (Ex. 32:1-8; 1 Cor. 10:14). Wanting another's possessions is a form of idolatry (Col. 3:5).

**I AM.** Name that God used to refer to Himself: "I AM THAT I AM" (Ex. 3:14). Compare Jesus' expressions in John's Gospel (8:24,58; 18:5).

**ICONIUM** (igh KOH nih uhm). City in Galatia, Asia Minor, presently Turkey (Acts 13:51). Paul preached in Iconium on his missionary journeys.

**IDLE.** Lazy, unprofitable (Ex. 5:17; Matt. 20:3).

*Probable Hittite idols, one of gold and the other of stone, found at Bogaskoy.*

● *Who or what has first place in your life?*

**IMAGE.** Likeness (Gen. 1:26; 2 Cor. 3:18). God created us to be like Him-able to think, feel, and decide. When we sin, this image is not destroyed; but it is marred. Christ is the perfect *image of God* (2 Cor. 4:4), and God is molding us back into that perfect image (Rom. 8:28-30).

**IMMANUEL** (ih MAN yoo el). "God is with us" (Isa. 7:14; Matt. 1:23). In the OT this name was announced to Ahaz as God's deliverer from the enemies. In the NT it is the name applied to the coming Messiah, Jesus. Also spelled Emmanuel.

**IMMORTALITY.** Living forever, life after death (1 Cor. 15:53- 54; 2 Tim. 1:10). A Christian is promised eternal life through personal faith in Jesus Christ (Rom. 6:23). Eternal life is not simply existence but a quality relationship with God and other Christians. People are not immortal. We die. God then raises the dead to eternal life or immortality.

**IMPART.** To give a share or portion to (Job 39:17; Rom. 1:11).

**IMPORTUNITY.** Persistence, shameless pleading (Luke 11:8).

**IMPUTE.** Count, assign to the account of another (Ps. 32:2; Rom. 4:8).

■ **INCARNATION.** Literally, *in flesh.* Technical theological term used to describe God's taking on human flesh and living as a person on earth. Christ became human and took an earthly body but still kept the perfectness of His divine and sinless nature (John 1:14; Phil. 2:5-8).

**INCENSE.** Perfume (Ex. 30:1; Luke 1:9). Sweet-smelling spices burned as an offering in worship. Used as symbols to acknowledge God's presence or prayers going up to God (Ps. 141:2). See **CENSER.**

▼ *The recipe for incense was specified in Exodus 30:34-37.*

*Incense bowl from the island of Malta.*

*Incense altar from the site of ancient Hazor.*

**INCLINE.** Stretch out, turn toward (Ps. 119:36).

**INCREASE.** Noun: Fruit, produce (Lev. 26:4). Verb: To grow, multiply (Pro. 1:5; Acts 6:7).

**INDIGNATION.** Anger (Ps. 69:24; Rev. 14:10).

■ **INERRANT.** Free from error or mistake. A confession used to describe the Bible as the work of the perfect God.

**INFIRMITY.** Sickness, disease, weakness (Prov. 18:14; John 5:5).

**INHABITANT.** Someone who dwells or lives in a place (Gen. 19:25; Rev. 17:2).

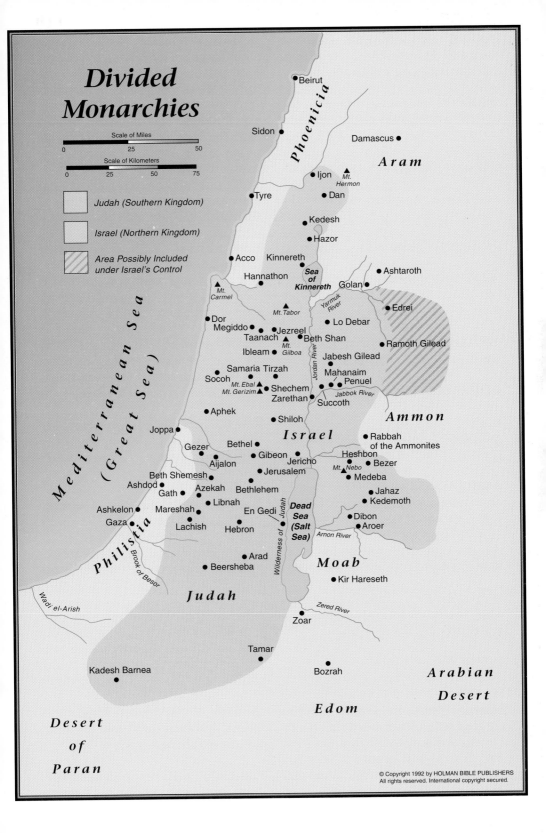

# Divided Monarchies

Scale of Miles

0     25     50

Scale of Kilometers

0     25     50     75

Judah (Southern Kingdom)

Israel (Northern Kingdom)

Area Possibly Included under Israel's Control

*Mediterranean Sea (Great Sea)*

*Phoenicia*

*Aram*

• Beirut

Sidon •

Damascus •

• Ijon   ▲ Mt. Hermon

• Tyre   • Dan

• Kedesh

• Hazor

• Acco   Kinnereth

Hannathon •   *Sea of Kinnereth*   Golan •

• Ashtaroth

▲ Mt. Carmel

▲ Mt. Tabor

*Yarmuk River*

• Edrei

• Dor   • Lo Debar

Megiddo •

Taanach •   • Jezreel   Beth Shan •

Ibleam •   ▲ Mt. Gilboa

• Ramoth Gilead

Jabesh Gilead •

Samaria • Tirzah •   Mahanaim •

Socoh •   Mt. Ebal ▲   • Penuel

Mt. Gerizim ▲   • Shechem

Zarethan •   *Jabbok River*

Succoth •

*Jordan River*

• Aphek   • Shiloh

*Israel*

*Ammon*

Joppa •

Gezer •   Bethel •

Aijalon •   • Gibeon

Beth Shemesh •   • Jericho

Ashdod •   Azekah •   • Jerusalem

Gath •   Bethlehem •

Ashkelon •   • Libnah

Gaza •   Mareshah •

Lachish •   En Gedi •

Hebron •

• Rabbah of the Ammonites

Heshbon •

Mt. ▲ Nebo   • Bezer

• Medeba

• Jahaz

• Kedemoth

• Dibon

• Aroer

*Dead Sea (Salt Sea)*

*Arnon River*

*Wilderness of Judah*

*Philistia*

*Brook of Besor*

*Wadi el-Arish*

• Arad

• Beersheba

*Judah*

*Moab*

• Kir Hareseth

Zoar •

*Zered River*

• Tamar

Kadesh Barnea •

• Bozrah

*Edom*

*Arabian Desert*

*Desert of Paran*

**INHERIT, INHERITANCE.** To possess (Gen. 15:7; Luke 10:25). To receive something from an ancestor (Deut. 21:16).

**INIQUITY.** Sin, wrong, corruption, lawlessness, wickedness, the opposite of what is right (Ps. 25:11; Luke 13:27; 2 Thess. 2:7).
● *What iniquity do you have in your life?*

**INJUSTICE.** A wrong, an injury (Job 16:17).

**INNOCENT.** Guiltless (Matt. 27:4).

**INSPIRATION.** Breath, God-breathed (Job 32:8; 2 Tim. 3:16). God inspired people to write the Scriptures.

**INSTRUCT.** Discipline, train, teach, nurture (Deut. 4:36; 2 Tim. 2:25).

**INSURRECTION.** Rebellion, uprising (Ezra 4:19; Mark 15:7).

**INTEGRITY.** Innocence, blamelessness (Ps. 26:1).

■ **INTERCESSION.** Praying or pleading on someone else's behalf (Isa. 53:12; Heb. 7:25). An intercessor serves as a go-between. Jesus and the Holy Spirit intercede for Christians (Rom. 8:26-27,34). Christians are to intercede for one another (1 Tim. 2:1).
● *How could your prayer help someone else? What do you think about Jesus interceding for you?*

**INTEREST.** See **USURY**.

**ISAIAH** (i ZAY uh). Old Testament prophet of Judah. He prophesied during the reign of four kings. He began his ministry the year King Uzziah died about 740 B.C. (Isa. 6:1). He continued until 701 B.C. or slightly later. See **King Chart** page 141.

**ISAIAH, BOOK OF.** God's messages about Judah and Jerusalem as revealed to Isaiah are recorded in this OT book. Isaiah is called a major prophet book because of its length. Isaiah focuses on sincere religion that shows itself in action not lip service. The Book calls God's people to use power to help rather than harass those weaker than you.

The first thirty-nine chapters of Isaiah emphasize the importance of obeying God, no matter what other people choose to do. As recorded in chapters 40-55, many people of Judah were held captive in Babylon. Isaiah gave the people hope that God would work in history to set them free and give them a mission. These chapters include beloved descriptions of Jesus, the "Servant of the Lord" (see example in Isa. 53). In chapters 56-66, the people of Judah were back home but needed assurance that God would fulfill His promises. Isaiah emphasizes the importance of righteousness, justice toward others, sabbath observance, and prayer.
▼ *Jesus used Isaiah 61:1-2 to express His calling.*

**ISHMAEL** (ISH may el). Son of Abraham by Hagar, Sarah's maid (Gen. 16:15). He was forced to leave home because of Sarah's jealousy and desire to have her own son, Isaac, receive the inheritance (Gen. 21).

**ISRAEL** (IZ ray el). The new name given to Jacob, which means *ruling with God* (Gen. 32:28). Israel had twelve sons whose descendants became the twelve tribes. The tribes were collectively known as the nation Israel. Israel later became the name of the Northern Kingdom. In the NT, *Israel* was a term used to refer to the true and obedient people of God.

**ISRAELITE.** A Hebrew, a descendant of Abraham; same as a Jew (Rom. 11:1).

**JAMES, BOOK OF.** New Testament book. Probably written by the half-brother of Jesus between A.D. 40 and 60. The book, written to Christians, focuses on matching beliefs with actions.
● *How would the world be different if we all lived by James 1:22-26?*

**JAPHETH** (JAY feth). One of the sons of Noah (Gen. 5:32). He and his wife were among the eight survivors of the great Flood.

**JAVELIN.** Spear (1 Sam. 18:10).

**JEALOUS.** Intolerant of rivalry or unfaithfulness (Ex. 20:5); zealous or ardent. God declared Himself to be a jealous God demanding the faithfulness of His people.
● *How is God's jealousy different from and similar to human jealousy?*

**JEBUSITE** (JEB yoo sight). A tribe of Canaanite people who lived in and around Jerusalem (Judg. 1:21).

**JEHOIACHIN** (jih HOY uh kin). Son of King Jehoiakim (2 Kings 24:6). At his father's death, Jehoiachin was eighteen and became king of Judah. His evil reign lasted only three months. See the **King Chart** page 141.

**JEHOIADA** (jih HOY uh duh). 1. High priest at the Temple in Jerusalem and active in political affairs (2 Kings 11:4). He and his wife rescued the child Joash from being murdered and hid him six years. When Joash was finally placed on the throne, Jehoida helped him rule until Joash became older. 2. The father of one of David's officers (2 Sam. 8:18). 3. Priest in the time of Jeremiah (Jer. 29:25-26).

**JEHOIAKIM** (jih HOY uh kim). Son of Josiah and king of Judah 609-598 B.C. (2 Kings 23:34-36). His evil reign of eleven years was marked by heavy taxation, reli-

**JACOB** (JAY kuhb). Name means *who schemes to take the place of another* (Gen. 25:26). Jacob later became Israel (see **ISRAEL**). Son of Isaac and Rebekah. He had a twin brother Esau whom he tricked and defrauded out of his birthright (the father's blessing to the oldest son). He ran away to escape his brother's anger but was later reconciled to him. He married sisters, Leah and Rachel, and fathered twelve sons, the ancestors of Israel's twelve tribes.
● *How may Jacob's family situation be similar to and different from yours?*

**JAIRUS** (JIGH ruhs). He was a ruler of a synagogue (Mark 5:22). Jesus brought his daughter back to life.

**JAMES** (JAYMZ). 1. Son of Zebedee and brother of John (Matt. 4:21). He and his brother were fishermen called to follow Jesus. James became one of the twelve apostles. 2. Son of Alphaeus and one of the twelve apostles (Matt. 10:3). 3. Half brother of Jesus, probably the author of the Book of James (Matt. 13:55). He rejected Jesus' earthly ministry but later believed and became a leader in the church at Jerusalem. 4. James the Little or James the Less, also translated as James the Younger (Mark 15:40) may be the son of Alphaeus. 5. Brother (KJV) or Son (Modern translations) of the apostle Judas (Greek text simply has Judas of James-Luke 6:16).

Reconstruction of Herod the Great's Winter Palace at Jericho. Situated at the mouth of the Wadi (dry creek) Kelt along the lower slope of the western ridge of the Jordan valley, the palace had a commanding view of New Testament Jericho and the arid, fertile Jordan river valley.

*Reconstruction of New Testament Jericho based on home, shop, and building architecture of the period.*

gious decay, and murder. See the **King Chart** page 141.

**JEHORAM** (jih HOH ruhm). Son of Jehoshaphat and king of Judah 850-843 B.C. (1 Kings 22:50). He was a wicked king who had his six brothers put to death and practiced idolatry. 2. Son of Ahab who ruled the Northern Kingdom Israel 851-842 B.C. (2 Kings 3:1). Same as Joram. See the **King Chart** page 141.

**JEHOSAPHAT** (jih HAHSH uh fat). King of Judah, the Southern Kingdom (1 Kings 15:24). He reigned twenty-five years and was a good king who tried to do away with places of idol worship and see that the people were taught the Law. See the **King Chart** page 141. Other royal officials were also named Jehosaphat (2 Sam. 8:16; 1 Kings 4:17; 2 Kings 9:2,14).

**JEHU** (JEE hyoo). Tenth king of Israel, the Northern Kingdom (1 Kings 19:16). He killed his predecessor's family and the king of the Southern Kingdom. He killed many followers of Baal but was not a true follower of God. See the **King Chart** page 141. Others named Jehu include a prophet (1 Kings 16), a soldier (1 Chron. 12:3), and a tribal leader (1 Chron. 4:35).

**JEREMIAH** (jer ih MIGH uh) (sometimes **JEREMY** JER uh mih and **JEREMIAS** jer ih MIGH uhs). One of the greatest OT prophets (Jer. 1:1). He was born into a priestly family near Jerusalem. He prophesied to Judah, the Southern Kingdom, under the reign of the last five kings. Jeremiah preached judgment for the sins of the people, but his warnings were not heeded. He cried out to God seeking to understand why he had to be a prophet (11:18-12:6; 15:10-21; 17:14-18; 18:18-23; 20:7-18). While in Jerusalem, he was taken as a captive to Egypt where he died. Several other Jeremiahs are mentioned one time each.

**JEREMIAH, BOOK OF**. Old Testament book the prophet Jeremiah dictated to his secretary, Baruch. The book contains Jeremiah's life and work and his message to the people of Judah, the Southern Kingdom. Jeremiah showed loyalty to God above nation, above other prophets, and above his own desires. He pointed to a new covenant (31:31).

**JERICHO** (JER ih koh). An ancient city located a few miles west of the Jordan River and north of the Dead Sea (Josh. 2:1; Matt. 20:29). Jericho is known for its falling walls as Joshua and the Israelites attacked the city. In the NT it is the home of Zacchaeus (Luke 19:1-2).

**JEROBOAM** (jer uh BOH uhm). 1. First king of the Northern Kingdom-about 931-

*Modern Arab citrus and vegetable vendor in the city of Jericho.*

*Round Neolithic (New Stone Age) defense (or gate) tower at Old Testament Jericho, from ca. 7000 B.C.*

910 B.C. (1 Kings 11:26). He built rival places of worship at Dan and Bethel and encouraged pagan idolatry. 2. Jeroboam II

*The Wailing Wall, for centuries revered by Jews as the only remaining wall of the ancient Temple area.*

was the thirteenth king of Israel (2 Kings 13:13). Although he was successful by human standards, he was not true to God. See the **King Chart** page 141.

**JERUBBAAL** (jer uh BAY uhl). Name given to Gideon by his father, Joash (Judg. 6:32).

**JERUSALEM** (jih ROO suh lem). Capital city and center of worship for united kingdom and then for Southern Kingdom. David captured it from Jebusites (2 Sam. 5:1-10). It was located in the hills of Judah between the Mediterranean Sea and the Dead Sea. Solomon built the Temple there. The city was taken by Babylon in 598 B.C. and destroyed in 587. It was rebuilt from 538 to 440. In Jesus' day it was the center of Jewish worship and life though ruled by the Romans.

**JESSE** (JES ih). The grandson of Boaz and the father of David (1 Sam. 16:1).

■ **JESUS** (JEE zuhs). Savior. Name prophesied and given to Christ when He was

# JERUSALEM

Jerusalem in the Time of Jesus
1. The Temple (Herod's Temple)
2. Women's Court
3. The Soreg
4. The Court of the Gentiles
5. Royal Porch
6. Eastern Gate (the present-day Golden Gate)
7. Antonia Fortress
8. The Double Gate (the Western Huldah Gate)
9. The Triple Gate (the Eastern Huldah Gate)
10. Monumental Herodian Staircase (sections still remain today)
11. The City of David (established by David, the oldest part of the city)
12. Earliest defense wall (destroyed and constructed many times)
13. Herodian outer defense wall around the expanded city

14. Herodian wall separating the Upper City (or affluent district) from the Lower City (or lower economic district)
15. The Second North Wall (possible location)
16. Garden of Gethsemane (the west side of the Mount of Olives)
17. Mount of Olives
18. Kidron Valley
19. Gihon Spring
20. Pool of Siloam
21. Tyropoeon Valley (Lower City)
22. Herodian aqueduct (possible location)
23. Shops and marketplace of Jesus' day
24. Additional shops and marketplace (probably added at a later time)
25. Staircase (Robinson's Arch) leading up from the Lower City

# A.D. 30

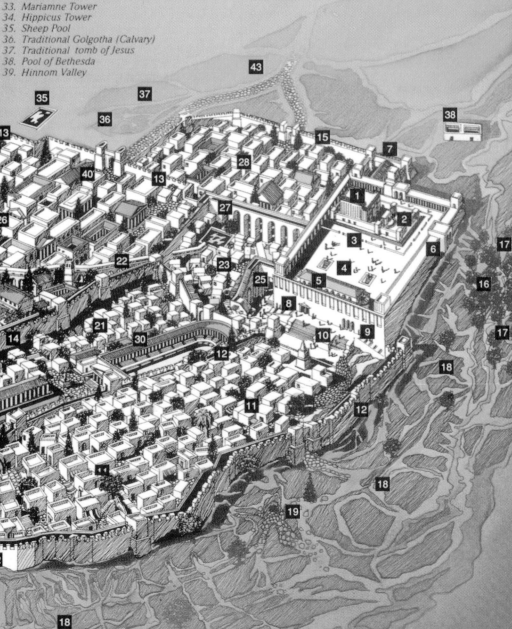

born to Mary (Matt. 1:21; Luke 1:31). Jesus is the divine Son of God; He is God the Son (Matt. 3:17). He is eternal; that means He always was, is, and will be. He existed and was active with God the Father in creation (Col. 1:15-16).

His earthly ministry began when He was about thirty years old and lasted for three years (Luke 3:23). In obedience to God the Father, Jesus lived a sinless life, suffered an agonizing death, and provided salvation for mankind (Eph. 1:4; Phil. 2:5-11). God raised Jesus from death to reign with Him forever.

● *Jesus died for everyone. Do you know how a person receives eternal life? Believe that Jesus is God's Son and that He can save you from your sins. Repent by turning from your sins to Jesus. Trust Him to save you from your sins and to eternal life. Ask Him to do this. Confess to others that Jesus is Lord of your life. See* **CONFESS**, **REPENT** *to better understand the process.*

### NAMES FOR JESUS
Jesus Christ called Himself many names and was called by many names in the Bible.

● What do each of these names teach you about Him?

**The Way** (John 14:6)
**The Truth** (John 14:6)
**The Life** (John 14:6)
**Good Shepherd** (John 10:11)
**The Light** (John 1:7)
**Bread of Life** (John 6:35)
**Immanuel** (Isa. 7:14)
**Savior** (2 Pet. 3:18)
**Wonderful Counselor** (Isa. 9:6)
**Mighty God** (Isa. 9:6)
**Everlasting Father** (Isa. 9:6)
**Prince of Peace** (Isa. 9:6)
**The Word** (John 1:1)
**The Resurrection** (John 11:25)
**Lord** (Matt. 8:8)
**Son of Man** (Mark 2:28)

**Son of God** (1 John 4:15)
**God** (John 20:28)

**JETHRO** (JETH roh). Father-in-law of Moses and a priest of Midian (Ex. 3:1). Also called Reuel (Ex. 2:18).

**JEW**. The term first applied to an inhabitant of Judah (2 Kings 16:6). Later it came to refer to all descendants of Abraham who were also called Israelites or Hebrews.

**JEZEBEL** (JEZ uh bel). Wife of Ahab, king of Israel, the Northern Kingdom (1 Kings 16:31). She was a wicked woman who led the Israelites deeper into idolatry using treachery and murder to get her way. She died a horrible death. See **AHAB**. She was so wicked her name was used to condemn a prophetess in Thyatira (Rev. 2:20).

**JEZREEL** (JEZ reel). 1. City in the hill country of Judah (1 Sam. 29:1). 2. City between Megiddo and Bethshean protecting northeast entrance to valley of same name; a favorite place of King Ahab and his family (1 Kings 18:45).

**JOAB** (JOH ab). Nephew of King David who became commander of David's army (2 Sam. 2:13). Although a competent mili-

*Jesus teaching from a boat on the Sea of Galilee.* ▶

# TITLES FOR JESUS IN SCRIPTURE

| TITLE | SIGNIFICANCE | REFERENCE |
|---|---|---|
| Alpha and Omega | The Beginning and Ending of all things | Rev 21:6 |
| Bread of Life | The one essential food | John 6:35 |
| Chief Cornerstone | A Sure Foundation of life | Eph 2:20 |
| Chief Shepherd | Gives guidance and protection | 1 Pet 5:4 |
| Christ | The Anointed One of God foreseen by Old Testament prophets | Matt 16:16 |
| Firstborn from the Dead | Leads us into resurrection | Col 1:18 |
| Good Shepherd | Gives guidance and protection | John 10:11 |
| High Priest | The Perfect Mediator | Heb 3:1 |
| Holy One of God | Perfect and sinless | Mark 1:24 |
| Immanuel | God with us | Matt 1:23 |
| Jesus | His personal name meaning Yahweh Saves | Matt 1:21 |
| King of Kings, Lord of Lords | The Sovereign Almighty | Rev 19:16 |
| Lamb of God | Offered His life as a sacrifice for sins | John 1:29 |
| Light of the World | One who brings hope and gives guidance | John 9:5 |
| Lord | Sovereign Creator and Redeemer | Rom 10:9 |
| Lord of Glory | The power of the Living God | 1 Cor 2:8 |
| Mediator | Redeemer who brings forgiven sinners into the presence of God | 1 Tim 2:5 |
| Prophet | One who speaks for God | Luke 13:33 |
| Rabbi/Teacher | A title of respect for one who taught the Scriptures | John 3:2 |
| Savior | One who delivers from sin | John 4:42 |
| Son of David | One who brings in the Kingdom | Matt 9:27 |
| Son of God | A title of Deity signifying Jesus' unique and special intimacy with the Father | John 20:31 |
| Son of Man | A divine title of suffering and exaltation | Matt 20:28 |
| Word | Eternal God who ultimately reveals God | John 1:1 |

*The Valley of Jezreel (or Esdraelon, or Megiddo) as viewed from the top of the Megiddo tel.*

tary man and loyal to the king, he was very cruel. He murdered David's rebellious son, Absalom, even though David had instructed that Absalom be spared.

**JOASH** (JOH ash). 1. Son of Ahaziah and the ninth king of Judah, the Southern Kingdom (2 Kings 11:2). Spared of murder as an infant, he was hidden and placed on the throne at age seven by the high priest Jehoiada. He reigned forty years and directed the people back toward God. However, at Jehoiada's death, Joash let the nation fall back into idolatry.

2. Son of Johoahaz and the twelfth king of Israel, the Northern Kingdom. He had a successful reign and was befriended by the prophet Elisha. See the **King Chart** page 141. Six other minor Bible characters bore the name Joash.

**JOB** (JOHB). Old Testament character whose story is told in the book of Job (Job 1:1; Jas. 5:11). Job lived in the land of Uz, apparently about the same time as Jacob, the patriarch. Although he is usually referred to as having great patience, he questioned God and demanded answers. Job demonstrated persistent trust and steadfastness (Job 13:15).

**JOB, BOOK OF.** Old Testament book included in the poetry division. The book focuses on God's arrangement with Satan concerning Job, Job's many trials and sufferings, the responses of his wife and friends, and Job's steadfastness toward God. God's presence, not answers to questions, proved to be what Job needed.

*Job being consoled by his friends.*

## COMPARISON OF THE GOSPELS

| Event or Point of Comparison | In Synoptic Gospels? | In Gospel of John? | Scripture Reference |
|---|---|---|---|
| Wedding at Cana | No | Yes | John 2:1-11 |
| Encounter with Nicodemus | No | Yes | John 3:1-14 |
| Encounter with Woman at the Well | No | Yes | John 4:1-45 |
| Washing of the Disciples' Feet | No | Yes | John 13:1-17 |
| Last Supper | Yes | No | Luke 22:7-23 |
| Jesus' Final Priestly Prayer | No | Yes | John 17:1-26 |
| Extensive Prologue to the Gospel | No | Yes | John 1:1-18 |
| Concluding Epilogue to the Gospel | No | Yes | John 21:1-25 |
| Birth Narratives | Yes | No | Luke 2:1-20 |
| Jesus' Use of Parables | Yes | No | Matt 13:1-52 |
| Casting Out Demons | Yes | No | Mark 1:21-28 |
| Jesus with Tax Collectors | Yes | No | Luke 6:27-32 |
| Jesus Heals Lepers | Yes | No | Luke 17:11-17 |
| Jesus with Children | Yes | No | Mark 10:13-16 |
| Sermon on the Mount | Yes | No | Matt 5:1–7:27 |
| Discourses on the End Times | Yes | No | Matt 24:1-51 |
| Emphasis on Miracles | Yes | No | Matt 8:1–9:8 |
| Emphasis on Interpretation of Miracles/Signs | No | Yes | John 5:1-47 |
| Jesus' Teaching on Hell | Yes | No | Matt 23:1-39 |
| Temptations of Jesus | Yes | No | Matt 4:1-11 |
| "I AM" Sayings | No | Yes | John 14:6 |

**JOEL** (JOH el). 1. Author of OT book listed with the minor prophets; son of Pethuel (Joel 1:1). We know nothing else about him. 2. Thirteen other Joels are mentioned in the OT.

**JOEL, BOOK OF.** Old Testament book of sermons of Joel, son of Pethuel. The book looks upon destruction caused by a plague of locusts as the judgment of God upon sin. Joel prophesied that further judgment of God would be much worse than the locusts. He pointed ahead to the coming of God's Spirit (2:28-29; compare Acts 2:16-21).

**JOHN, APOSTLE.** Son of Zebedee and a fisherman by trade (Matt. 4:21). He was one of the twelve disciples and among the closest to Jesus. Most scholars credit him with writing the Gospel of John, 1, 2, and 3 John, and Revelation.

**JOHN, 1, 2, 3, BOOKS.** New Testament letters written by John, sometimes called the Johannine Epistles. First John warns Christians of false teachers and urges them to show love to others. Second John also warns of false teachers. Third John is written to an individual, Gaius, to express appreciation for his Christian life and hospitality.

**JOHN, BOOK OF.** New Testament book that focuses on Jesus as the Son of God, His miracles or signs, and His teachings to individuals and groups. The purpose of this Gospel is to lead people to accept Christ as Lord and Savior (John 20:30-31). Most scholars believe John the apostle wrote this book about A.D. 90.

**JOHN THE BAPTIST.** Son of Elisabeth and Zacharias (also spelled Zachariah) and a cousin of Jesus (Luke 1:13). His birth was an answer to the prayers of his elderly parents. He grew up in the isolation of the desert. He came out of seclusion to preach a message of repentance and to prepare the way for Jesus. He is called the forerunner of Jesus. He was eventually imprisoned and put to death for preaching against the sins of Herod Antipas.

**JONAH** (JOH nuh). Son of Amittai and a prophet of Israel (Jonah 1:1) about 750 B.C. He lived in a town near Nazareth and gave good advice to King Jeroboam II of Israel (2 Kings 14:23-29). He is sometimes credited with being the first recorded missionary to a heathen or Gentile (nonJewish) nation.

● *Jonah resisted God's command to preach to Nineveh (Jonah 1:3ff.). Why?*

*Jonah running from God's call.*

**JONAH, BOOK OF.** This OT book tells how Jonah reluctantly went to preach the message of God's judgment to the people of Nineveh. Jonah was disappointed when the judgment did not come about after the people repented. The book is listed in the division of minor prophets. The book is unusual among the prophets, having only one brief sermon (3:4), telling an extensive story about a prophet, and making the prophet the villain rather than the hero. It emphasizes God's great love for all people (4:10-11).

**JONATHAN** (JAHN uh thuhn). Son of King Saul and loyal friend to David (1 Sam. 14:1). Jonathan defended David to Saul and helped spare David's life. He died with his father in battle against the Philistines. Fourteen other Jonathans appear in the Bible.

**JOPPA** (JAHP uh). Town where Peter raised Dorcas to life and received his vision to preach to the Gentile Cornelius (Acts 9:36-43). Seacoast city thirty-five miles northwest of Jerusalem. Cedar logs for King Solomon's Temple were shipped here (2 Chron. 2:16). Israel contested the Philistines and Phoenicians for control of Joppa.

**JORAM** (JOH ruhm). Wicked king of Judah (same as Jehoram). See the **King Chart** page 141.

**JORDAN** (JAWR d'n). River of Palestine that played an important role in biblical history (Josh. 1:2; Mark 1:9). The Jordan originates above the Sea of Galilee and ends in the Dead (Salt) Sea. Although it is only seventy miles from the Sea of Galilee to the Dead Sea, the Jordan meanders two hundred miles. It is three to ten feet deep and about one hundred feet wide. The Israelites

*The green waters of the Jordan River as it meanders through Israel.*

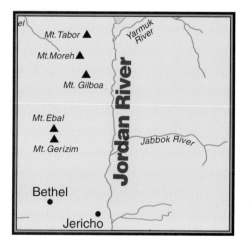

crossed over the Jordan River to enter the Promised Land. John baptized Jesus in the Jordan.

**JOSEPH** (JOH zif). 1. Son of Rachel and Jacob and the favorite of his father's twelve sons (Gen. 37:3). Joseph's jealous brothers sold him into Egyptian slavery. He found favor in Pharaoh's eyes and became second in authority in Egypt. He rescued his family in a time of famine and brought them to live in Egypt.

2. A carpenter who was the husband of Jesus' mother, Mary (Matt. 1:18). Joseph was engaged to Mary when she conceived Jesus by the Holy Spirit; then Joseph took Mary as his wife to save her from public disgrace.

3. A Jew of Arimathea, member of the Sanhedrin, and secret disciple of Jesus. He came forward after the crucifixion to ask for Jesus' body to bury it in his own tomb.

*The children of Israel crossing the Jordan River.*

The Old Testament mentions four other Josephs, and the New Testament, six.

● *Each Joseph faced a difficult situation with God's help. Which situation is most like one you face or have faced?*

**JOSHUA** (JAHSH yoo uh). Son of Nun, assistant and successor to Moses (Ex. 17:9). Joshua and Caleb differed from the other ten spies by being confident that the Israelites could conquer the land of Canaan. After forty years of wilderness wanderings and Moses' death, Joshua led the Israelites into the Promised Land in victory over the inhabitants.

**JOSHUA, BOOK OF.** This OT book tells how Israel entered, conquered, and divided Canaan. In the closing chapter, Joshua calls the people to absolute faithfulness to God and renews covenant with them.

**JOSIAH** (joh SIGH uh). Sixteenth king of Judah, he began to rule at age eight, succeeding his evil father, Amon (2 Kings 22:1). Josiah was known for his good reforms: repairing the Temple, discovering and implementing the lost book of Law, and abolishing idolatry. See the **King Chart** page 141.

**JOT.** The reference is to the smallest letter in an alphabet-the Greek *iota* or the Hebrew *yod* (Matt. 5:18).

**JOY.** Gladness, rejoicing (Ps. 16:11; Matt. 2:10). An evidence of a Holy Spirit-filled life (Gal. 5:22).
● *How is joy similar to and different from happiness?*

**JUBILEE, YEAR OF.** An OT celebration held every fifty years (Lev. 25:10ff.).

*Joshua challanging the people of Israel.* ➤

*The Wilderness of Judea as viewed toward the Dead Sea (left center) from atop the Herodium.*

During this time of thanksgiving the land was not planted in crops; Hebrews enslaved for debt were freed; and property went back to its original owners.

**JUDAH** (JOO duh). Fourth son of Jacob and Leah (Gen. 29:35). Judah's descendants became the tribe of Judah, and the land they occupied was known as Judah. When the Hebrew kingdom divided, Judah was the Southern Kingdom.

**JUDAS** (JOO duhs). Judas was a common name. Those with that name included: 1. A disciple of Jesus (John 6:71) called Judas Iscariot, who betrayed Jesus and later hanged himself. 2. A brother of Jesus (Matt. 13:55), probably the same as the brother of James and author of the Book of Jude. New Testament mentions at least five other Judases.

**JUDE, BOOK OF.** New Testament book written by Jude, brother of James, to combat false teachings in the early Christian church. The author was probably also the brother of Jesus.

**JUDEA** (joo DEE uh). Land located between the Dead Sea and the Mediterranean Sea (Matt. 3:1). Earlier this area was called Judah after the Israelite tribe that claimed it, but after the return from Babylonian captivity it became Judea. Spelled Judaea in KJV.

**JUDGE.** Noun: A public official who helps interpret the laws (Ezra 7:25; Matt. 5:25). The judges from the time of Joshua to Samuel were also spiritual and military leaders. Verb: To discern or criticize (Gen. 15:14; Matt. 7:1). The Bible cautions us not to judge others because only God is qualified to do so. We are responsible to Him for our beliefs and actions (Rev. 20:12-13).

● *How may human motives for judging be different from God's motives for judging? When is judgment destructive? Constructive?*

**JUDGES, BOOK OF.** Old Testament book that deals with the history of the Israelites from the time of Joshua to the time of Samuel. The author is not known. It shows how lack of godly leadership destroys a nation.

■ **JUDGMENT.** Pronouncement of a decision (Josh. 20:6). Often used to refer to God's discipline of His people (Ps. 9:16; Rom. 2:2). The Bible also speaks of a future and final judgment (Rev. 14:7).

**JUST.** Righteous, fair, right—especially in God's eyes (Gen. 6:9; Rom. 1:17).

**JUSTICE.** Rightness, fairness (Isa. 59:4).
● *With what actions do you show justice?*

■ **JUSTIFICATION.** God's act of declaring and making a repentant person right with Him (Rom. 4:24-25; 5:17; 1 Cor. 1:30). Remember the definition by recalling that justification = just-as-if-I-had-not-sinned.

**JUSTIFIED.** To be made right-as in being made right with God (Ps. 143:2; Gal. 2:16).

| JUDGES OF THE OLD TESTAMENT | | |
|---|---|---|
| NAME | REFERENCE | IDENTIFICATION |
| Othniel | Judg 1:12-13; 3:7-11 | Conquered a Canaanite city |
| Ehud | Judg 3:12-30 | Killed Eglon, king of Moab, and defeated Moabites |
| Shamgar | Judg 3:31 | Killed 600 Philistines with an oxgoad |
| Deborah | Judg 4–5 | Convinced Barak to lead an army to victory against Sisera's troops |
| Gideon | Judg 6–8 | Led 300 men to victory against 135,000 Midianites |
| Tola | Judg 10:1-2 | Judged for 23 years |
| Jair | Judg 10:3-5 | Judged for 22 years |
| Jephthah | Judg 11:1–12:7 | Defeated the Ammonites after making a promise to the Lord |
| Ibzan | Judg 12:8-10 | Judged for 7 years |
| Elon | Judg 12:11-12 | Judged for 10 years |
| Abdon | Judg 12:13-15 | Judged for 8 years |
| Samson | Judg 13–16 | Killed 1,000 Philistines with a donkey's jawbone; was deceived by Delilah; destroyed a Philistine temple; judged 20 years |
| Samuel | 1 and 2 Sam | Was the last of the judges and the first of the prophets |

## KIN, KINSMAN, KINDRED

**KIDRON** (KID ruhn) **CEDRON** (KE druhn). A brook and valley along the east side of Jerusalem. During the time of the kings, idolatrous items were burned or destroyed there.

**KIN, KINSMAN, KINDRED.** Family member, relative, of the same tribe or race (Gen. 12:1; Luke 14:12). The Hebrew culture provided many marriage guidelines

**KADESH** (KAY desh) **KADESH-BARNEA** (KAY desh BAHR nee uh). Place in the wilderness area seventy miles south of Hebron (Num. 13:26). Moses sent the twelve spies from here to check out the Promised Land.

**KERYGMA** (KEH rig muh). Greek word for a proclamation. Scholars often use this word to refer to the thing preached-the content rather than the act of preaching.

*Iron age fortress in the area of ancient Kadesh-Barnea.*

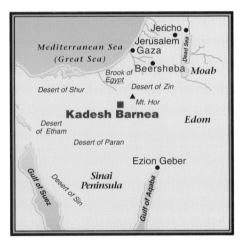

*The Kidron Valley in Jerusalem.*

and family responsibilities relating to relatives.

**KINDLE**. To light or cause to burn (Ex. 35:3; Acts 28:2).

**KINE**. Cows (Amos 4:1).

**KING**. Ruler of a nation (Ex. 1:8; Matt. 2:1). During the time of Samuel, at the Israelites' insistence, God allowed the Israelites to have their first king, Saul. A king was mainly looked upon as a military leader, but most of Israel's kings also influenced the people spiritually, both good and bad. See **King Chart** on facing page.

■ **KINGDOM**. Refers to a king's authority or rule over a territory or over the hearts of people (as in the kingdom of God; 1 Sam. 10:16; Matt. 6:10).

**KINGDOM OF GOD, KINGDOM OF HEAVEN**. A kingdom is a territory ruled over by a king (Gen. 10:10). The term kingdom of God (or heaven-used interchangeably) refers to when and where God rules, both present and future (Mark 1:15; Matt. 6:10). The Kingdom is also considered to be a place where God's reign is complete (Rev. 12:10).
● *What expressions of the kingdom of God do you see today? How do you show membership in it?*

**KINGS, 1, 2, BOOKS OF**. Old Testament books of history. They covered the last days of David through the division of Israel and down to the fall of the Northern and Southern Kingdoms (in 722 B.C. and 587 B.C.). The books deal with God's judgment of His rebellious people.
● *Some people think persons in Bible times were better than people today. What does 1 and 2 Kings say about this?*

**KISH**. Father of Saul (1 Sam. 9:1-2). Four other Bible personalities were named Kish.

**KISHON** (KIGH shahn). A stream flowing from Mount Tabor westward toward the Mediterranean (Judg. 4:7).

**KNEEL**. Bend the knee or bow in a sign of worship, reverence, or subjection (Ps. 95:6; Acts 9:40).

**KNIT**. Joined together, bound (1 Chron. 12:17; Acts 10:11).

**KNOW**. Understand intimately. Biblical term for sexual intercourse (Gen. 4:1,25; Luke 1:34).
● *How would knowing your spouse emotionally and spiritually make physical knowledge more intimate and satisfying?*

**KNOWLEDGE**. Understanding (Prov. 1:7; Phil. 1:9).

**KORAH** (KOH ruh). Man who led a rebellion against Moses and Aaron (Num. 16:19). Four other people and a town bear the name.

# RULERS OF ISRAEL AND JUDAH

## RULERS OF THE UNITED KINGDOM

Saul  1 Sam 9:1–31:13
David  1 Sam 16:1–1 Kgs 2:11
Solomon  1 Kgs 1:1–11:43

## RULERS OF THE DIVIDED KINGDOM

| RULERS OF ISRAEL | | RULERS OF JUDAH | |
| --- | --- | --- | --- |
| Jeroboam I | I Kgs 11:26–14:20 | Rehoboam | 1 Kgs 11:42–14:31 |
| | | Abijah (Abijam) | 1 Kgs 14:31–15:8 |
| Nadab | 1 Kgs 15:25-28 | Asa | Kgs 15:8-24 |
| Baasha | 1 Kgs 15:27–16:7 | | |
| Elah | 1 Kgs 16:6-14 | | |
| Zimri | 1 Kgs 16:9-20 | | |
| Omri | 1 Kgs 16:15-28 | | |
| Ahab | 1 Kgs 16:28–22:40 | Jehoshaphat | 1 Kgs 22:41-50 |
| Ahaziah | 1 Kgs 22:40–2 Kgs 1:18 | Jehoram | 2 Kgs 8:16-24 |
| Jehoram (Joram) | 2 Kgs 1:17–9:26 | Ahaziah | 2 Kgs 8:24–9:29 |
| Jehu | 2 Kgs 9:1-10:36 | Athaliah | 2 Kgs 11:1-20 |
| Jehoahaz | 2 Kgs 13:1-9 | Joash | 2 Kgs 11:1–12:21 |
| Jehoash (Joash) | 2 Kgs 13:10–14:16 | Amaziah | 2 Kgs 14:1-20 |
| Jeroboam II | 2 Kgs 14:23-29 | Azariah (Uzziah) | 2 Kgs14:21; 15:1-7 |
| Zechariah | 2 Kgs 14:29–15:12 | | |
| Shallum | 2 Kgs 15:10-15 | Jotham | 2 Kgs 15:32-38 |
| Menahem | 2 Kgs 15:14-22 | | |
| Pekahiah | 2 Kgs 15:22-26 | | |
| Pekah | 2 Kgs 15:25-31 | Ahaz (Jehoahaz) | 2 Kgs 16:1-20 |
| Hoshea | 2 Kgs 15:30–17:6 | Hezekiah | 2 Kgs 18:1–20:21 |
| | | Manasseh | 2 Kgs 21:1-18 |
| | | Amon | 2 Kgs 21:19-26 |
| | | Josiah | 2 Kgs 21:26–23:30 |
| | | Jehoahaz II (Shallum) | 2 Kgs 23:30-33 |
| | | Jehoiakim (Eliakim) | 2 Kgs 23:34–24:5 |
| | | Jehoiachin (Jeconiah) | 2 Kgs 24:6-16; 25:27-30 |
| | | Zedekiah (Mattaniah) | 2 Kgs 24:17–25:7 |

# RULERS OF OLD TESTAMENT PAGAN NATIONS
## (Listed Alphabetically)

| NAME | REFERENCE | NATIONALITY |
| --- | --- | --- |
| Abimelech | (1) Gen 20 | Philistine |
| | (2) Gen 26 | Philistine |
| Achish | 1 Sam 21:10-14; 27–29 | Philistine |
| Adoni-Zedek | Josh 10:1-27 | Canaanite |
| Agag | 1 Sam 15:8-33 | Amalekite |
| Ahasuerus | See Xerxes I | |
| Ammon, King of (Unnamed) | Judg 11:12-28 | Ammonite |
| Artaxerxes | Ezra 4:7-23; 7; 8:1; Neh 2:1-8 | Persian/Mede |
| Ashurbanipal (also known as Osnapper) | Ezra 4:10 | Assyrian |
| Baalis | Jer 40:14 | Ammonite |
| Balak | Num 22–24 | Moabite |
| Belshazzar | Dan 5; 7:1 | Babylonian |
| Ben-Hadad I | 1 Kgs 20:1-34 | Syrian |
| Ben-Hadad II | 2 Kgs 6:24 | Syrian |
| Bera | Gen 14:2-24 | Canaanite |
| Cyrus the Great | 2 Chron 36:22-23; Ezra 1; Isa 44:28; 45:1; Dan 1:21; 10:1 | Persian/Mede |
| Darius the Great | Ezra 4–6; Neh 12:22; Hag 1:1; Zech 1:1,17 | Persian/Mede |
| Darius the Mede | Dan 11:1 | Persian/Mede |
| Edom, King of (Unnamed) | Num 20:14-21 | Edomite |
| Eglon | Judg 3:12-30 | Moabite |
| Egypt, Pharaoh of (Unnamed) | (1) Gen 12:18-20 | Egyptian |
| | (2) Gen 41:38-55 | Egyptian |
| | (3) Exod 1:8 | Egyptian |
| | (4) Exod 2:15 | Egyptian |
| | (5) Exod 3:10; 5:1 | Egyptian |
| | (6) 1 Kgs 3:1 | Egyptian |
| Esarhaddon | Ezra 4:2 | Assyrian |
| Evil-Merodach | 2 Kgs 25:27-30; Jer 52:31-34 | Babylonian |
| Hanun | 2 Sam 10:1-4 | Ammonite |
| Hazael | 1 Kgs 19:15; 2 Kgs 8:7-15 | Syrian |
| Hiram | 1 Kgs 5:1-18 | Tyrian |
| Hophra | Jer 44:30 | Egyptian |
| Jabin | (1) Josh 11:1-11 | Canaanite |
| | (2) Judg 4:2 | Canaanite |
| Jericho, King of (Unnamed) | Josh 2:2 | Canaanite |
| Merodach-Baladan | 2 Kgs 20:12; Isa 39:1 | Babylonian |
| Mesha | 2 Kgs 3:4-27 | Moabite |
| Nahash | 1 Sam 11:12 | Ammonite |
| Nebuchadnezzar | 2 Kgs 24–25; Dan 1–4 | Babylonian |
| Neco | 2 Kgs 23:29-30 | Egyptian |
| Nergal-Sherezer | Jer 39:3,13 | Babylonian |
| Osnapper | SEE Ashurbanipal | |
| Pul | SEE Tiglath-Pileser III | |
| Rezin | 2 Kgs 15:37; 16:5-9 | Syrian |
| Sargon II | Isa 20 | Assyrian |
| Sennacherib | 2 Kgs 18–19; Isa 36–37 | Assyrian |
| Shalmaneser V | 2 Kgs 17:1-6 | Assyrian |
| Shishak | 1 Kgs 14:25-26; 2 Chr 12:2-9 | Egyptian |
| Tiglath-Pileser III | 2 Kgs 15:19,29; 16:7-10 | Assyrian |
| Tyre, Prince of (Unnamed) | Ezek 28:1-10 | Tyrian |
| Xerxes I (also known as Ahasuerus) | Ezra 4:6; Esth | Persian/Mede |

**LAMENTATIONS, BOOK OF.** Old Testament book in the division of major prophets. Jeremiah is traditionally recognized as the author. The book mourns the capture of Jerusalem in 587 B.C. It is written in a poetic style with the first four chapters in an acrostic pattern (in this case, the pattern uses the letters of the Hebrew alphabet).

**LABAN** (LAY buhn). Brother of Rebekah and father of Leah and Rachel (Gen. 29:16ff.). Laban tricked Jacob into marrying Leah-instead of Rachel-at the end of seven years of labor. Laban then required Jacob to serve him for seven more years to have Rachel for his wife. The strife between the men was eventually settled through a covenant (Gen. 31:44-54).

**LABOUR, LABOR.** Work (Gen. 31:42; 1 Cor. 3:8).

**LAD.** Young person, child, servant (Judg. 16:26; John 6:9).

**LAMB.** A young sheep used as offerings in the Jewish sacrificial system (Ex. 29:38). Jesus is our sacrificial Lamb in the sense that He died as a sacrifice in our place (Rev. 7:14).

**LAMB OF GOD.** Title John the Baptist called Jesus (John 1:29), pointing to His sacrificial death.

**LAME.** Limping, crippled (Deut. 15:21; Matt. 11:5).

**LAMECH** (LAY mek). Descendant of Cain, son of Methusulah (Gen. 4:18). Father of Noah (Gen. 5:30).

**LAMENT.** Mourn or show deep sorrow (Jer. 4:8; John 16:20).

**LANGUISH.** Become weak, fade (Hos. 4:3).

**LAODICEA** (lay ahd ih SEE uh). Chief commercial city of Asia Minor (Col. 4:15). The city was a banking center and was known for its black woolen garments and medicines.

■ **LASCIVIOUSNESS.** Shameless immorality, conduct shocking to public decency (Eph. 4:19).

**LATIN.** Language of the Romans (John 19:20).

**LAVER.** Large brass bowl containing water; used in the tabernacle and Temple for ceremonial cleansing (Ex. 30:18; 1 Kings 7:38).

**LAW.** Teaching, commandment (Ps. 19:7). 1. God's rules or commandments. 2. First five books of OT; division of OT. 3. Part or all of the OT. 4. Rules made by human (Esther 1:19).

**LAWFUL.** Authorized, allowed or permitted by law (Ezek. 18:19; Matt. 12:2).

**LAWLESS.** Unauthorized, unguided by the law, unruly, disorderly (1 Tim. 1:9).

**LAY HANDS ON.** Symbolic act of dedication and consecration (Lev. 4:4; Acts 6:6).

**LAZARUS** (LAZ uh ruhs). 1. Brother of Mary and Martha (John 11:1-2). Jesus

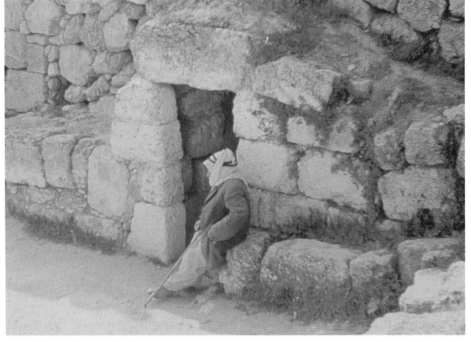

*The traditional site of the tomb of Lazarus in Bethany.*

raised this close friend from the dead. 2. Name of the beggar in a parable Jesus told (Luke 16:20).

**LEAH** (LEE uh). Laban's older daughter who became Jacob's first wife as the result of trickery (Gen. 29:16).

**LEARN**. Grow in knowledge and understanding (Deut. 5:1; Matt. 11:29).

**LEAVEN**. Substance which makes bread rise (Ex. 12:15; Luke 13:21). Usually a small portion of dough was saved to add and mix with the next batch. Unleavened bread was often used with OT worship and was a part of the Passover meal. Symbolically, anything that influences something far larger than itself (Matt. 13:33). Leaven can mean either good or bad influence (Luke 12:1). See **PASSOVER**.

**LEBANON** (LEB uh nuhn). A mountain range extending one hundred miles along the Mediterranean Sea (Deut. 1:7). It was heavily wooded in Bible times and known especially for its magnificent cedar trees.

**LEES**. Sediment from wine (Isa. 25:6).

**LEFT SIDE**. Along with the right-hand side, a position of honor next to a king (Matt. 20:21-27).

**LEGION**. A Roman army division of six thousand men that sometimes included a cavalry unit. Name given to the Gadarene demoniac because of the large number of demons possessing him (Mark 5:9).

**LENTILS**. Pea-like seeds used in stew or soup (2 Sam. 17:28).

**LEPER, LEPROSY**. A sufferer and the cause of suffering, namely skin diseases which took several forms in biblical times (2 Kings 5:1; Matt. 8:3). Many times the leper was removed from his or her family and society and was considered ceremonially unclean.

**LEST.** For fear that (Gen. 4:15; Matt. 7:6).

**LET.** Usually permit or allow (Ex. 3:19; Matt. 8:22), but can mean hinder, forbid, prevent, or restrain (Isa. 43:13; Rom. 1:13; 2 Thess. 2:6-7).

**LETTER.** Same as epistle (Acts 15:30), compare KJV and RSV. About half the NT books were letters.

**LEVI** (LEE vigh). Jacob's third son by Leah (Gen. 29:34).

**LEVITE** (LEE vight) **LEVITICAL** (leh VIT ih kuhl) **PRIESTHOOD.** Descendants of Levi-one of the twelve tribes (Num. 3:6). The Levites did not receive a territorial assignment but were allowed to live in fourty-eight cities (Josh. 21). They performed duties in the tabernacle and, later, in the Temple. They received support from the tithes and offerings. The Levitical priesthood consisted of Aaron and his descendants.

**LEVIATHAN** (lih VIGH uh thuhn). Large water creature-possibly a crocodile (Job 41:1-34) or a whale (Ps. 104:26).

**LEVITICUS, BOOK OF.** Third book of the OT. It outlines the duties of the Levitical priesthood and guidelines for the sacrificial system, purification, and feasts.
● *Read about the Day of Atonement in Leviticus 16. What does the word* scapegoat *mean in the KJV?*

**LEVY.** Refers to men forced into slave labor (1 Kings 5:13; 9:15). May also refer to what is taken in war (livestock, slaves, and other things) and turned over to tabernacle service (1 Kings 9:15-23; Num. 31:28).

**LEWD.** Wicked (Acts 17:5), lustful (Ezek. 16:27; 23:44).

**LIBERAL.** Noble, free, willing (Isa. 32:8). Single-minded, sincerety (2 Cor. 9:13).

**LIBERTY.** Physical, mental, and spiritual freedom (Isa. 61:1; Gal. 5:1). Liberty brings responsibility (Gal. 5:13).

**LIBYA** (LIB ih uh). A region west of Egypt (Ezek. 30:5; Acts 2:10). Ancient Greek name for North Africa.

**LICENTIOUS.** Immoral (2 Pet. 2:18, NRSV).

**LIFE, BOOK OF.** God's record of those who belong to Him (Rev. 3:5).

**LIGHT.** Opposite of darkness (Gen. 1:3-4). Radiance (Matt. 17:2). Spiritual awareness and right living (1 John 1:7). Characteristic of God (Ps. 27:1). See **DARKNESS.**
● *Jesus is somtimes called the Light (John 1:9). Why do you like this name for Him?*

**LIKENESS.** In the image of, made like another (Gen. 1:26; Rom. 8:3).
● *How do you view yourself? Read Genesis 1:26-28; Psalm 8; Romans 8:28-29; 12:1-3. Now, how do you view yourself?*

**LO**. Look, see, behold (Dan. 7:6; Matt. 2:9).

**LOATHE, LOATHSOME**. Verb: Despise (Job. 7:16). Adjective: Rejected (Prov. 13:5).

**LOCUST**. Insect with an enormous appetite in all stages of maturity (Joel 2:25). One of the ten plagues God sent upon the Egyptians (Ex. 10:14). John the Baptist ate locusts (Matt. 3:4).

**LODGE**. Rest, spend the night (Ruth 1:16; Luke 13:19).

**LOFTY**. High (Isa. 57:7), self-centered and proud (Isa. 2:12).

**LOINS**. Area of the body between the waist and the knees, clothed for modesty's sake (2 Kings 1:8; Mark 1:6). Sometimes used for the reproductive organs (Gen. 35:11).

**LOINCLOTH**. (Job 12:18, NIV). Piece of clothing worn by men next to the skin and around their waist; made of leather or animal skin and used to gird up the loins, that is tie the long flowing robe up around the waist for easy travel. For comfort could be loosened at night or when resting. Priests were to have their hips and thighs covered so as not to be exposed when in service to Yahweh.

**LONGING**. Desire (Ps. 119:20).

■ **LORD**. Master, sir, title of respect (Ruth 2:13; Luke 12:46). The title is used for God the Father and God the Son (Ex. 15:2; Luke 2:11). Accepting Jesus as our Lord and Master is essential for salvation (Rom. 10:9-10).
● *Is Jesus your Lord? How do you know? Do otheers know?*

**LORD'S PRAYER**. Prayer Jesus gave to His disciples as an example of how to pray (Matt. 6:9-13; Luke 11:2-4). Also called The Model Prayer.
● *Have you memorized this prayer? What does each sentence of it teach you about how to pray?*

**LORD'S SUPPER**. A memorial observance Jesus instituted with His disciples to point toward His sacrificial death (Matt. 26:26-29). Today Christians participate in this observance (1) to recall Christ's death, (2) to focus on the salvation He brings, (3) and to anticipate His return. A Christian should examine his or her life before God and then participate in a worthy manner (1 Cor. 11:27-32).
● *Have you taken the Lord's Supper? What does the experience mean to you?*

**LOST**. Used to describe people without God (Jer. 50:6; Luke 19:10).
● *Are you lost? Do you know someone who is?*

**LOT**. Nephew of Abraham (Gen. 12:4). Lot lived with his uncle in Canaan. When Abraham's servants and Lot's servants had a dispute over land, Lot chose the best land near Sodom. His choice had disastrous consequences (Gen. 19).

**LOTS**. Objects, probably stones, used to reach a decision (Josh. 19:51; Acts 1:26); sometimes used in OT to determine God's will in a matter. Jesus' garments were divided by lots at His crucifixion (Ps. 22:18; Matt. 27:35).

■ **LOVE**. Deep, enduring concern for others' welfare; affection, friendship (Gen. 37:3; Matt. 5:46). An essential characteristic of God that comes only as a gift (John 3:16). Two different Greek words for *love* are used as synonyms (see John 16:27; 15:9; 21:15-17).

*Jesus and His disciples at the last supper.* ▶

**LOVINGKINDNESS**. Merciful and steadfast love; God's kind of love (Ps. 17:7). Covenant love that calls for commitment and mutual faithfulness.

**LOW, LOWLY**. Humble (Isa. 2:12; Luke 1:52). See **HUMILITY**.

**LUCIFER** (LYOO sih fur). Literally, *shining one*. The name came from the Latin translation of Isaiah 14:12 and was actually given to the king of Babylon to refer to his glory and splendor. Early Christian commentators interpreted this name as a reference to the archangel hurled from heaven for his wickedness. Modern translations usually read Morning Star or its equivalent.

**LUKE** (LYOOK). Physician, co-worker and companion of Paul. Author of Luke and Acts. Luke was apparently the only Gentile (non-Jewish) writer of the Bible. His sources were other written accounts, eyewitnesses, and his own personal experiences (Luke 1:1-4). Luke accompanied Paul on some of his journeys and was with Paul shortly before his martyrdom (2 Tim. 4:11).

**LUKE, BOOK OF (GOSPEL OF)**. New Testament book written by Luke, Gentile physician and companion of Paul. Luke points to Jesus Christ as the Son of God and Redeemer of all people who accept Christ as Lord and Savior. Luke's writings focus on healing, prayer, parables, Gentiles, and the status of women.

**LURK**. To hide, watch secretly (Prov. 1:11).

■ **LUST**. Desire that turns bad when it wants something besides what God wants. Self-seeking craving for a person, thing, or experience (Rom. 1:27; 7:7). Lust is a sin of attitude that becomes more serious if it leads to action (Jas. 1:14-15). Lust never satisfies (Jas. 4:2).

● *We can't always keep lustful thoughts from coming, but we can get rid of them once they arrive. Walking in the Holy Spirit's power (Gal. 5:16-21) and enjoying sex within marriage are ways to do this (1 Cor. 7:9). What are some problems lust creates? How does the Holy Spirit help you recognize lust and deal with it? (See 1 John 2:16-17; Col. 3:2.)*

**LUZ** (LUHZ). 1. City of the Canaanites later called Bethel (Gen. 28:19). 2. City of unknown location (Judg. 1:26).

**LYDIA** (LID ih uh). 1. A woman of Thyatira. She became Paul's first European convert to Christianity in Philippi. Lydia was the head of her household and a businesswoman dealing in a famous purple dye. She opened her home to Paul and his companions (Acts 16:14-15). 2. Country in Asia Minor with Sardis as capital (Ezek. 30:5).

**LYRE**. A small harp.

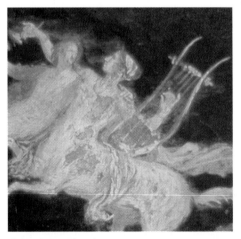

*A lyre being played.*

**LYSTRA** (LISS truh). City in Lycaonia in Asia Minor (Acts 14:6). Timothy joined Paul on one of his missionary journeys there.

# MACEDONIA

**MAGISTRATE**. Judge, ruler (Ezra 7:25; Luke 12:11).

**MAGNIFY**. To praise highly, exalt (Ps. 69:30; Luke 1:46).
● *How do you magnify the Lord?*

**MAGOG** (MAY gahg). Second son of Japheth (Gen. 10:2) Land and residents of this land (Ezek. 38:2; Rev. 20:8).

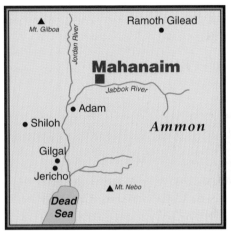

**MACEDONIA** (mass uh DOH nih uh). Country north of Greece. In NT times it was a Roman province. Paul responded to a vision to come and help in Macedonia (Acts 16:9), beginning the church in Europe.

**MAHANAIM** (may huh NAY im). A town east of Jordan (Gen. 32:2).

**MAIMED**. Deprived of a limb, crooked, distorted, crippled (Mark 10:43; Luke 14:13-14).

**MAKER**. One who forms; creator (Hab. 2:18). The Bible often refers to God as Creator (Job 35:10).

**MAD, MADNESS**. Insane, raving, foolish (1 Sam. 21:13; Eccl. 1:17; John 10:20). These words are used to describe various degrees of mental derangement or unhealthy behavior that might be permanent or temporary.

**MAGDALENE** (MAG duh leen). Resident of the city of Magdala, as in Mary Magdalene (Matt. 27:56). Mary was one of the women who came to the tomb to anoint Jesus and discovered that He had risen. See **MARY**.

**MALACHI**. Old Testament prophet whose sermons produced the Book of Malachi. He questioned priests and people about their unfaithfulness. His name means *my messenger*. He preached about 450 B.C.

**MALACHI, BOOK OF** (MAL uh kigh). Old Testament book; one of the minor prophets; last book of OT. The themes of the book are Israel's sin and God's judgment.

**MALCHUS** (MAL kuhs). Servant of the high priest (John 18:10). Malchus' ear was cut off by Peter during Jesus' arrest. Then Jesus healed Malchus.

**MALEFACTOR.** Evildoer, criminal (Luke 23:33).

**MALICE, MALICIOUSNESS.** Evil (1 Cor. 5:8; Rom. 1:29).

**MAMMON.** Wealth, riches, possessions (Matt. 6:24).

**MAMRE** (MAM rih). A place located two miles north of Hebron (Gen. 13:18).

**MAN.** Human being created in God's image (Gen. 1:26), including male and female. To be created in God's image includes freedom of choice and responsibility for creation. Humans choose to sin (Gen. 3) and thus need salvation (Rom. 3). See **IMAGE.**

**MANASSEH** (muh NASS uh). 1. Firstborn son of Joseph (Gen. 41:51). Also refers to the tribe descended from Manasseh. 2. Son of Hezekiah. Manasseh succeeded Hezekiah as fourteenth king of Judah (2 Kings 20:21). Manasseh was an evil and cruel king. See the **king chart** following **KING.**

**MANDRAKES.** Wild plants with edible berries and roots that were supposed to help women bear children (Gen. 30:14-16).

**MANGER.** Feeding trough for animals (Luke 2:7).

**MANIFEST.** Reveal, uncover, openly show, make visible (John 1:31).

**MANIFOLD.** Many, abundant (Neh. 9:19; Eph. 3:10).

*A stone manger still in place in the archaeological excavations at ancient Megiddo.*

**MANNA.** A whitish substance of nourishment that God provided for the Israelites during their forty years in the wilderness (Ex. 16:15). It remained after the morning dew evaporated and usually spoiled after one day. God instructed the Israelites to gather enough for one day with extra on the sixth day to provide for the sabbath. Although the Israelites became tired of this and complained, God continued to provide. This helped the Israelites to learn daily dependence on and obedience to God.

● *What are the results of being completely obedient to God?*

**MANTLE.** Covering, robe (2 Kings 2:8).

**MARK.** Nephew of Barnabas (Col. 4:10) and author of the Gospel of Mark. While accompanying Paul on his first missionary journey, Mark left and went home to Jerusalem. After Paul later refused to take him on another journey, Mark traveled with Barnabas. Paul later forgave Mark and affirmed his value in the ministry.

● *What can we learn from Mark about dealing with our fears and mistakes?*

**MARK, BOOK OF (GOSPEL OF).** Second Bible book of NT. Written by Mark. It may have been the first Gospel written. Its clear and fast-moving style focuses on Jesus' ministry and miracles.

■ **MARRIAGE.** Commitment of a man and woman to wed their lives together lovingly in a union that is total: spiritual, mental, physical (Matt. 19:5-6; Mark 10:7-9; 2 Cor. 11:2-3; Eph. 5:21-25). God created marriage, encourages it, and commands unity in it as a lifelong relationship (Gen. 2:24-25). It was the first institution.
● *Why is marriage best between two Christians? (See 2 Cor. 6:14-15.)*
● *Why do you think God wants us to love the same person for life?*

**MARTHA** (MAHR thuh). Older sister of

*"Mary's House" in Ephesus where tradition says that Mary the mother of Jesus lived out her last days.*

Mary and Lazarus (Luke 10:38). Jesus enjoyed visiting in their Bethany home.

**MARVEL.** Wonder, admire, be amazed (Matt. 8:10).

**MARY** (MAY rih). 1. Mother of Jesus (Luke 2:16). Mary was a young Jewish girl engaged to the carpenter Joseph when God revealed to her that she was to be the mother of the Messiah. Joseph, advised of these events in a dream and knowing Mary was miraculously pregnant, took Mary as his wife. Toward the end of her pregnancy, the couple from Nazareth traveled to Bethlehem for a taxation census, and Jesus was born there. Mary was present at Jesus' crucifixion and became one of His followers after His resurrection.

2. Mary Magdalene, healed by Jesus, became one of His close followers (Luke 8:1-2). She was present at Jesus' crucifixion and a witness of His resurrection.

3. Sister of Martha and Lazarus (John 11:1). Mary and her family were close to Jesus. Mary seemed spiritually aware of

Jesus' destiny as she demonstrated in her act of anointing Jesus with oil (John 12:3-8).

4. Mary, the mother of James and Joses (Matt. 27:56); the mother of John Mark (Acts 12:12); the wife of Cleophas (John 19:25); and a female believer who helped Paul (Rom. 16:6).

**MASTER.** Lord, ruler, sir, teacher (Gen. 24:12; Matt. 8:19).

**MATTHEW** (MATH yoo). A tax collector who responded to Jesus' call to become a disciple (Matt. 9:9). Also was known as Levi. Wrote the Gospel of Matthew.

**MATTHEW, BOOK OF (GOSPEL OF).** First Bible book of the NT; written by Matthew. The book focuses on Jesus as the supreme Teacher and the promised Messiah. It climaxes with Christ's Great Commission (28:18-20).

**MATTHIAS** (muh THIGH uhs). A disciple of Jesus chosen to replace Judas as the twelfth apostle (Acts 1:21-26).

**MEASURE.** As a noun in OT, refers to various dry or liquid weights such as *ephah* (Deut. 25:14), *cor* (1 Kings 4:22), or *seah* (Gen. 18:6). In the NT it can refer to this type of measure or to length or capacity (Matt. 7:2). See **WEIGHTS AND MEASURES**.

**MEAT OFFERING** (KJV; grain offering in NASB and NIV; cereal offering in RSV). An offering presented to God in response to His command (Lev. 2). Consisted of flour, baked cakes, or raw grain combined with oil and frankincense. It could accompany burnt offerings and peace offerings (Num. 15:1- 9). Also used without the frankincense as a substitute for an animal sacrifice by those who could not afford an animal (Lev. 5:11-13). Giving one's best grain during worship was part of a ceremony that represented removal of past sins.

**MEDE** (MEED). Inhabitant of the land of Media, which was located west and south of the Caspian Sea (Isa. 13:17). The Medes were a strong power. They were known as a rude and uncultivated race. Joined with Babylon to destroy Assyrian kingdom about 612 B.C.

**MEDIATOR.** One who reconciles or brings people back into a right relationship (Heb. 12:24). A go-between. Jesus is the Mediator between God and humans.

**MEDITATE.** Consider, study thoughtfully (Ps. 1:2; 1 Tim. 4:15).

■ **MEEK.** Humble, having a gentle and disciplined spirit (Ps. 25:9; Matt. 5:5). Meek does not mean weak. See **HUMILITY**.

**MEET.** Besides the common meaning, *meet* can also mean right or proper (Ex. 8:26); necessary or for a good reason (Luke 15:32); qualified or sufficient (Col. 1:12).

*◀ Mary with baby Jesus and Joseph fleeing to Egypt.*

**MEGIDDO** (mih GID oh). City west of

Jordan in the plain of Jezreel. An important city and the scene of several OT battles. Kings Ahaziah and Josiah died here (2 Kings 9:27; 23:29).

**MELCHISEDEC** (mel KIZ uh dek). Priest and king of Salem (same as Jerusalem). He blessed Abraham (Gen. 14:18-19). The writer of Hebrews referred to Christ as being like Melchizedec-a high priest (Heb. 5:6-10).

▼ *Read the Bible references to note similarities between Melchisedec (also spelled Melchizedek) and Christ: Genesis 14:18-20; Psalm 110:4; Hebrews 5:6-20; 7:1-21.*

**MELODY.** To make melody meant to play on a harp or other stringed instrument (Isa. 23:16; Eph. 5:19).

**MEMORIAL.** A reminder or token of remembrance (Ex. 3:15; Matt. 26:13).

**MENE** (MEE nih) **MENE, TEKEL** (TEE k'l), **UPHARSIN** (yoo FAR sin). Aramaic words that appeared on the wall of Belshazzar's banquet hall (Dan. 5:25). Daniel interpreted the words to mean that Belshazzar's kingdom was judged by God, found lacking, and would be divided and given to his enemies, the Medes and Persians (Dan. 5:26-28). It happened that night (Dan. 5:30-31).

**MEPHIBOSHETH** (me FIB oh sheth). A crippled son of Jonathan (2 Sam. 4:4; 9; 16; 21:7).

■ **MERCY.** Compassion, love, sympathy, deep caring, forgiveness (Ps. 145:9; Eph. 2:4-5). Giving or receiving care when it isn't deserved. Mercy may withhold or ease expected punishment.

▼ *The OT usage especially links mercy to God's covenant grace which treats people kindly.*

**MERCY SEAT.** Gold covering on the ark of the covenant. God commanded His people to build the mercy seat and later met with them there (Ex. 25:17-22; Lev. 16:2). Blood was sprinkled on it to symbolize forgiveness of sins (Lev. 16:15). It bordered by statues of cherubim (angelic beings). See **ARK OF THE COVENANT.**

**MESHACH** (MEE shak). New name given to Mishael, friend of Daniel. Ate healthy food with Daniel, Shadrach, and Meshach and entered fiery furnace with the latter two friends because he obeyed God rather than the king (Dan. 1:6,15; 3:16-30).

**MESOPOTAMIA** (MESS uh puh TAY mih uh). Area between the Tigris and Euphrates Rivers (Gen. 24:10; Acts 2:9). Babylonia, Assyria, and Sumeria were located there.

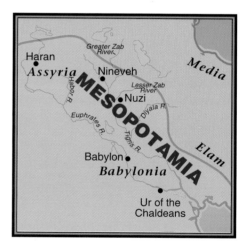

**MESSAGE, MESSENGER.** Word, promise (Judg. 3:20; 1 John 1:5). One who brings a word. Angel is the Greek word for *messenger*, and angels were often messengers.

**MESSIAH.** Literally *Anointed One* (Dan. 9:25; John 1:41; Matt. 16:16). *Messiah* transliterates the Hebrew word that refers to the ruling King or coming Savior. *Christ* transliterates the Greek word for the

*Rotary mills at Capernaum.*

Anointed One or Messiah. See **ANOINT, CHRIST**.

**METHUSELAH** (mih THYOO zuh luh). Son of Enoch and grandfather of Noah (Gen. 5:21). Best known for his long life of 969 years.

**MICAH** (MIGH kuh). 1. An OT prophet who prophesied during the reigns of Jotham, Ahaz, and Hezekiah (Mic. 1:1). 2. An Ephramite who hired a Levite to be priest to his idol (Judg. 17:7-13). 3. Several other Micahs are mentioned in the Bible.

**MICAH, BOOK OF.** Old Testament book in minor prophets. Micah preached about 735 B.C. to 715 B.C. and denounced the rich who mistreated the poor, the busi-nessmen who were dishonest, and the rulers who were unjust. Micah prophesied God's judgment on Israel, and the suffer-ing and restoration of Jerusalem. He called for justice and righteousness (6:8).

**MICAIAH** (migh CAY yuh). Prophet in Samaria. Ahab disliked Micaiah because Micaiah told the truth: he predicted the death of King Ahab (1 Kings 22:8).

**MICHAEL** (MIGH kuhl). 1. A messenger of God (Dan. 10:13; Rev. 12:7). Referred to in Jude 9 as the archangel. 2. There were also several other Michaels.

**MICHAL** (MIGH kuhl). Youngest daugh-ter of Saul who became David's wife (1 Sam. 14:49).

**MIDIAN, MIDIANITES** (MID ih uhn,

MID ih uhn ight). Abraham's son; Midian's land and descendants (Gen. 25:2; 37:28; Ex. 2:15).

**MIDWIFE.** A person who helps with the birth of a baby (Gen. 35:17).

■ **MILLENNIUM.** A thousand years. Though not in the Bible, *millennium* is used to refer to a thousand-year period in relation to Christ's return (see Rev. 20:2-7). Scholars differ on whether the number is literal or symbolic and on other matters in reference to the return of Christ.

**MILLSTONE.** Stones used to grind grain into flour (Deut. 24:6). Smaller ones were used by individuals, while larger ones were pulled by animals (Matt. 18:6).

■ **MINISTER, MINISTRY.** Serve, service (Ex. 28:35; Mark 10:45; Eph. 4:12). A primary goal of Jesus and Christians is to minister to people in need.

**MIRACLE.** God's intervention in humanity, nature, and history (Num. 14:22; John 2:11). Sometimes translated as signs, wonders, or mighty acts. Miracles carry out God's purpose or reveal God.

**MIRE.** Thick mud, filth (Jer. 38:22; 2 Pet. 2:22).

**MIRIAM** (MIR ih uhm). Older sister of Moses and Aaron (Ex. 15:20). She helped save Moses' life when he was an infant (Ex. 2:4-9) and celebrated the victory at the Sea (Ex. 15:20-21). As adults, she and her brother Aaron criticized Moses' marriage to an Ethiopian woman (Num. 12:1-15).

**MIRTH.** Joy, gladness (Isa. 24:8).

**MISCHIEF.** Wickedness, injury, evil thought (Ps. 36:4; Acts 13:10).

**MISHAEL** (MISH ih uhl). Daniel's friend who was renamed Meshach. Ate healthy food with Daniel and entered fiery furnace (Dan. 1:6,15; 3:16-30).

**MISTRESS.** Woman in charge of household, owner (1 Kings 17:17).

**MIZPAH** (MIZ pah). Name of various sites and towns. In one location, east of the Jordan River, Jacob and Laban made a covenant of peace there. Jacob set up a stone altar (Gen. 31:44-50).

▼ *Have you ever seen or worn a necklace that says "The Lord watch between me and thee, when we are absent one from another" (Gen. 31:49)? It is based on Jacob and Laban's covenant and is used today as a symbol of love. Originally it was a promise to keep these two enemies from fighting!*

**MOAB, MOABITE** (MOH ab, MOH uh bight). Grandson of Lot. The land east of the Dead Sea that Moab's descendants occupied. Resident of Moab (Gen. 19:37; 36:35). The Moabites were usually enemies of the Israelites. Ruth was a Moabitess.

**MOCK.** Scorn, insult, laugh at (Job 11:3; Gal. 6:7).

**MOLECH** (MOH lek), **MOLOCH** (MOH lahk). A god worshiped by the Ammonites (Lev. 18:21). The rituals included sacrificing children by fire.

**MOLTEN.** Melted (Ezek. 24:11). A molten image is metal poured into a form or mold (Ex. 32:4).

**MONEY.** Israelites did not have coined money and so used a system of weights in transactions (Gen. 23:16; 1 Chron. 21:25). Early a shekel and a talent were weights rather than monetary values. By New Testament times, coins

## MIRACLES OF JESUS

| MIRACLE | BIBLE PASSAGES | | | |
|---|---|---|---|---|
| Water Turned to Wine | | | | John 2:1 |
| Many Healings | Matt 4:23 | Mark 1:32 | | |
| Healing of a Leper | Matt 8:1 | Mark 1:40 | Luke 5:12 | |
| Healing of a Roman Centurion's Servant | Matt 8:5 | | Luke 7:1 | |
| Healing of Peter's Mother-in-law | Matt 8:14 | Mark 1:29 | Luke 4:38 | |
| Calming of the Storm at Sea | Matt 8:23 | Mark 4:35 | Luke 8:22 | |
| Healing of the Wild Men of Gadara | Matt 8:28 | Mark 5:1 | Luke 8:26 | |
| Healing of the Lame Man | Matt 9:1 | Mark 2:1 | Luke 5:18 | |
| Healing of a Woman with a Hemorrhage | Matt 9:20 | Mark 5:25 | Luke 8:43 | |
| Raising of Jairus's Daughter | Matt 9:23 | Mark 5:22 | Luke 8:41 | |
| Healing of Two Blind Men | Matt 9:27 | | | |
| Healing of a Demon-possessed Man | Matt 9:32 | | | |
| Healing of Man with a Withered Hand | Matt 12:10 | Mark 3:1 | Luke 6:6 | |
| Feeding of 5,000 People | Matt 14:15 | Mark 6:35 | Luke 9:12 | John 6:1 |
| Walking on the Sea | Matt 14:22 | Mark 6:47 | | John 6:16 |
| Healing of the Syrophoenician's Daughter | Matt 15:21 | Mark 7:24 | | |
| Feeding of 4,000 People | Matt 15:32 | Mark 8:1 | | |
| Healing of an Epileptic Boy | Matt 17:14 | Mark 9:14 | Luke 9:37 | |
| Healing of Two Blind Men at Jericho | Matt 20:30 | | | |
| Healing of a Man with an Unclean Spirit | | Mark 1:23 | Luke 4:33 | |
| Healing of a Deaf, Speechless Man | | Mark 7:31 | | |
| Healing of a Blind Man at Bethesda | | Mark 8:22 | | |
| Healing of Blind Bartimaeus | | Mark 10:46 | Luke 18:35 | |
| A Miraculous Catch of Fish | | | Luke 5:4 | John 21:1 |
| Raising of a Widow's Son | | | Luke 7:11 | |
| Healing of a Stooped Woman | | | Luke 13:11 | |
| Healing of a Man with the Dropsy | | | Luke 14:1 | |
| Healing of Ten Lepers | | | Luke 17:11 | |
| Healing of Malchus's Ear | | | Luke 22:50 | |
| Healing of a Royal Official's Son | | | | John 4:46 |
| Healing of a Lame Man at Bethesda | | | | John 5:1 |
| Healing of a Blind Man | | | | John 9:1 |
| Raising of Lazarus | | | | John 11:38 |

*A coin from Pamphylia (190—36 B.C.).*

were in use. Because the value of money changes over time, it is difficult to give present day equivalents. Perhaps it is better to note what each could buy. A denarius (same as a drachma) equaled a day's pay for a Roman soldier or an ordinary laborer. The KJV translates it "penny." A talent was about six thousand Denarii. Other money values:

*Roman coins in a bowl of the same period at Caesarea Maritima on the coast of Israel.*

Lepton = widow's mite = fraction of a cent

Denarius = one day's pay (translated *penny* in KJV)

Drachma (Greek) = denarius (Roman)

Stater = 4 denarii (plural of denarius)

Aureus = 25 denarii

Talent = 6000 denarii

**MONOGAMY.** A marriage with one mate. God's ideal plan for marriage is one wife for one husband throughout life. God designed us to be happiest in this relationship.

● *Why do you think monogamy is best? Our yearning for lifelong love and faithfulness are two of the many reasons.*

**MONEYCHANGER.** A person who exchanged foreign currency at a profit. The temple moneychangers made exchanges from Roman coins to the half shekel required for the Temple offering (Matt. 21:12).

**MONTH.** Hebrew months began with the new moon. See the **Calendar Chart** pages 228 & 229. Some of these

*Rock traditionally considered the Rock of Rephidim that Moses struck to get water for the Israelites.*

and their approximate modern equivalents are:

1. Nisan (Abib) = March/April
2. Iyyar (Ziv) = April/May
3. Sivan = May/June
4. Thammuz = June/July
5. Ab = July/August
6. Elul = August/September
7. Tishri (Ethanim) = September/October
8. Marchesvan (Buf) = October/November
9. Chislev = November/December
10. Tebeth = December/January
11. Shebat = January/February
12. Adar = February/March

**MORDECAI** (MAWR dih kigh). Means *little man.* Cousin and guardian of Esther (Esther 2:5-7). He was a Jewish exile who became an official in the Persian palace. Mordecai worked with Esther to save the Jewish people from slaughter.

**MORTAL**. Human, subject to death (Job 4:17; Rom. 6:12).

**MOSES** (MOH ziss). A Hebrew born into Egyptian slavery (Ex. 2:1-2). Spared from death as an infant and raised in the palace by Pharaoh's daughter, Moses fled Egypt after committing murder. Later God called him

*Moses breaking the tables of the law.*

to return to Egypt to lead the Hebrew people from captivity. During the journey to the Promised Land, God gave Moses the Law by which the people were to live and worship.

Moses was able to view the Promised Land but not to enter it because of his sin. Moses is traditionally held to be the author of the Book of the Law, the first five books of the Bible.

**MOST HIGH**. Name to describe God or used for God (Gen. 14:18-22; Acts 7:48). See **GOD**.

**MOST HOLY PLACE**. The innermost part of the tabernacle or Temple. Only the high priest could enter the most holy place, and he could enter only once a year. There he made a sacrifice for the sins of the people (Ex. 26:34). The only item in the holy of holies was the ark of the covenant, a small wooden structure covered with gold and containing the Ten Commandments, a pot of manna, and Aaron's rod (Ex. 25). See **HOLY OF HOLIES** and **ORACLE**.

**MOUNT, MOUNTAIN**. The land in and around Palestine is made up of many hills and mountains, the highest of which is about 9,100 feet above sea level in Syria. Mountains had great significance as places of defense, refuge, and worship. They are symbols of eternity, stability, obstacles, and difficulty.

**MOUNT OF OLIVES**. A mile-long ridge of hills east of Jerusalem (Matt. 21:1). Also called Olivet (Acts 1:12).

**MOURN**. To show pain, grief, sorrow (2 Sam. 13:37; Matt. 5:4). In the Bible death was often associated with weeping, tearing of clothing, and putting on sackcloth and ashes. A period of mourning could last up to seven days, and sometimes a professional mourner was hired to help.

Mourning was also an expression of grief over sin and of repentance.

**MULTIPLY**. To heap up, make abundant, increase (Gen. 1:22; Acts 6:7).

**MULTITUDE**. Great crowd (Judg. 4:7; Matt. 4:25).

**MURMUR**. Grumble, speak with discontent (Ex. 15:24; John 6:41).

**MUSTARD SEED**. An annual plant that grew quite fast and was popularly thought to have been the smallest of all seeds. However, positive identification cannot be made of the plant Jesus made reference to in His parable of the mustard seed (Matt. 13:31-32). Christ used the parable to illustrate something that starts small and grows rapidly such as the kingdom of God.

**MUSTER**. Cause to assemble, gather (2 Kings 25:19).

**MUTE**. Silent, voiceless, cannot talk (Mark 7:37, NIV). Does not mean stupid or unable to learn (dumb in KJV.)

**MUZZLE**. Stop, gag (Deut. 25:4; 1 Cor. 9:9).

**MYRRH**. Gum extracted from a shrub used for anointing oil, women's purification, and burial (Gen. 37:25; Matt. 2:11). Known for its pleasing odor, it was one of the gifts of the Magi to Jesus.

**MYRTLE**. A shrub with good-smelling leaves and white flowers. The Hebrews often used this shrub for shelter in the fields at the Feast of Tabernacles (see Lev. 23:40; Neh. 8:15).

**MYSTERY**. A special revelation of God that was once hidden but is now revealed to His followers (Matt. 13:11; Eph. 3:3-5; 1 Cor. 2:7-8).

See the **Names for Jesus** following **JESUS** and the **Names for God** following **GOD**.

**NAOMI** (nay OH mih). Wife of Elimelech (Ruth 1:2). During a famine they left their home of Bethlehem to live in Moab. After Naomi became a widow and her two sons died, she returned to her homeland with her Moabite daughter-in-law, Ruth.
● *Read Ruth 1-4. What tips for family relationships does Naomi's relationship with her daughter give you?*

**NAAMAN** (NAY uh muhn). Commander under Ben-hadad, king of Syria (2 Kings 5:1). Naaman was healed of leprosy when he obeyed God's message that came through Elisha (2 Kings 5:8-14).

**NAPHTALI** (NAF tuh ligh). Sixth son of Jacob (Gen. 30:8); name of Naphtali's descendants and their territory.

**NABOTH** (NAY bahth). An Israelite vineyard owner (1 Kings 21:1). Jezebel plotted to have Naboth killed so her greedy husband, Ahab, could have Naboth's vineyard.

**NATHAN** (NAY thuhn). 1. Prophet of OT who counselled King David (2 Sam. 7:2) saying the king would not be allowed to build the temple; rather, God would build David's house to rule His people (2 Sam.

**NADAB** (NAY dab). 1. Aaron's oldest son (Ex. 6:23). Together with his father, brother, and uncle he saw the glory of God (Ex. 24:1,9-10). Later ordained into the Aaronic priesthood (Ex. 29), Nadab and his brother offered a strange or unholy fire to God, which resulted in their deaths (Lev. 10:1-2). 2. King of Israel briefly about 900 B.C. (1 Kings 15:25-28). See **Kings Chart** under **KINGS**. 3. Two other Old Testament personalities.

**NAHUM**. Old Testament prophet who preached against Nineveh and Assyria about 620 B.C.

**NAHUM** (NAY huhm), **BOOK OF**. Old Testament book containing sermons by Nahum, a prophet of Elkosh (Nahum 1:1). The book tells of God's judgment on wickedness, especially on the city of Nineveh.

**NAMES FOR CHRIST AND FOR GOD.**

*The Church of the Annunciation in Nazareth built over the caves where tradition says Mary and Joseph lived.*

7:12-13). Nathan boldly confronted David with his sins of adultery and murder by use of a parable. 2. Nathan was a popular biblical name that others also bore (including a son of David).

● *How do you think Nathan got the courage to confront David? Why did a story work better than direct accusation?*

**NAVE.** Ring or hub of a wheel (1 Kings 7:33).

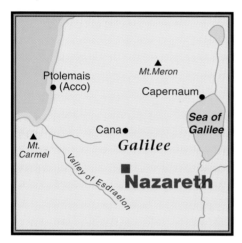

*The modern city of Nazareth.*

**NAZARENE** (naz uh REEN). Person from the city of Nazareth (Matt. 2:23). In Acts 24:5 Nazarenes refers to a group of Christians. *Nazarene* was apparently a term of scorn and ridicule.

**NAZARETH** (NAZ uh reth). A town in Galilee located seventy miles north of Jerusalem (Matt. 2:23). Nazareth is where Jesus grew up.

**NAZARITE** (NAZ uh right). A person, dedicated to God, who vowed to abstain from certain practices such as having a haircut and drinking alcohol (Num. 6:2-8). The most famous Nazarite is Samson (Judg. 16:17).

● *Would you consider taking a vow not to drink alcohol?*

**NEBO** (NEE boh). 1. Name of cities within the territories of Reuben and Judah (Num. 32:38; Ezra 2:29). 2. Mountain (east of the Jordan River) where Moses viewed the Promised Land (Deut. 34:1).

**NEBUCHADNEZZAR** (neb yoo kad

*View of the Jordan Valley from the top of Mt.
Nebo looking toward Jericho.*

NEZZ ur). King of Babylon who conquered Judah, the Southern Kingdom (2 Kings 24:10). He captured Jerusalem and carried many of its inhabitants into captivity in Babylon. He was the king who ordered the three young men into the fiery furnace (Dan. 3:19-20). See the **King Chart** page 142.

**NECROMANCER.** A person who tries to contact the dead. God's law forbids this practice (Deut. 18:10-12).

**NEEDLE, EYE OF.** Expression Jesus used

*Relief of a bull in glazed brick from the famous Ishtar Gate of Babylon built by Nebuchadnezzar in about 580 B.C.*

to point out the difficulty of a rich person entering the kingdom of God (Matt. 19:24). Often a rich person's priority is riches, not God. It is a false teaching that "eye of a needle" refers to a narrow gate or opening in Jerusalem.
● *What has first place in your life?*

**NEEDS.** Used as a phrase: must needs (Luke 14:18), meaning to be necessary.

**NEGLECT.** Disregard, overlook (Acts 6:1).

**NEHEMIAH.** Jew who served Persian King Artaxerxes I as cupbearer or personal taster and server of royal food. He received leaves of abscences to lead team to Jerusalem to rebuild the city's fallen walls about 445 B.C. and to purify temple practices about 432. He exemplified godly servant leadership. He brought revival and covenant renewal to a dispirited people.

**NEHEMIAH, BOOK OF** (nee huh MIGH uh). Old Testament book that tells of Nehemiah's return to Jerusalem, his leadership in the rebuilding of the city walls, the dedication of the walls, and other reforms he carried out.

*Nehemiah secretly viewing the ruins of the walls of Jerusalem.*

**NEPHILIM** (NEF uh lim). Used in some contemporary Bible translations to refer to a variety of unusual people (NIV: Gen. 6:4; Num. 13:33).

**NETHER.** Lower, under (Ex. 19:17).

**NETTLES.** Thorns, shrubs (Job 30:7).

**NETWORK.** Ornamental grill used on the altar of burnt offering (Ex. 27:4). It possibly served as a vent as well as a decoration.

**NEW TESTAMENT.** This second part of the Bible contains twenty-seven books: the four Gospels, the Book of Acts, twenty-one epistles or letters, and Revelation. The NT tells of Jesus' birth, life, death, resurrection; the growth of the church; instructions, warnings, and encouragements to the church; and prophecy of the end of time. *Testament* means covenant or agreement. The NT tells of God's new covenant through Jesus Christ (Heb. 8:6-10).
● *Check the table of contents in your Bible for the names of the NT Bible books. Memorize them.*

**NICODEMUS** (nik uh DEE muhs). A Pharisee and member of the Sanhedrin (John 3:1). He came to Jesus at night searching for answers to eternal questions and learned he needed to be born again. Nicodemus later spoke in Jesus' defense and brought spices to anoint his body (John 19:39-41). See **BORN AGAIN**.
● *Can you tell a friend how to be born again?*

**NIGER** (NIGH JUR). Also called Simeon (Acts 13:1). Leader of the church at Antioch.

**NIGH.** Near (Ps. 145:18; Matt. 24:32).

**NIMROD** (NIM rahd). Son of Cush (Gen. 10:8). Nimrod's name means *strong* or *valiant,* and he was known as a mighty hunter.

**NINEVEH** (NIN uh vuh). The last and most important capital of Assyria (Gen. 10:11), located on the Tigris River. God sent Jonah to warn the people of Nineveh of His judgment, and they repented and were spared. Babylon destroyed the city in 612 B.C.
▼ *God does not change, but He changes His intentions based on people's responses to His word.*

**NISAN** (NIGH san). First month of the Jewish year beginning at the end of March

(Neh. 2:1). See **MONTH** and **Calendar Chart** pages 228 & 229.

**NOAH** (NO uh). A righteous man who lived during a time of evil and corruption (Gen. 6:8). God instructed Noah to build an ark, which God used to save a small number of people and animals while He destroyed the rest with a great flood.

**NORTHERN KINGDOM.** Refers to the northern ten tribes of Israel after the division of the kingdom (about 922-912 B.C.). This area included all the tribal lands except Judah, which became known as the Southern Kingdom, and Benjamin. Israel was one nation before about 950 B.C. After Solomon's death a division occurred (1 Kings 14:19-30). Israel continued until 722 B.C. Judah continued until 587 B.C. See the **King Chart** page 141.

**NUMBERS.** Besides the normal usage of

*Restored gate at the site the ancient city of Nineveh of Assyria.*

numbers in the Bible, there is also a symbolic usage. Some of these numbers and their meanings are:

One=unity and uniqueness

Four, five, seven, ten=completion or perfection

Six=association with humans

Twelve=elective purposes of God

Forty=new developments of God's mighty acts in history.

Ten and twelve with their multiples may be literal or may symbolize completion (for example: one thousand years-Rev. 20:2-7; or 144,000 people-Rev. 14:1).

**NUMBERS, BOOK OF.** Old Testament book included in the five books of the Law. The book contains the census of the tribes, the wilderness wanderings, the murmuring of the people, Levitical and other laws, and preparation for the conquest of the Promised Land.

**NUN** (NUN). Father of Joshua (Num. 14:6).

# ANCIENT NUMBER SYSTEMS

| AMERICAN | SUMERIAN | EARLY EGYPTIAN (HIEROGLYPHIC) | LATER EGYPTIAN (HIERATIC) | CANAANITE (and PHOENICIAN) | POST-EXILIC HEBREW | EARLY GREEK | LATER GREEK (IONIC) | ANCIENT ROMAN (LATIN) |
|---|---|---|---|---|---|---|---|---|
| 1 | Y (or ˅) | I | I | I | א | I | A | I |
| 2 | YY (or ˅˅) | II | q | II | ב | II | B | II |
| 3 | YYY (or ˅˅˅) | III | III | III | ג | III | Γ | III |
| 4 | YYYY (or ˅˅˅˅) | IIII | IIII | IIII | ד | IIII | Δ | IIII (or IV) |
| 5 | YYY / YY (or ˅˅˅˅˅) | IIIII | ן | I IIII | ה | ΓI | E | V |
| 6 | YYY / YYY (or ˅˅˅) | III / III | ٢ | II III | ו | ΓII | F | VI |
| 7 | YYYY / YYY (or ˅˅˅˅) | IIII / III | ے | III IIII | ז | ΓII | Z | VII |
| 8 | YYYY / YYYY (or ˅˅˅˅) | IIII / IIII | ₁ | II III III | ח | ΓIII | H | VIII |
| 9 | YYYYY / YYYY (or ˅˅˅˅˅) | IIIII / IIII | ₃ | III III III | ט | ΓIIII | Θ | VIIII (or IX) |
| 10 | ‹ (or ◀) | ∩ | ٨ | ⌐ | י | Δ | I | X |
| 20 | ‹‹ (or ◀◀) | ∩∩ | ٦ | ⌐⌐ | כ | ΔΔ | K | XX |
| 50 | | ⌒ | ⌒ | ξ | נ | | N | L |
| 100 | | ⊙ | ٦ | | ק | H | P | C |
| 200 | | ⊙⊙ | ٦ | | ר | HH | Σ | CC |
| 1,000 | | 𓆼 | ᓭ | | ן | X | /A | M |

**OATH.** Solemn promise of commitment (Gen. 26:28; Matt. 5:33).

**OBADIAH** (oh buh DIGH uh). Governor under Ahab (1 Kings 18:3). Also, the Prophet whose sermons comprise the OT book of Obadiah (Obad. 1). Over ten other Obadiahs appear in the Bible.

**OBADIAH, BOOK OF.** Old Testament Bible book; fourth of the minor prophets. This shortest book of the OT tells of the judgment of Edom and the restoration of Israel.

**OBED** (OH bed). Son of Ruth and Boaz; grandfather of King David and ancestor of Jesus (Ruth 4:17; Matt. 1:5-6). Four other Obeds appear in Scripture.

■ **OBEDIENCE.** Believing and doing what God says; living like Him (Rom. 6:14-17). Obeying God shows our trust in God and His will. It is also true freedom of choice (Ex. 24:7; 1 John 3:23-24; Jas. 3:3).

**OBEISANCE.** To bow down in respect or submission (Gen. 43:28).

**OBLATION.** Offering (Jer. 14:12).

**OBSERVE.** Besides meaning *to watch*, it also means *to keep* or *to practice*-such as observing the sabbath (Deut. 5:32). *Observe* in the KJV may carry the idea of to treat with respect (Mark 6:20).

● *How do you observe Sunday? Do you think this is the way God intended? Why or why not?*

**OCCASION.** Besides the usual meaning, it also means *opportunity* (Dan. 6:4; Rom. 14:13; 2 Cor. 5:12).

**OCCUPY.** Do business (Luke 19:13); trade (Ezek. 27:9); use (Judg. 16:11).

**ODIOUS.** Hated, detestable (Prov. 30:23; 1 Chron. 19:6).

**ODOR, ODOUR.** Smell, incense, perfume (Rev. 5:8).

**OFFENCE, OFFEND.** Besides its usual meaning, a trap or a cause for stumbling (Isa. 8:14; Matt. 16:23). The verb form means *to cause to stumble* (Mark 9:42).

**OFFER, OFFERING.** Verb: To give freely as a gift or a sacrifice, as in worship (Gen. 31:54; Heb. 9:14). Noun: Gift or present. Biblical offerings include animals, birds, produce, or incense. The nation or individuals made offerings that symbolized the repentance and faith required to have a right relationship with God.

**OFFICE.** Position of service or calling (1 Chron. 6:32; Rom. 11:13; 12:4; 1 Tim. 3:1).

**OFFSPRING.** Children (Job 5:25; Acts 17:28).

**OG** (AHG). Amorite king of Bashan (Num. 21:33). He was of the giant race of Rephaim and was defeated and killed during the conquest of Palestine.

**OIL.** Usually the product of olive trees, oil was an essential part of everyday life in biblical times (2 Kings 18:32; Matt. 25:3). It was used in trade, religious ceremonies,

# COMPARISON OF LISTS OF THE OLD TESTAMENT BOOKS

| RABBINIC CANON 24 BOOKS | SEPTUAGINT 53 BOOKS | ROMAN CATHOLIC OLD TESTAMENT 46 BOOKS |
|---|---|---|
| **The Law** | **Law** | **Law** |
| Genesis | Genesis | Genesis |
| Exodus | Exodus | Exodus |
| Leviticus | Leviticus | Leviticus |
| Numbers | Numbers | Numbers |
| Deuteronomy | Deuteronomy | Deuteronomy |
| **The Prophets** | **History** | **History** |
| The Former Prophets | | |
| Joshua | Joshua | Joshua |
| Judges | Judges | Judges |
| 1-2 Samuel | Ruth | Ruth |
| 1-2 Kings | 1 Kingdoms (1 Samuel) | 1 Samuel (1 Kingdoms) |
| The Latter Prophets | 2 Kingdoms (2 Samuel) | 2 Samuel (2 Kingdoms) |
| Isaiah | 3 Kingdoms (1 Kings) | 1 Kings (3 Kingdoms) |
| Jeremiah | 4 Kingdoms (2 Kings) | 2 Kings (4 Kingdoms) |
| Ezekiel | 1 Paralipomena (1 Chronicles) | 1 Chronicles (1 Paralipomena) |
| The Twelve | 2 Paralipomena (2 Chronicles) | 2 Chronicles (2 Paralipomena) |
| Hosea | 1 Esdras (Apocryphal Ezra) | Ezra (1 Esdras) |
| Joel | 2 Esdras (Ezra-Nehemiah) | Nehemiah (2 Esdras) |
| Amos | Esther (with Apocryphal additions) | Tobit |
| Obadiah | Judith | Judith |
| Jonah | Tobit | Esther |
| Micah | 1 Maccabees | 1 Maccabees |
| Nahum | 2 Maccabees | 2 Maccabees |
| Habakkuk | 3 Maccabees | |
| Zephaniah | 4 Maccabees | **Poetry** |
| Haggai | | Job |
| Zechariah | **Poetry** | Psalms |
| Malachi | Psalms | Proverbs |
| | Odes (including the prayer of Manasseh) | Ecclesiastes |
| **The Writings** | Proverbs | Song of Songs |
| Poetry | Ecclesiastes | Wisdom of Solomon |
| Psalms | Song of Songs | Ecclesiasticus (The Wisdom of |
| Proverbs | Job | Jesus the son of Sirach) |
| Job | Wisdom (of Solomon) | |
| Rolls—"the Festival Scrolls" | Sirach (Ecclesiasticus or The Wisdom | **Prophecy** |
| Song of Songs | of Jesus the son of Sirach) | Isaiah |
| Ruth | Psalms of Solomon | Jeremiah |
| Lamentations | | Lamentations |
| Ecclesiastes | **Prophecy** | Baruch (including the Letter |
| Esther | The Twelve Prophets | of Jeremiah) |
| Others (History) | Hosea | Ezekiel |
| Daniel | Amos | Daniel |
| Ezra-Nehemiah | Micah | Hosea |
| 1–2 Chronicles | Joel | Joel |
| | Obadiah | Amos |
| | Jonah | Obadiah |
| | Nahum | Jonah |
| | Habakkuk | Micah |
| | Zephaniah | Nahum |
| | Haggai | Habakkuk |
| | Zechariah | Zephaniah |
| | Malachi | Haggai |
| | Isaiah | Zechariah |
| | Jeremiah | Malachi |
| | Baruch | |
| | Lamentations | **Appendix** |
| | Letter of Jeremiah | The Prayer of Manasseh |
| | Ezekiel | The two apocryphal books of |
| | Daniel (with apocryphal additions, including the Prayer of Azariah and the Song of the Three Children, Susanna, and Bel and the Dragon) | Esdras |

The Canonical Books of the Old Testament ✱

- Books of Law
- Books of History
- Books of Poetry and Wisdom
- Books of the Major Prophets
- Books of the Minor Prophets

✱ Grouped according to the Christian canon

food preparation, cosmetics, as medicine, and for lamplight. Oil was used in the consecration of priests and kings. Among other things, oil symbolized joy (Isa. 61:3; Ps. 45:7).

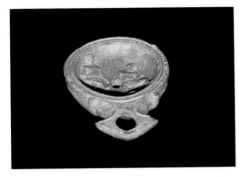

*Ancient oil lamp decorated with two human figures.*

*Olive trees provide fruit for the valuable olive oil of the Middle East.*

**OINTMENT.** Usually a perfumed oil (Ps. 109:18; Luke 7:46). Ointments were often kept in alabaster containers and were used as cosmetics, in religious ceremonies, and for anointing the dead. Aging and the use of certain ingredients made some ointments very valuable.

**OLD TESTAMENT.** The OT is made up of thirty-nine books: five books of Law; twelve of history; five of poetry; five major prophets; and twelve minor prophets. Major and minor prophets are named that because of the length of the books not their importance.

● *Look in front of your Bible at list of Bible books. Memorize the names of the Old Testament books.*

**OLIVE TREE.** A slow-growing, crooked

tree of immense value in biblical times (Deut. 6:11; Rom. 11:17). A cultivated tree grows to about twenty feet in height and can live several hundred years. Oil made from the tree's fruit has many uses (see **OIL**). The olive tree is a symbol of fruitfulness, and the branch of the olive tree is a symbol of peace.

**OMEGA** (oh MEE guh). Last letter of the Greek alphabet. *Alpha* is the first letter. Together, the two letters are used symbolically to refer to Christ as the beginning and the end (Rev. 1:8).

**OMER.** A dry measure equal to one-tenth of an ephah, four pints, or about two liters (Ex. 16:16). See **Weights and Measures Chart** pages 244 & 245.

**OMRI** (AHM righ). Powerful and evil king of Israel, the Northern Kingdom about 885-874 B.C. (1 Kings 16:25). He moved the capital to Samaria. Omri was the father of the wicked Ahab who succeeded him. See **King Chart** page 141.
● *Name of three other Bible characters.*

**ONESIMUS** (oh NESS ih muhs). A runaway slave of Philemon (Col. 4:9). Paul converted Onesimus to Christianity and sent him back to his master with a letter that became the NT Bible book of Philemon.

**ONYX.** Either a green stone or translucent (see-through) agate with layers of black and white (Ex. 25:7).

**OPPRESS.** Bruise, crush, overpower, put down, or burden (Ex. 3:9; Prov. 14:31).

**ORACLE.** 1. Holy of holies (1 Kings 6:16). 2. divine words or utterances (2 Sam. 16:23; Heb. 5:12). May sometimes be translated burden (NASB: Jer. 23:33-34). **See HOLY OF HOLIES; PROPHET.**

**ORDAIN.** To appoint (Dan. 2:24); establish (Ps. 8:3); set aside (1 Tim. 2:7).

**ORDER.** Most common use means to put in arrangement or array (Job 10:22; 1 Cor. 14:40).

**ORDINANCE.** Decree, law (Ex. 12:24; Luke 1:6). God gave many ordinances for the Hebrew people to observe in the OT. Some churches today refer to baptism and the Lord's Supper as NT ordinances. See **BAPTISM, LORD'S SUPPER.**

**OTHNIEL** (AHTH nih el). First of the judges. He restored authority and order after the death of Joshua and judged for fourty years (Josh. 15:17; Judg. 1:11-15; 3:8-11).

**OUTCAST.** Person driven or forced away (Ps. 147:2).

**OVERCOME.** Prevail or gain victory (Num. 13:30; Rev. 2:7).

**OVERFLOW.** To flood or spill over (Ps. 69:2).

**OVERLAID.** Covered (Ex. 26:32; Heb. 9:4).

**OVERSEER.** Inspector, administrator (Gen. 39:4; Acts 20:28). The Greek word for overseer is also translated as *bishop* (Phil. 1:1).

**OVERSIGHT.** 1. Error (Gen. 43:12). 2. Have responsibility for, be in charge of (2 Kings 12:11; 1 Peter 5:2).

**OVERWHELM.** To cover or overflow (Ps. 55:5).

**OX, OXEN.** Cow, cattle (Gen. 12:16). Important in agriculture and sacrificial worship. The "stalled ox" was a symbol of luxury (Prov. 15:17).

# P

Palestine was about 70 miles wide and 150 miles long. It has a variety of landscape from seacoast to desert to mountains. See map on next page.

**PALM TREE.** The date palm grows in the Jordan Valley (1 Kings 6:29). The palm symbolized grace and elegance. Palm branches were used to symbolize praise as Jesus entered Jerusalem (John 12:13).

**PALACE.** Residence of the royal family (2 Chron. 9:11) or the high priest (Matt. 26:3). It could also refer to a fortress or the most prominent or important building in a city.

**PALESTINE** (PAL uhs tighn). Area east and west of the Jordan River to the Mediterranean Sea. Palestine was also called the Promised Land, Caanan, Israel, Judea, and (today) the Holy Land. In NT times it was divided into Galilee, Samaria, and Judea (west of the Jordan) and the Decapolis and Perea (east of the Jordan).

**PALSY.** Paralysis (Luke 5:18).

*The road north from Anatolia Isparta in the Roman province of Pamphylia (modern Turkey).*

**PAMPHYLIA** (pam FIL ih uh). A Roman province Paul visited on his missionary journeys (Acts 13:13). It was a

*Palm trees in the Wadi Feiran on the Sinai peninsula.*

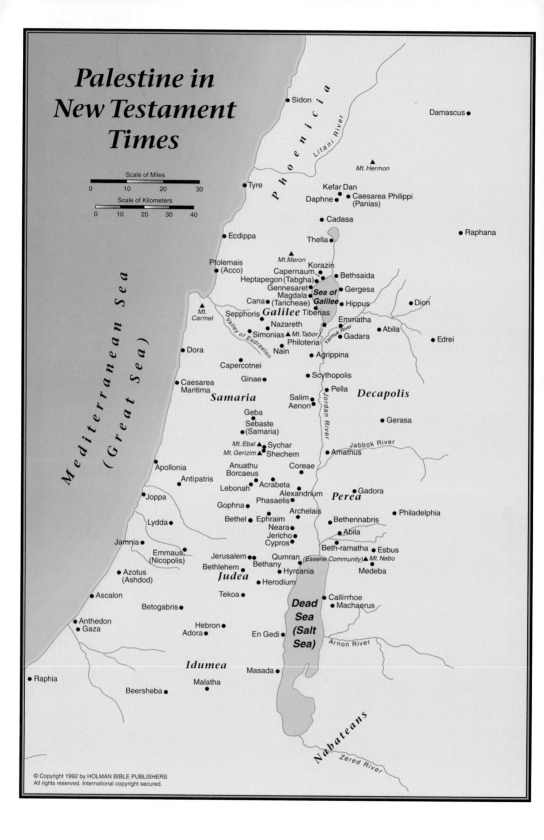

# Palestine in New Testament Times

Scale of Miles
0   10   20   30

Scale of Kilometers
0   10   20   30   40

Sidon

Damascus

*P h o e n i c i a*

Litani River

Mt. Hermon

Tyre

Kefar Dan
Daphne   Caesarea Philippi
(Panias)

Cadasa

Ecdippa

Thella

Raphana

Ptolemais
(Acco)

Mt. Meron

Korazin
Capernaum
Heptapegon (Tabgha)   Bethsaida
Gennesaret   Gergesa
Magdala   *Sea of*
Cana (Taricheae)   *Galilee*   Hippus
Sepphoris   *Galilee*   Tiberias   Dion
Mt. Carmel   Nazareth   Emmatha
Simonias   Mt. Tabor   Gadara   Abila
Philoteria   Edrei
Nain   Agrippina

Valley of Esdraelon

Yarmuk River

Dora

Capercotnei

Ginae   Scythopolis

Caesarea
Maritima

*Samaria*

Pella   *Decapolis*

Geba
Sebaste
(Samaria)

Salim
Aenon

Jordan River

Gerasa

Mt. Ebal   Sychar
Mt. Gerizim   Shechem

Amathus   Jabbok River

Apollonia
Antipatris

Anuathu
Borcaeus

Coreae

Gadora

Joppa

Lebonah   Acrabeta
Alexandrium
Phasaelis

*Perea*

Philadelphia

Lydda

Gophna

Archelais

Bethel   Ephraim
Neara
Jericho
Cypros

Bethennabris
Abila

Jamnia

Emmaus
(Nicopolis)

Jerusalem   Qumran (Essene Community)   Mt. Nebo
Bethlehem   Bethany   Beth-ramatha   Esbus
Hyrcania   Medeba

Azotus
(Ashdod)

*Judea*   Herodium

Ascalon

Tekoa

*Dead
Sea
(Salt
Sea)*

Callirrhoe
Machaerus

Betogabris

Anthedon
Gaza

Hebron
Adora

En Gedi

Arnon River

*Idumea*   Masada

Raphia

Malatha

Beersheba

*N a b a t e a n s*

Zered River

*Mediterranean Sea
(Great Sea)*

Mediterranean coastal area in south Asia Minor.

**PANGS**. Pain, distress; used to describe the pain of childbirth (Isa. 26:17).

**PAPHOS** (PAY fahs). A city located on the western side of the island of Cyprus, which Paul visited (Acts. 13:6).

**PAPYRUS**. A tall plant that grows in water. Papyrus also refers to writing paper made from the plant. Much of the biblical material was recorded on papyrus.

▼ *To make paper, thin strips of the papyrus stem were laid side by side and overlapped on a hard surface. Then another layer was added crossways. These strips were molded together by beating with a hard instrument. Individual sheets could then be pasted together to form long rolls or scrolls.*

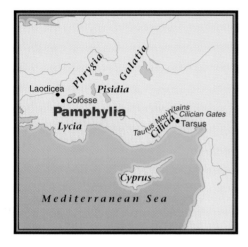

*A papyrus plant from whose stalks writing material was made.*

**PARABLE**. Something laid alongside of-parallel to (Num 23:7; Mark 4:2). A parable is an earthly story that has a heavenly meaning (Luke 15). It is an everyday truth that has a spiritual application. Jesus used parables as a major teaching method.

**PARACLETE**. An advocate; helper, someone who stands beside you or acts in your behalf. The apostle John used this Greek word to refer to the Holy Spirit as the Comforter (John 14:16). See **HOLY SPIRIT**.

▼ *You will find the word* paraclete *in your English dictionary.*

# PARABLES OF JESUS

| PARABLE | OCCASION | LESSON TAUGHT | REFERENCES |
|---|---|---|---|
| 1. The speck and the log | When reproving the Pharisees | Do not presume to judge others | Matt 7:1-6; Luke 6:37-43 |
| 2. The two houses | Sermon on the Mount, at the close | The strength conferred by duty | Matt 7:24-27; Luke 6:47-49 |
| 3. Children in the marketplace | Rejection by the Pharisees of John's baptism | Evil of a fault-finding disposition | Matt 11:16; Luke 7:32 |
| 4. The two debtors | A Pharisee's self-righteous reflections | Love to Christ proportioned to grace received | Luke 7:41 |
| 5. The unclean spirit | The scribes demand a miracle in the heavens | Hardening power of unbelief | Matt 12:43-45; Luke 11:24-26 |
| 6. The rich man's meditation | Dispute of two brothers | Folly of reliance upon wealth | Luke 12:16 |
| 7. The barren fig tree | Tidings of the execution of certain Galileans | Danger in the unbelief of the Jewish people | Luke 13:6-9 |
| 8. The sower | Sermon on the seashore | Effects of preaching religious truth | Matt 13:3-8; Mark 4:3-8; Luke 8:5-8 |
| 9. The tares | The same | The severance of good and evil | Matt 13:24-30 |
| 10. The seed | The same | Power of truth | Mark 4:20 |
| 11. The grain of mustard seed | The same | Small beginnings and growth of Christ's kingdom | Matt 13:31-32; Mark 4:31-32; Luke 13:19 |
| 12. The leaven | The same | Dissemination of the knowledge of Christ | Matt 13:33; Luke 13:21 |
| 13. The lamp | To the disciples alone | Effect of good example | Matt 5:15; Mark 4:21; Luke 8:16 11:33 |
| 14. The dragnet | The same | Mixed character of the church | Matt 13:47-48 |
| 15. The hidden treasure | The same | Value of religion | Matt 13:44 |
| 16. The pearl of great value | The same | The same | Matt 13:45-46 |
| 17. The householder | The same | Varied methods of teaching truth | Matt 13:52 |
| 18. The marriage | To the Pharisees, who censured the disciples | Joy in Christ's companionship | Matt 9:15; Mark 2:19-20; Luke 5:34-35 |
| 19. The patched garment | The same | The propriety of adapting actions to circumstances | Matt 9:16; Mark 2:21; Luke 5:36 |
| 20. The wine bottles | The same | The same | Matt 9:17; Mark 2:22; Luke 5:37 |
| 21. The harvest | Spiritual wants of the Jewish people | Need of labor and prayer | Matt 9:37; Luke 10:2 |
| 22. The opponent | Slowness of the people to believe | Need of prompt repentance | Matt 5:25; Luke 12:58 |
| 23. Two insolvent debtors | Peter's question | Duty of forgiveness | Matt 18:23-35 |

| PARABLE | OCCASION | LESSON TAUGHT | REFERENCES |
|---|---|---|---|
| 24. The good Samaritan | The lawyer's question | The golden rule for all | Luke 10:30-37 |
| 25. The three loaves | Disciples ask lesson in prayer | Effect of importunity in prayer | Luke 11:5-8 |
| 26. The good shepherd | Pharisees reject testimony of miracle | Christ the only way to God | John 10:1-16 |
| 27. The narrow gate | The question, Are there few who can be saved? | Difficulty of repentance | Matt 7:14; Luke 13:24 |
| 28. The guests | Eagerness to take high places | Chief places not to be usurped | Luke 14:7-11 |
| 29. The marriage supper | Self-righteous remark of a guest | Rejection of unbelievers | Matt 22:2-9; Luke 14:16-23 |
| 30. The wedding clothes | Continuation of the same discourse | Necessity of purity | Matt 22:10-14 |
| 31. The tower | Multitudes surrounding Christ | Need of deliberation | Luke 14:28-30 |
| 32. The king going to war | The same | The same | Luke 14:31 |
| 33. The lost sheep | Pharisees objected to His receiving the wicked | Christ's love for sinners | Matt 18:12-13; Luke 15:4-7 |
| 34. The lost coin | The same | The same | Luke 15:8-9 |
| 35. The prodigal son | The same | The same | Luke 15:11-32 |
| 36. The unjust steward | To the disciples | Prudence in using property | Luke 16:1-9 |
| 37. The rich man and Lazarus | Derision of the Pharisees | Salvation not connected with wealth | Luke 16:19-31 |
| 38. The importunate widow | Teaching the disciples | Perseverance in prayer | Luke 18:2-5 |
| 39. The Pharisee and tax-gatherer | Teaching the self-righteous | Humility in prayer | Luke 18:10-14 |
| 40. The slave's duty | The same | Man's obedience | Luke 17:7-10 |
| 41. Laborers in the vineyard | The same | The same further illustrated | Matt 20:1-16 |
| 42. The talents | At the house of Zaccheus | Doom of unfaithful followers | Matt 25:14-30; Luke 19:11-27 |
| 43. The two sons | The chief priests demand His authority | Obedience better than words | Matt 21:28 |
| 44. The wicked vine-growers | The same | Rejection of the Jewish people | Matt 21:33-43; Mark 12:1-9; Luke 20:9-15 |
| 45. The fig tree | In prophesying the destruction of Jerusalem | Duty of watching for Christ's appearance | Matt 24:32; Mark 13:28; Luke 21:29-30 |
| 46. The watching slave | The same | The same | Matt 24:43; Luke 12:39 |
| 47. The man on a journey | The same | The same | Mark 13:34 |
| 48. Character of two slaves | The same | Danger of unfaithfulness | Matt 24:45-51; Luke 12:42-46 |
| 49. The ten virgins | The same | Necessity of watchfulness | Matt 25:1-12 |
| 50. The watching slaves | The same | The same | Luke 12:36-38 |
| 51. The vine and branches | At the last supper | Loss and gain | John 15:1-6 |

**PARADISE**. A park or garden ground; sometimes used to refer to the Garden of Eden. The NT term indicates an eternal dwelling place for those who trust in God (Luke 23:43).

**PARAMOUR**. Male or female lover who is not one's husband or wife (Ezek. 23:20).

**PARAN** (PAY ruhn). Wilderness area in the Sinai Peninsula (between Egypt and Edom); sometimes referred to as Mount Paran (Gen. 21:21).

**PARCHED**. Burnt (Jer. 17:6). Roasted, as in cooking (Ruth 2:14).

**PARCHMENT**. Writing material made from specially prepared animal skins (2 Tim. 4:13).

**PARDON**. Cover or pass over; forgive the guilty (Ps. 25:11).

**PARTAKE**. To join in or have in common (Ps. 50:18; Heb. 3:1).

**PARTIALITY**. Bias. Using the wrong basis for a judgment. Showing favoritism (1 Tim; 5:21; Jas. 3:17).
● *What's wrong with partiality?*

**PASCHAL**. Passover. Paul referred to Christ as our paschal or sacrificial lamb (1 Cor. 5:7 RSV). See **PASSOVER.**

**PASSAGE**. A crossing place (Judg. 12:5). Also, used today to refer to a section of Scripture, one or more verses.

**PASSION**. Suffering; refers to Christ's crucifixion and death on the cross (Acts 1:3).

**PASSOVER**. Feast instituted the night before God delivered His people from Egyptian slavery (Ex. 12). God instructed the Israelites to mark their doorposts with the blood of a lamb so the death angel would pass over their home and spare their oldest child. Also called the Feast of Unleavened Bread and the Feast of Firstfruits, this feast is still used to celebrate and remember God's deliverance and provision.

In the NT Christ became our sacrificial or passover lamb (1 Cor. 5:7). His shed blood and death on the cross delivers us from the stranglehold of sin. See the **Feast Chart** page 92 and the **Calendar Chart** pages 228 & 229.

**PASTOR**. Shepherd; one who feeds, leads, and oversees (Jer. 2:8; Eph. 4:11).

**PATIENCE**. Longsuffering or enduring; continuing even in the face of difficulties (Rom. 5:3).

**PATMOS** (PAT muhs). Small island off the coast of Asia Minor in the Aegean Sea. It was here that John received his vision from God and wrote the Book of Revelation (1:9).

**PATRIARCH**. Literally, *chief father* or *ruling father.* Name given to the founding fathers of the Hebrew race (Abraham, Isaac, Jacob); Jacob's twelve sons and other great leaders of the OT—such as David (Acts 2:29; 7:8-9).

*The island of Patmos on which John was probably exiled by the Romans.*

**PAUL**. An apostle of Jesus Christ. Strong leader of the early Christian church and writer of almost half of the NT. Originally called Saul, he was first a dedicated Pharisaic Jew who persecuted Christians. He considered this persecution part of his religious responsibility (Acts 8:1-3; 26:10-11; 23:6).

While traveling to Damascus, Paul encountered Jesus and was dramatically converted to Christianity (Acts 9:1-30;

22:1-21). He then gave his life to teaching and writing and to starting and strengthening churches.

▼ *Paul's inspired letters to churches and individual Christians became books of the NT. See **PAULINE EPISTLES**. Imprisoned for his preaching, Paul wrote a number of his letters from jail (Col. 4:18).*

● *God used Paul's strong will and stubbornness in positive ways. How might He use your characteristics for His good?*

**PAULINE EPISTLES**. Paul's letters to churches or individuals which have become books of the Bible. They are: Romans, 1 and 2 Corinthians, Galatians, Ephesians, Philippians, Colossians, 1 and 2 Thessalonians, 1 and 2 Timothy, Titus, and Philemon. Each was named for the church or individual to whom it was written.

▼ *Paul typically began each letter by identifying himself and the recipient of the letter; then he gave a greeting, usually "grace to you and peace" (Rom.*

*1:1-7) and a thanksgiving for the church. See **PAUL***

**PAVILION**. 1. Hiding or sheltering place; cover. Movable tent, booth, or canopy (1 Kings 20:12). Figuratively used to mean a protective hiding place that God provided (Ps. 18:11; 27:5; 31:20). 2. Nebuchadnezzar spread a royal canopy (translated "pavilion" in KJV) as a sign of God's sovereignty (Jer. 43:10). See **CANOPY**.

■ **PEACE**. Absence of inner or outer conflict, unity, wholeness (Lev. 26:6; Luke 1:79). **Peace** (Hebrew *shalom*) was a common biblical greeting that meant both the absence of conflict and God's highest blessing.

**PEACE OFFERING**. Animal sacrifice to thank or express love to God (Ex. 20:24).

**PEARL**. In the OT probably some type of precious stone (Job 28:18). In the NT, *pearl* refers to the product of the clam.

*A tent is one type of pavilion.*

Pearl was used for jewelry and decoration (1 Tim. 2:9). It was also used for a symbol of spiritual truth (Matt. 13:46).

**PENTATEUCH**. The first five books of the Bible, the books of Law. These are Genesis, Exodus, Leviticus, Numbers, and Deuteronomy. The Sadducees accepted only these books as Holy Scripture. Other Jews accepted all of the Old Testament as Holy Scripture.

■ **PENTECOST**. Fifty days. Originally a yearly Jewish celebration of harvest; also called the Feast of Weeks (Deut. 16:9-10; Acts 20:16; 1 Cor. 16:8) and the Feast of Harvest. On the first Pentecost after Christ's resurrection, the Holy Spirit uniquely came upon believers (Acts 2:1-16). For that reason, Christians connect Pentecost with the coming of the Holy Spirit. See the **Feast Chart** page 92 and the **Calandar Chart** pages 228 & 229.

● *How would you have reacted to the Holy Spirit's arrival on Pentecost? (See Acts 2:6-11.) Did you know that he arrived in your life the moment you*

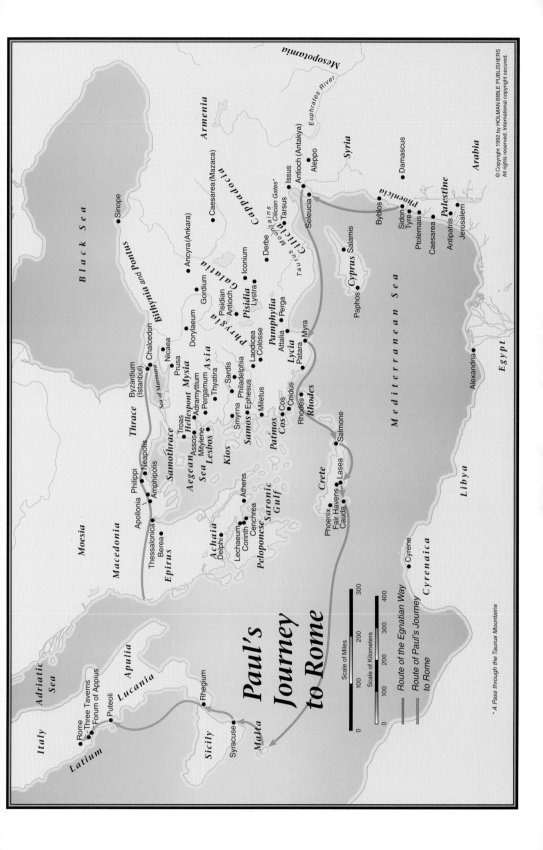

# Paul's Journey to Rome

Scale of Miles

Scale of Kilometers

___ Route of the Egnatian Way

___ Route of Paul's Journey
to Rome

* A Pass through the Taurus Mountains

**Italy** · Rome · Three Taverns · Forum of Appius · Puteoli

**Latium** · **Apulia** · **Lucania** · Rhegium · **Sicily** · Syracuse · **Malta**

**Adriatic Sea**

**Moesia** · **Macedonia** · Thessalonica · Berea · **Epirus** · Apollonia · Philippi · Neapolis · Amphipolis

**Thrace** · **Samothrace** · Byzantium (Istanbul) · Chalcedon · Nicaea · Prusa · Dorylaeum

**Bithynia and Pontus** · Sinope

**Black Sea**

Sea of Marmara

**Mysia** · Troas · Assos · Mitylene · Adramyttium · Pergamum · **Lesbos** · Thyatira · Sardis

**Aegean Sea** · **Kios** · Smyrna · Ephesus · Philadelphia · Laodicea · Colosse · Miletus · **Samos** · **Patmos** · **Cos** · Cos · Cnidus

**Achaia** · **Hellespont** · **Asia** · **Phrygia** · Gordium · Pisidian Antioch · **Pisidia** · Iconium · Lystra · Derbe

**Galatia** · Ancyra (Ankara) · Caesarea (Mazaca) · **Cappadocia** · **Armenia**

**Athens** · Lechaeum · Corinth · Cenchrea · Delphi · **Peloponese** · **Saronic Gulf**

**Pamphylia** · Perga · Attalia · **Lycia** · Patara · Myra

**Rhodes** · Rhodes

**Crete** · Phoenix · Fair Havens · Lasea · Cauda · Salmone

**Mediterranean Sea**

Tarsus · **Cilicia** · Mt. Taurus · "Cilician Gates*" · Issus · Antioch (Antakya) · Aleppo · Seleucia · **Syria** · Damascus

**Euphrates River** · **Mesopotamia**

**Phoenicia** · Byblos · Sidon · Tyre · Ptolemais · Caesarea · Antipatris · Jerusalem · **Palestine** · **Arabia**

**Cyprus** · Salamis · Paphos

**Libya** · **Cyrenaica** · Cyrene · **Egypt** · Alexandria

became a Christian? (See Eph. 1:13; 4:30.) See **HOLY SPIRIT.**

**PERCEIVE.** To know, see, understand (1 Sam. 3:8; John 4:19).

**PERDITION.** Death, destruction, loss (1 Tim. 6:9).

**PEREZ** (PEE rez). Son of Judah, who was conceived through the trickery of Tamar, Judah's daughter-in-law (Gen. 38, RSV).

**PERFECT.** Whole, complete, mature (Gen. 6:9; Matt. 19:21).

**PERFORM.** Besides having the usual meaning of *to do*, the word also means *to confirm* (Deut. 9:5) and *to complete* (Rom. 15:28).

**PERGA** (PUR guh). Important city in Pamphylia (Acts 13:13). It was here that John Mark left Paul and Barnabas on their first missionary trip and returned home.

**PERGAMOS** (PUR guh mahs). A wealthy

city in Asia Minor (Rev. 2:12). Also spelled Pergamum.

*Carved reliefs found among the ruins of the stadium at ancient Perga.*

*The Temple of Athena at ancient Pergamum.*

**PERISH.** Be lost or destroyed (Ps. 1:6; John 3:15).

**PERIZZITES** (PER ih zight). A tribe that opposed Israel and was driven out of Canaan (Gen. 13:7; Josh. 9:1-2).

**PERPETUAL.** Unending; indefinite time (Gen. 9:12).

**PERPLEXED.** Confused, puzzled (Esther 3:15; Luke 9:7).

**PERSECUTE.** Treat badly, harass, cause to suffer (Jer. 29:18; Matt. 5:10).

■ **PERSEVERANCE.** Keeping on, not giving up, lasting consistency, endurance (Eph. 6:18).

**PERSIA** (PUR zhuh). A large empire that had great effect on ancient history. Located in what is now mostly Iran, Persia's boundaries changed and expanded through the centuries. In 559 B.C. Cyrus became the king of Persia, and in 539 B.C. he conquered Babylon. He inherited the Jewish captives and allowed them to return to begin rebuilding the Temple destroyed by the Babylonians (Ezra 1:1-4). See map on next page.

**PERTAIN.** Besides the usual meaning, can also mean *belong* (1 Sam. 27:6).

**PERVERSE.** Twisted out of proper shape, evil, deceitful, devious, rebellious, obstinate, misguided (Prov. 14:2; Matt. 17:17).

**PERVERT.** Twist, distort, turn aside (Ex. 23:8; Acts 13:10).

**PESTILENCE.** Plague, devastating epidemic (Ex. 5:3; Luke 21:11).

**PETER** (PEE tur). Greek for *rock* (Aramaic for *rock* is Cephas, John 1:42). Disciple of Jesus whose name was Simon until Jesus gave him the name Peter (Mark 3:16; Matt. 4:18). He was a fisherman. His brother Andrew introduced him to Jesus.

Peter is always first in the listing of the disciples and was one of the three closest to Jesus during His ministry. Peter often acted impulsively. Although he verbally denied Christ during His time of arrest and trial, Peter became a bold and dynamic leader of the early church. He preached the Pentecost sermon (Acts 2). Tradition says he was put to death during the time of Nero's persecution of Christians.

**PETER, 1, 2 BOOKS OF.** New Testament books (letters) written by Peter to the Christians in Asia Minor. First Peter sets forth the purpose and privileges of God's people, thoughts on relationships to others, and encouragement in the time of suffering. Second Peter includes guidelines for the Christian life, warnings against false prophets, and thoughts on the second coming of Christ.

**PHARAOH** (FAY roh). Egyptian ruler or king (Gen. 12:15). A pharaoh invited the family of Jacob (Israel) to Egypt during a famine. Later generations of the Israelites were enslaved by a succeeding pharaoh.

*The funerary mask of King Tut (Pharaoh Tutankhamun) of Egypt.*

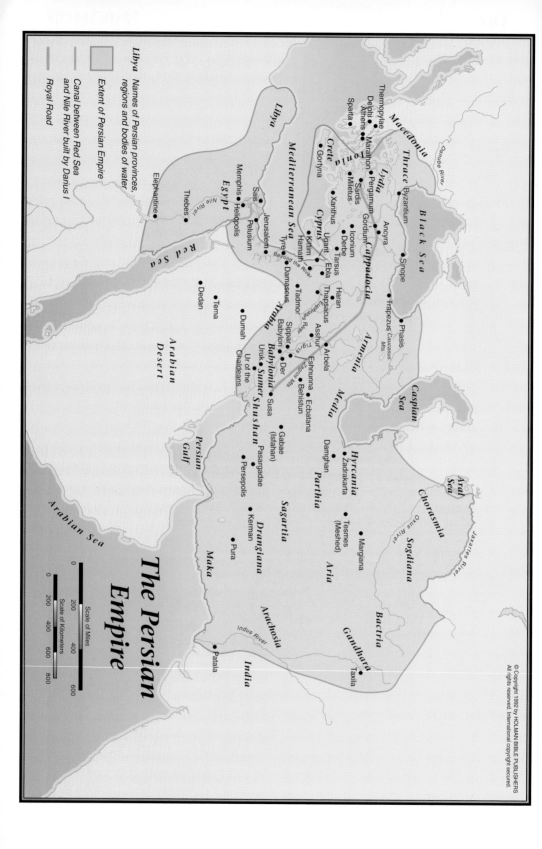

# The Persian Empire

Libya — Names of Persian provinces, regions and bodies of water.

☐ Extent of Persian Empire

— Canal between Red Sea and Nile River built by Darius I

— Royal Road

Scale of Miles
0    200    400    600

Scale of Kilometers
0    200    400    600    800

Libya
Macedonia
Thrace
Thermopylae
Delphi
Athens
Sparta
Marathon
Crete
Gortyna
Ionia
Byzantium
Lydia
Pergamum
Sardis
Miletus
Anoyra
Cappadocia
Black Sea
Sinope
Phasis
Trapezus
Caucasus Mts.
Danube River
Xanthus
Cyprus
Gordium
Iconium
Derbe
Tarsus
Mediterranean Sea
Ugarit
Kittim
Ebla
Haran
Armenia
Arbela
Asshur
Caspian Sea
Elephantine
Thebes
Memphis
Sais
Heliopolis
Pelusium
Jerusalem
Tyre
Damascus
Hamah
Beyond the River
Tadmor
Thapsacus
Euphrates River
Eshunna
Behistun
Media
Ecbatana
Egypt
Nile River
Red Sea
Dedan
Tema
Aram
Sippar
Babylon
Der
Babylonia
Uruk
Ur of the Chaldeans
Sumer
Susa
Shushan
Gabae
(Isfahan)
Pasargadae
Persepolis
Damghan
Zadrakarta
Hyrcania
Tesmes
(Meshed)
Parthia
Sagartia
Kerman
Drangiana
Aria
Margiana
Chorasmia
Sogdiana
Oxus River
Jaxartes River
Aral Sea
Arabian Desert
Dumah
Zagros Mts.
Tigris
Arabian Sea
Persian Gulf
Maka
Pura
Arachosia
Bactria
Gandhara
Taxila
India
Patala
Indus River

*Valley of the Kings, containing tombs of pharaohs, across the Nile River from Luxor (at ancient Thebes).*

■ **PHARISEE** (FER uh see). Influential group of Jews whose name means *separated ones* (Matt. 23; Luke 5:30-32; 14:1-6). Sincere but misled, they believed that religious ritual and separation from common sinners was the way to please God and to prepare for His coming. As a rule, they did not accept Jesus as the Messiah (Mark 3:6).

▼ *Pharisees followed the traditions of the prophets, while Sadducees followed the traditions of the priests.*

**PHILADELPHIA** (fil uh DEL fih uh). City in Asia Minor (Rev. 1:11); name means *brotherly love*. It was a wealthy commercial city known for its temples and religious festivals.

*Temple ruins at the site of the ancient city of Philadelphia in Asia Minor (modern Turkey).*

**PHILEMON** (figh LEE muhn). Owner of the slave Onesimus, a Christian, and fellow worker with Paul. Receiver of Paul's letter to Philemon.

**PHILEMON, BOOK OF.** New Testament book; a letter Paul wrote from prison. Paul encouraged Philemon to receive and forgive his runaway slave Onesimus as a new believer in Christ.

**PHILIP** (FILL ip). 1. One of Jesus' disciples (Matt. 10:3). Philip was from Bethsaida. He brought his brother Nathanael to Jesus, helped with the feeding of the multitudes, and brought Gentiles (non-Jews) to Jesus. 2. One of seven set aside for deacon-like service (Acts 6:5). 3. Two of the Herods (Matt. 14:3; Luke 3:1).

**PHILIPPI** (FILL ih pigh). A city in the Roman province of Macedonia (Acts 16:12). The apostle Paul extended his missionary journey to this city after receiving the vision of the Macedonian call (Acts 16:9-10).

*The agora (marketplace) in the ancient city of Philippi in Macedonia.*

**PHILIPPIANS, BOOK OF** (fih LIP ih uhns). New Testament book Paul wrote while he was in prison. Paul wrote the church at Philippi to express joy and gratitude for their help and to encourage them in their faith and witness.

**PHILISTIA** (fih LIST ih uh). Territory along the Mediterranean seacoast extending from Joppa to Gaza (Ps. 60:8). Sometimes referred to as Palestina (Ex. 15:14).

**PHILISTINE** (fih LISS teen). Inhabitant of the territory of Philistia (Gen. 21:32). Although the Philistines are mentioned during the Old Testament time of the patriarchs, they came onto the biblical scene in full force as enemies of Israel during the time of the judges and the reigns of Saul and David. They originated around the Aegean Sea.

**PHILOSOPHY.** Literally, love or study of wisdom; also, a way of thought (Acts 17:18). Paul warned the Colossian Christians to beware of any philosophy that contradicted the gospel (Col. 2:8).

**PHINEHAS** (FIN ih uhs). 1. Grandson of Aaron (Ex. 6:25). 2. Sinful son of Eli (1 Sam. 1:3). 3. A third Phinehas was the Father of Eleazar. He returned from exile with Ezra (Ezra 8:33).

**PHOEBE** (FEE bih). Deaconess of the church at Cenchrea. Paul commended her to the church at Rome (Rom. 16:1-2).

**PHOENICIA** (fuh NISH ih uh). Also called Phenice (KJV Acts 11:19; 27:12). A narrow strip of land between the Mediterranean Sea and the Lebanon Mountains. The Phoenicians were known for their colorful dyes, seamanship, ship-building, and carpentry. Their cedar forests provided material for Solomon's Temple (1 Kings 5:8-10). Phoenicia's two principal cities were Tyre and Sidon.

**PHRYGIA** (FRIG ih uh). An area of land that was a large part of Asia Minor (Acts 2:10). Paul began churches in several cities of this area on his second missionary journey (Acts 16:5-6).

**PHYLACTERIES**. Small leather cases

*An orthodox Jewish man wearing the traditional phylactery (frontlet) on his forehead.*

worn on the foreheads of Jewish men during prayer times. The following Scriptures were written on parchment and placed inside the phylacteries: Exodus 13:1-10,11-16; Deuteronomy 6:4-9; 11:13-21. Jesus condemned men who wore large phylacteries for show (Matt. 23:5). In OT called frontlets (Ex. 13:16).

● *Identify any of your practices that could be more for a show of religion than for true expression.*

● *What are your feelings about wearing a cross?*

**PIETY**. Reverence, religious worship (1 Tim. 5:4).

**PILATE, PONTIUS** (PIGH luht, PAHN shuhs). Roman governor of Judea (Matt. 27:2). Even though Pilate did not find Jesus guilty of any crime, Pilate yielded to pressure and allowed Jesus to be put to death (Luke 23:4,14,22; John 18:38; 19:4,6). See next page.

**PILLAR**. 1. Stone monuments set up for memorials or as places of worship for God or idols (Gen. 35:20; 28:18; Deut. 12:3). 2. Structural supports (1 Kings 10:12). 3. Pillars of cloud and fire were the visual expressions of God as He led the children of Israel through the wilderness (Ex. 13:21).

**PINE**. Adjective: Type of tree (Isa. 41:19). Verb: Be sick of heart or waste away (Ezek. 24:23).

**PINNACLE**. Highest point of a building (Matt. 4:5).

**PIPE**. Musical instrument, flute (1 Sam. 10:5).

**PISGAH** (PIZ guh). Mountain or mountain ridge (Num. 21:20). Place where

*Pilate questioning Jesus.* ▶

| THE TEN PLAGUES OF EGYPT | |
|---|---|
| **PLAGUE** | **SCRIPTURE** |
| 1. WATER TO BLOOD—The waters of the Nile turned to blood. | Exod 7:14-25 |
| 2. FROGS—Frogs infested the land of Egypt. | Exod 8:1-15 |
| 3. GNATS (Mosquitoes)—Small stinging insects infested the land of Egypt. | Exod 8:16-19 |
| 4. FLIES—Swarms of flies, possibly a biting variety, infested the land of Egypt. | Exod 8:20-32 |
| 5. PLAGUE ON THE CATTLE—A serious disease, possibly anthrax, infested the cattle belonging to Egyptians. | Exod 9:1-7 |
| 6. BOILS—A skin disease infected the Egyptians. | Exod 9:8-12 |
| 7. HAIL—A storm that destroyed the grain fields of Egypt but spared the land of Goshen inhabited by the Israelites. | Exod 9:13-35 |
| 8. LOCUSTS—An infestation of locusts stripped the land of Egypt of plant life. | Exod 10:1-20 |
| 9. DARKNESS—A deep darkness covered the land of Egypt for three days. | Exod 10:21-29 |
| 10. DEATH OF THE FIRSTBORN—The firstborn of every Egyptian family died. | Exod 11:1–12:30 |

Moses went to view the Promised Land (Deut. 34:1).

**PISIDIA** (pih SID ih uh). Province in Asia Minor (Acts 13:14). The main city of the province was Antioch.

**PIT**. Hole or well (Gen. 37:20); grave, death, or Sheol (Job 33:18).

**PITCH**. Verb: Make a camp, set up a tent (Ex. 17:1; Heb. 8:2); Noun: Black tar or asphalt-like material (Ex. 2:3).

**PITY**. Loving-kindness, concern, compassion (Job 19:21; Matt. 18:33).

**PLAGUE**. Deadly disease or destruction (Ex. 9:14; Rev. 9:20). God sent the ten plagues upon Egypt to show His power and to persuade Pharaoh to free His people from slavery. The plagues were water turned to blood, frogs, lice, flies, cattle disease, boils, hail, locusts, darkness, and death of the firstborn.

**PLAISTER, PLASTER**. 1. A wall covering usually made of clay (Deut. 27:2). 2. A mixture made from plant products used medically for warmth, relieving pain, and as an antiseptic (Isa. 38:21).

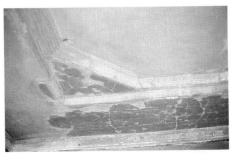
*Corner of a room in Pompeii showing the decorative way in which plaster was used in the first century.*

**PLEDGE**. Item of personal property given as a guarantee for payment of a debt (Ezek. 18:12).

**PLEIADES** (PLIGH uh deez). A grouping of several stars in the constellation Taurus (Job 9:9).

■ **PLENARY VERBAL INSPIRATION**. Full word-for-word inspiration of the Bible as a God-breathed book. (The phrase is not used in the Bible.)

**PLENTY**. Abundance, fullness (Gen. 27:28).

**PLOWSHARE**. Cutting edge of a plow (Isa. 2:4). Beating swords into plowshares symbolizes a time of peace.

*Arab farmer plowing his field wiith a simple double-yoked plow and team of two donkeys.*

**PLUCK.** Snatch, take away (2 Sam. 23:21; John 10:28).

**PLUMBLINE, PLUMMET.** A measuring

*Roman bronze plumb bob which attached to a plumbline.*

device to test the up-and-down straightness of a wall (2 Kings 21:13). It was usually a cord with a stone or metal weight at the end. *Plumbline* is also used symbolically for God's test of His people (Amos 7:7-8).

**POLLUTE.** Profane, defile, make unclean (Mal. 1:7; Acts 21:28).

**POLYGAMY.** The practice of having more than one spouse at a time. (The word is not used in the KJV.)

**POLYTHEISM.** The belief or worship of more than one god. (The word is not used in the KJV.)

**POMEGRANATE.** Small tree or fruit of the tree (Ex. 28:33). The fruit has many seeds and red pulp.

**POMP.** Pride, show (Isa. 14:11; Acts 25:23).

**POSSESSED.** Besides the usual meaning of acquired or taken over, to be possessed also means under the control of the devil or a demon (Matt. 4:24).

*The pomegranate is one of the many fruits found in the Middle East.*

● *If a Christian is filled with the Holy Spirit, can he or she be possessed by a demon? (See Eph. 4:30.)*

**POSTERITY**. Descendants, sons (Dan. 11:4).

**POTIPHAR** (POT ih fur). Egyptian official under Pharaoh (Gen. 37:36). After

*Potsherds from the Sudan area south of Egypt.*

Joseph's brothers sold him into slavery to the Midianites, the Midianites sold Joseph to Potiphar. Potiphar's wife tried to seduce Joseph, but he remained pure (Gen. 39:7-20).

● *How would you have reacted in Joseph's situation? Why?*

**POTSHERD**. Piece of broken pottery (Job 2:8).

**POTTAGE**. A thick vegetable soup (Gen. 25:29).

**POTTER'S FIELD**. Piece of land in the Hinnom Valley used as a burial ground for strangers (Matt. 27:3-10; Acts 1:18-19). The money Judas received for the betrayal of Jesus was used to buy the field.

**POUND**. A pound weight varied from about twelve ounces in the Roman system (John 12:3) to about twenty ounces in the Hebrew-Greek system (Ezra 2:69). In terms of money, a pound was about one hundred days' wages (Luke 19:13). See **Weight and Measures**

## BIBLICAL PRAYERS

| Type of Prayer | Meaning | Old Testament Example | New Testament Example | Jesus' Teaching |
|---|---|---|---|---|
| Confession | Acknowledging sin and helplessness and seeking God's mercy | Ps 51 | Luke 18:13 | Luke 15:11-24 Luke 18:10-24 |
| Praise | Adoring God for who He is | 1 Chr 29:10-13 | Luke 1:46-55 | Matt 6:9 |
| Thanksgiving | Expressing gratitude to God for what He has done | Ps 105:1-7 | 1 Thess 5:16-18 | Luke 17:11-19 |
| Petition | Making personal request of God | Gen 24:12-14 | Acts 1:24-26 | Matt 7:7-12 |
| Intercession | Making request of God on behalf of another | Exod 32:11-13, 31-32 | Phil 1:9-11 | John 17:9,20-21 |
| Commitment | Expressing loyalty to God and His work | 1 Kgs 8:56-61 | Acts 4:24-30 | Matt 6:10 Luke 6:46-49 |
| Forgiveness | Seeking mercy for personal sin or the sin of others | Dan 9:4-19 | Acts 7:60 | Matt 6:12 Luke 6:27-36 |
| Confidence | Affirming God's all-sufficiency and the believer's security in His love | Ps 23 | Luke 2:29-32 | Matt 6:5-15; 7:11 |
| Benediction | A request for God's blessing | Num 6:24-26 | Jude 24 | Luke 11:15-13 |

**Chart**, pages 244 & 245, and **Money Chart** page 158.

**POWER.** Strength, authority (Ps. 111:6; Matt. 9:6; 6:13). God revealed His power through history, acts of nature, individual lives, and the Holy Spirit. Jesus revealed God's power through His miracles and forgiveness.
● *How do you see God's power at work today?*

**PRAETORIUM** (prih TAWR ih uhm). Barracks or building that housed the Roman soldiers (Mark 15:16).

■ **PRAISE.** Express honor and gratitude to God through worship, words, attitudes, actions (Ps. 69:30; Luke 19:37).

■ **PRAYER.** Talking and listening to God, an intimate fellowship with God (1 Kings 8:28; Matt. 21:22). Calls for faith and a right relationship with God (Ps. 66:18; Jas. 5:16). May include praising, thanking, confessing, asking, interceding (praying for someone else), and receiving.
● *Try each of the types of prayer. What do you like about each?*

**PREACH.** To proclaim, to tell or announce good news about the kingdom of God (Isa. 61:1; Luke 4:43).

**PREACHER.** One who proclaims or shares the good news (Eccl. 1:1; Rom. 10:14).
● *How does one become a preacher? Might you be a preacher?*

**PRECEPT.** Teaching, command (Ps. 119:4; Mark 10:5).

■ **PREDESTINATION.** Choice or selection beforehand (Rom. 8:29-30). God, in His supreme authority and wisdom, chooses those who will trust in Him and be saved. God's predestination occurs in Christ and one's response to Him (Eph. 1:4-5,11). Predestination does not remove each person's responsibility for accepting Jesus Christ as Lord and Savior (Rom. 10:9-10).

**PREEMINENCE.** First place (Col. 1:18).

**PREPARATION, DAY OF.** This was the day set aside for getting ready for the sabbath (Matt. 27:62). Since no work was permitted on the sabbath, completion of work and food preparation was done the day before. The day of preparation began at 6 P.M. on Thursday and ended at 6 P.M. on Friday, the beginning of the sabbath.
See **SABBATH.**

**PRESCRIBE.** Write (Isa. 10:1).

**PRESENCE OF GOD.** God making Himself known and coming face to face with people. In the OT, some examples of God's presence are the burning bush (Ex. 3:2-5) and the cloud and pillar of fire (Ex. 40:34-38). In the NT God was visible in Jesus Christ (John 1:14). Throughout the Bible the Holy Spirit revealed the presence of God. His Spirit performs that same work today.
See **GOD, HOLY SPIRIT.**
● *How do you experience God's presence day by day?*

**PRESERVE.** Keep, save (Ps. 12:7; Luke 17:33).

*An ancient olive press.*

**PRESS**. Noun: An instrument for collecting juice from grapes or olives (Prov. 3:10). Also, a crowd of people (Mark 2:4). Verb: Strain (Phil. 3:14). Also, devoted entirely (Acts 18:5).

**PRESUMPTUOUS**. Filled with pride, bold, daring (Ex. 21:14; 2 Pet. 2:10).

**PRETENCE**. Act as a hypocrite or show off (Matt. 23:14).

**PREVAIL**. Become mighty or strong; conquer (Gen. 7:18; Matt. 16:18).

**PREVENT**. Anticipate (Ps. 119:147); precede (Matt. 17:25; 1 Thess. 4:15). In the KJV, *prevent* does not mean to keep from happening.

**PREY**. Victim (Num. 14:3); something taken in war, spoils (Judg. 5:30).

**PRIDE**. Arrogance, self-trust; opposite of humility (Prov. 29:23; Mark 7:22).

**PRIEST**. Someone who speaks to God or relates to God in behalf of others or for oneself. In the OT and early NT priests presented sacrifices to God for the people, taught them the Law, entered the holiest places of the tabernacle or temple, and met with God (Lev. 4:26; Ezek. 42:13-14; Luke 1:8-11). Two major lines of OT priests were the Aaronic (Ex. 28:1) and the Levitical (Heb. 7:11; Lev. 6:2-5).

Jesus became our once-and-for-all sacrifice and is now our High Priest (Heb. 4:14-16); therefore, we no longer need ceremonial sacrifices or priests to represent us to God. Every Christian is a priest (1 Pet. 2:5,9), needing only Jesus as Mediator before God. See **MEDIATOR, PRIESTHOOD OF THE BELIEVER.**

**PRIEST, HIGH**. Leader of worship in the temple or tabernacle (2 Kings 12:10; Matt. 26:3). Also called chief priest (2 Chron. 26:20; Matt. 2:4). The high priest participated in and supervised the priests in offering sacrifices and in other priestly functions. He alone had the privilege of going into the holy of holies (innermost part of the Temple or tabernacle) on the Day of Atonement (Lev. 16). Aaron was the first high priest (Ex. 28-29). See **HOLY OF HOLIES, LEVITES.**

■ **PRIESTHOOD OF THE BELIEVERS**. Each Christian can come directly into the presence of God without a mediator or priest (Eph. 2:18; 1 Pet. 2:5,9). Jesus provided for us to have this priesthood, and we work under His guidance (Rev. 1:6; 5:10).

▼ *Christians can interpret the Bible for themselves and speak to God themselves. They do not need to go through another believer to contact God, but they can certainly learn about God from other Christians such as pastors and teachers(Eph. 4:11-12).*

**PRINCIPALITIES**. Rulers, authorities (Titus 3:1). Also, angelic and demonic powers that could be good or evil (Rom. 8:38; 1 Cor. 15:24; Eph. 1:21).

**PRISCILLA** (prih SIL uh). Also called Prisca. Wife of Aquila. Together they worked beside and ministered with Paul (Acts 18:2-3,18; Rom. 16:3). They also helped a preacher named Apollos understand the way of God more perfectly. They had a church in their house (Acts 18:26; 1 Cor. 16:19). See **AQUILA.**

**PRISON, PRISONER**. In the OT, prisons were often small houses or rooms close to the palace (Judg. 16:21). Sometimes underground dungeons or cisterns (wells) were used. Most of the confinement was due to political offenses. In the NT, political offenses, unpaid debts, criminal acts, and some religious practices were causes for imprisonment (Acts 5:14-18). Famous

# THE PROPHETS IN HISTORY
## (9th—5th century B.C.)

| Prophet | Approximate Dates | Location/ Home | Basic Bible Passage | Central Teaching | Key Verse |
|---|---|---|---|---|---|
| Elijah | 875–850 | Tishbe | 1 Kgs 17:1–2 Kgs 2:18 | Yahweh, not Baal, is God | 1 Kgs 18:21 |
| Micaiah | 856 | Samaria | 1 Kgs 22; 2 Chr 18 | Proof of prophecy | 1 Kgs 22:28 |
| Elisha | 855–800 | Abel Meholah | 1 Kgs 19:15-21; 2 Kgs 2–9; 13 | God's miraculous power | 2 Kgs 5:15 |
| Jonah | 775 | Gath Hepher | 2 Kgs 14:25; Jonah | God's universal concern | Jonah 4:11 |
| Amos | 765 | Tekoa | Amos | God's call for justice and righteousness | Amos 5:24 |
| Hosea | 750 | Israel | Hosea | God's unquenchable love | Hos 11:8-9 |
| Isaiah | 740–698 | Jerusalem | 2 Kgs 19–20; Isaiah | Hope through repentance & suffering | Isa 1:18; 53:4-6 |
| Micah | 735–710 | Moresheth Gath Jerusalem | Jer 26:18; Micah | Call for humble mercy and justice | Mic 6:8 |
| Oded | 733 | Samaria | 2 Chr 28:9-11 | Do not go beyond God's command | 2 Chr 28:9 |
| Zephaniah | 630 | ? | Zephaniah | Hope for the humble humble righteous | Zeph 2:3 |
| Nahum | 625 | Elkosh | Nahum | God's jealousy protects His people | Nah 1:2-3 |
| Habakkuk | 625 | ? | Habakkuk | God calls for faithfulness | Hab 2:4 |
| Jeremiah | 626–584 | Anathoth/ Jerusalem | 2 Chr 36:12; Jeremiah | Faithful prophet points to new covenant | Jer 31:33-34 |
| Huldah (the prophetess) | 621 | Jerusalem | 2 Kgs 22; 2 Chr 34 | God's Book is accurate | 2 Kgs 22:16 |
| Ezekiel | 593–571 | Babylon | Ezekiel | Future hope for new community of worship | Ezek 37:12-13 |
| Joel | 588 (?) | Jerusalem | Joel | Call to repent and experience God's Spirit | Joel 2:28-29 |
| Obadiah | 580 | Jerusalem | Obadiah | Doom on Edom to bring God's kingdom | Obad 21 |
| Haggai | 520 | Jerusalem | Ezra 5:1; 6:14; Haggai | The priority of God's house | Hag 2:8-9 |
| Zechariah | 520–514 | Jerusalem | Ezra 5:1; 6:14; Zechariah | Faithfulness will lead to God's universal rule | Zech 14:9 |
| Malachi | 433 | Jerusalem | Malachi | Honor God and wait for His righteousness | Mal 4:2 |

*The traditional site of the prison of Paul and Silas at Philippi.*

biblical prisoners include Joseph, Samson, John the Baptist, Paul, and Silas.

**PRIZE.** A crown or garland awarded in athletic games (1 Cor. 9:24). Paul used *prize* to symbolize a spiritual award (Phil. 3:14).

**PROCLAIM.** To announce or make known (Ex. 33:19; Luke 12:3).

**PROCLAMATION.** Public announcement (Dan. 5:29).

**PROCONSUL.** Roman government official responsible for civil and military matters in a province (Acts 13:7, NIV; deputy in KJV).

**PROFANE.** Opposite of holy (Ezek. 44:23). Critical of God, destructive to God's purposes, having nothing to do with God, godless. Can be an action (Matt. 12:5), a person (Heb. 12:16), or a descriptive term (1 Tim. 6:20).

**PROMISE.** Agreement, pledge, contract (Acts 1:4). Obedient and faithful people receive the fulfillment of God's promises (Rom. 4:13-14).

**PRONOUNCE.** Speak (Jer. 11:17).

■ **PROPHECY** (noun), **PROPHESY** (verb). Speak for God. Tell God's truth (Mark 7:6; 2 Pet. 1:19-21; 1 Cor. 13:2). Prophets spoke God's Word to a present generation but with truths that often revealed the future (see Rev. 1:17-19).

**PROPHET, PROPHETESS.** One who speaks for God (Mic. 1:1; Judg. 4:4; Acts 21:9). A true prophet said exactly what God said. Both men and women served as prophets. Prophets were sometimes well-liked (except when they denounced people's sins). Nathan, Deborah, Daniel, and Anna were a few of God's many prophets. False prophets were not called by God and were not to be heeded (1 Kings 18:25-40).

■ **PROPITIATION** (pro PISH ee ay shun). Covering, atonement (1 John 2:2). In general, sacrifice that appeases a god. In Christianity, propitiation is Christ's sacrificial death on the cross that makes divine forgiveness possible (1 John 4:10). Propitiation is God's mercy and grace in action to put us in a right relationship with Him.

**PROSELYTE.** A person converted from one religion to another religion (Matt. 23:15).

**PROSTITUTE.** Verb: Defile or profane (Lev. 19:29). Noun: Person who performed sexual acts for personal reward. Some religions used acts with prostitutes in worship. Hosea's wife Gomer was a prostitute (Hos. 1). God forbid prostitution as part of His worship.

**PROVE.** To try or test (Ps. 17:3; Luke 14:19).

**PROVENDER.** Animal food made from grains and grasses (Judg. 19:21).

**PROVERB.** A short, pithy statement of truth (Prov. 1:1). Sometimes means an obscure saying or a parable.

**PROVERBS, BOOK OF.** Old Testament book that is a collection of practical truths

*The prophet Jonah preaching to the Ninevites.* ▶

about wisdom, moral values, and relationships.

▼ *The Book of Proverbs is full of useful information on such topics as friendship, family, and temptations. Proverbs 31:10-31 describes a godly woman.*

**PROVIDENCE**. Provision (Acts 24:2). The theme of God's providence runs throughout the Bible. God is seen not only as the Creator but as the One who plans for, cares for, and guides His creation. He knows the needs of His creation and provides for those needs.

**PROVINCE**. A political area or district (1 Kings 20:14; Acts 23:34). These areas were ruled by kings, emperors, senators, or procurators.

**PROVOCATION**. A reason that moves someone to anger (1 Kings 15:30; Heb. 3:8).

**PRUDENT**. Intelligent, wise (Prov. 18:15; Matt. 11:25).

**PSALM**. Song of praise (1 Chron. 16:9; Col. 3:16).

**PSALMS, BOOK OF**. Old Testament book of poems that were sung. The 150 psalms were and still are used in Hebrew and Christian worship. Psalms is the longest book in the Bible and is located approximately in the middle of the Bible. Psalms includes the longest chapter (Ps. 119) and the shortest chapter (Ps. 117) in the Bible. David and others are credited with writing the Psalms.

**PUBLICAN**. A tax collector who worked for the Roman government (Matt. 9:10). A publican usually collected more taxes than he had to so he could use the extra money for himself. Publicans were despised for their cheating and for serving the Roman government.

**PUBLISH**. Say, tell, cause to hear, proclaim (Neh. 8:15; Mark 1:45).

**PUFFED UP**. Proud, arrogant, boastful (1 Cor. 4:6).

**PULPIT**. Raised platform for a speaker to stand on (Neh. 8:4).

**PURE**. Clean, undefiled (Ps. 24:4; Matt. 5:8).

**PURGE**. Cleanse, purify (Ezek. 20:38; Heb. 9:14).

**PURIFICATION**. Cleansing (2 Chron. 30:19; Luke 2:22). In the Bible, ceremonial purification was an important element in worship. The Levites had to purify themselves for service. Individuals had to go through the ritual of purification after contact with a corpse, after menstruation or any other bloody discharge, after childbirth, and after the cure for leprosy. The ritual required a cleansing agent (water, blood, or fire) and a sacrifice (Num. 31:23). In the NT the emphasis is on personal, moral purity rather than on ceremonial purity (1 Pet. 1:22).

**PURIFY**. Make clean (Num. 19:12; Jas. 4:8).

**PURIM** (PYOO rim). Feast or Festival commemorating the efforts of Queen Esther to bring about the deliverance of the Jewish people from death (see the Book of Esther). It's a happy celebration held in the month of March and is also called the Feast of Lots since *purim* is the Hebrew term for *lots*. (The word purim itself does not appear in the KJV.) See the **Feast Chart** page 92 and the **Calendar Chart** pages 228 & 229.

**PURPLE**. A color that signified wealth or royalty (Judg. 8:26; Acts 16:14).

**QUAIL**. A spotted, brown migratory bird (Ex. 16:13). God provided quail for the Israelites to eat in the wilderness.

**QUAKE**. Tremble (Ex. 19:18; Matt. 27:51). Shake with fear (Heb. 12:21).

**QUARRIES**. Generally, a place where stones for building were available; but the term refers to idols or carved stones in the KJV (Judg. 3:19,26).

**QUARTER**. A fourth part; a corner, side, extreme end, or place (Jer. 49:36; Acts 28:7).

**QUENCH**. Extinguish, put out (2 Sam. 21:17; Matt. 12:20).

**QUICK, QUICKEN**. Alive (Num. 16:30; Acts 10:42). To quicken is to make alive (Ps. 71:20; John 5:21).

**QUIRINIUS** (kwi RIN ih uhs). Governor of Syria (Luke 2:2, NIV). In KJV, Cyrenius (sigh REE nih uhs).

**QUIVER**. Noun: Case for carrying arrows (Lam. 3:13). Verb: Tremble (Hab. 3:16).

**RABBI, RABBONI** (RAB igh; ra BOH nigh). Teacher, Master (John 1:38; 20:16).

**RABSHAKEH** (RAB-SHUH ke). An officer under Assyrian King Sennacherib (2 Kings 18:17).

**RACA**. Empty, worthless, ignorant (Matt. 5:22).

**RACHEL** (RAY chuhl). Younger daughter of Laban, favorite wife of Jacob (Gen. 29:5-6). Jacob was tricked into marrying Rachel's older sister Leah before he could marry Rachel. Rachel remained childless for many years but finally gave birth to Joseph and Benjamin. She died at Benjamin's birth.

*The traditional location of Rachel's tomb in Bethlehem.*

**RAHAB** (RAY hab). 1. Prostitute of Jericho who hid two Hebrew spies and provided escape for them (Josh. 2:1). Later she and her family were spared when the city was destroyed. Rahab was the mother of Boaz and the great grandmother of King David. 2. Poetic name for Egypt (NRSV: Ps. 87:4; Isa. 30:7; 51:9). 3. Poetic name for primeval sea monster representing forces God overcame in creation (Job 9:13; 26:12; Ps. 89:10).

**RAIL**. Verbally abuse or insult (Mark 15:29).

**RAIMENT**. Clothing (Gen. 24:53; Matt. 3:4).

**RAINBOW**. Symbol of God's covenant with Noah never again to destroy the earth with a flood (Gen. 9:8-17). The rainbow is mentioned in John's vision (Rev. 4:3; 10:1).

**RAM.** 1. Male goat; used frequently in animal sacrifices (Gen. 15:9). 2. A battering ram was a weapon made of wooden shaft with metal ends. It was rolled on wheels and used to break down gates or walls (Ezek. 4:2).

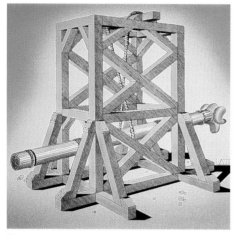

*Reconstruction of a Roman battering ram.*

**RAMA, RAMAH** (RAY mah). 1. City of Benjamin on the frontier between Israel and Judah (Josh. 18:25; Matt. 2:18). 2. City in Ephraim which was the birthplace of Samuel (1 Sam. 1:19). 3. Same as Ramoth-Gilead, an important city east of the Jordan River. King Ahab received his fatal wound here (2 Chron. 22:6).

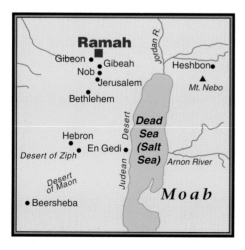

**RAMESES** (RAM uh seez). Prosperous Egyptian seaport city (Gen. 47:11). Also, the name of a line of Pharaohs but not mentioned in the Bible. Rameses II may have been the Pharaoh of the Exodus.

*The head of a monumental statue of Ramses the Great, builder of the store-city of Rameses.*

**RAMPART.** Fortification wall, usually made of earth (Lam. 2:8).

**RANK.** 1. Healthy and full (Gen. 41:5,7). 2. Line, arrangement, row (Joel 2:7; Mark 6:40).

**RANSOM.** Covering, price paid (Ex. 30:12; Matt. 20:28).
▼ *Christ gave His life as a ransom for our sins. The invitation to be Christ's disciple calls for a sacrifice on our part (Luke 9:23).*

■ **RAPTURE.** May mean either *ecstasy* or *to snatch from one place and put in another*. The Christian rapture refers to the second of these meanings. Jesus will come again with those who have died in Christ and join them in the air with those Christians who are still alive. The word *rapture* does not appear in the KJV Bible, but the concept does (Mark 13:26-27; 1 Thess. 4:16-17).
▼ *The idea of rapture as spiritual ecstasy is first recorded in Milton's "On The Morning of Christ's Nativity" (A.D. 1629).*

**RASH.** Impulsive, reckless, act hastily (Eccl. 5:2; Acts 19:36).

**RAVENING, RAVENOUS.** Devouring with greed (Isa. 35:9; Matt. 7:15).

**RAVISH.** Rape (Lam. 5:11; Isa. 13:16); also used to refer to passion (Prov. 5:19-20).

**REALM.** Kingdom (2 Chron. 20:30).

**REAP.** Gather in the harvest (Lev. 19:9; Gal. 6:7).

**REAR.** Raise, lift (Ex. 26:30; John 2:20).

**REBECCA, REBEKAH** (ruh BEK uh). Sister of Laban, wife of Isaac, and mother of Jacob and Esau (Gen. 24:29; Rom. 9:10).

**REBUKE.** Noun: Correction, reproof, strong disapproval (2 Sam. 22:16; Isa. 25:8). In Philippians 2:15, blameless: "without rebuke." Used similarly as a verb (Matt. 8:26; 2 Tim. 4:2).

**RECHAB** (REE kab), **RECHABITE** (REE kab ight). 1. A Benjaminite who, with his brother, murdered Ishbosheth, Saul's son (2 Sam. 4:2-12). 2. Father of Jehonadab (Jonadab). His descendants became the Rechabites (2 Kings 10:15). 3. Two other persons had the same name (1 Chron. 2:55; Neh. 3:14).

**RECKON.** Take into account, evaluate the character of, count, think, consider (Lev. 25:50; Luke 22:37; Rom. 4:4).

**RECOMPENSE.** Give or pay back, reward (Ruth 2:12; Luke 14:14).

**■ RECONCILE, RECONCILIATION.** Restore relationship (2 Cor. 5:18-20). Christ's death provided for the removal of the barrier of sin to bring people back into a right relationship with God. Renew friendship (Matt. 5:24; 1 Cor. 7:11). Form a unity (Col. 1:20).
● *In addition to reconciling us to Himself, God has given us the ministry of reconciliation. How do you fulfill this ministry?*

**RECORD.** Testimony or witness (Job 16:19; John 1:19).

*A serene view of the Red Sea.*

**RECOUNT.** Call, summon (Nah. 2:5).

**RED SEA.** Body of water between Arabia and northeastern Africa (Ex. 10:19; Acts 7:36). The Red Sea has two arms at its northern end: the Gulf of Suez and the Gulf of Aqaba. Although the exact location of the crossing is not known, God miraculously created an escape route across the Red Sea for the Israelites when they were pursued by the Egyptians (Ex. 14).

▼ Reed Sea *is often given as a literal rendering of the Hebrew term the KJV translates Red Sea.*

■ **REDEEM.** To buy back, to free or pay a price for (1 Chron. 17:21; Gal. 3:13). Christ's death paid for our sins and frees us from the bondage of sin upon our acceptance of Him. He is our Redeemer.

■ **REDEMPTION.** Release that occurs when a price is paid (Lev. 25:51-52; Num. 3:49; Heb. 9:12). Jesus paid the price for our release from sin (Rom. 3:24; Eph. 1:7).

**REDOUND.** Increase, overflow, be supremely great (2 Cor. 4:15).

**REED.** Several different types of stalk or cane plants that grow in shallow water (Isa. 19:6; Matt. 27:30). The stems of the plants were used in basket-making and in making paper.

**REEL.** Stagger like a drunk (Ps. 107:27; Isa. 24:20).

**REFINE.** Purify (Isa. 48:10; Mal. 3:2-3).

**REFRAIN.** Restrain, bridle, check, or keep back (Job 7:11; 1 Pet. 3:10). Keep away from (Acts 5:38).

▼ *Contemporary translations use* refrain *in the sense of abstaining or keeping oneself from doing something.*

**REFUGE.** Shelter or place of protection, safety zone (Ps. 46:1).

**REFUGE, CITY OF.** City designated by Hebrew law that provided safety for a person who had accidentally killed someone. This protected zone kept the victim's family from seeking revenge (Ex. 21:13; Num. 35:9-34). There were six cities of refuge, three on each side of the Jordan River (Num. 35:14; Josh. 20).

**REGENERATION.** Born again, a new creation (Matt. 19:28; Titus 3:5).

▼ *Spiritually speaking, this term reflects what happens when a person becomes a Christian (John 1:13; 3:3; 1 Pet. 1:23; 2 Cor. 5:17). The first birth is physical. Everyone becomes spiritually dead in sins and has to be made alive-regenerated, born again-by turning from sin and turning to Jesus in trust (Eph. 2:1–10).*

● *Evaluate your spiritual condition: Born? Dead? Born again? The Bible teaches that the answer to the first two questions is yes for everyone (Rom. 3:23). You have to own up to your sin, turn from it, and turn to Christ in faith to be able to answer yes to the last question. What is your answer? If it is anything besides yes, read the Scriptures listed, accept Christ, and change the no or maybe to yes!*

**REGISTER.** Written record (Ezra 2:62).

**REHOBOAM** (ree hoh BOH uhm). Son of King Solomon and successor to the throne (1 Kings 11:43; Matt. 1:7, NIV). Spelled Roboam in KJV in Matthew. Because of the heavy tax burden under Rehoboam, the ten northern tribes revolted, dividing the kingdom. Rehoboam was left with the two southern tribes of Judah and Benjamin. The divided kingdom became Israel (ten northern tribes) and Judah (two southern tribes). See the **king chart** following **KING.**

**REIGN.** Rule, act as a king (Gen. 36:31; Matt. 2:22).

**RELIEF.** Provision, aid, contribution, support (Acts 11:29).

**RELIGION, RELIGIOUS.** Belief in and worship of God or gods (Jas. 1:26-27). A person whose religion is genuine will show through attitude and actions a depth of commitment to the one worshiped.

**REMISSION.** Pardon, forgiveness (Matt. 26:28).

**REMNANT.** That which is left or remaining (Lev. 2:3; Matt. 22:6). In the Bible *remnant* especially refers to those who survived a political or military situation (2 Kings 25:11). Spiritually, *remnant* also means those who repent and survive God's judgment.

This is interpreted in different ways. Some feel it applies to those who returned from physical Babylonian captivity, while others apply the remnant to future generations. Some feel the remnant will be made up of Jewish people, while others interpret it to be a new community of people who trust in the Messiah (Rom. 9-11).

**REND, RENT.** Tear, rip, split (Gen. 37:29; Mark 15:38). The rending of garments was often a symbol for mourning or repentance.

**RENDER.** Repay or give back (Job 33:26; Matt. 22:21).

**RENOWN.** Fame (Ezek. 16:14).

■ **REPENT.** Change one's mind and heart (Ex. 13:17; Matt 3:2). Turn from life without God to life with Him. Repentance is the first step to becoming a Christian. It means to recognize that life without God is wrong, to be sorry for the pain caused by that godless life, and to change to God's way of living (Acts 2:38; 3:19). See **BORN AGAIN, REGENERATION.**

**REPENTANCE.** A godly grief that changes mind, heart, and life through trust in Christ (Jer. 26:3; 2 Cor. 7:8-10). May simply mean regret or change of mind (Matt. 27:3). God's repentance is not from sin but a judgment to undo what is done (1 Sam. 15:11,29,35). See **REGENERATION.**

**REPHIDIM** (REF ih dim). Location where the Hebrews camped during their wilderness wanderings (Ex. 17:1). When the people complained to Moses about their thirst, God instructed Moses to strike a rock to produce water (Ex. 17:2-7).

**REPORT.** Besides the usual meaning, means testimony, witness, reputation (Acts 6:3; 22:12).

**REPROACH.** Insult, disgrace (Gen. 30:23; Rom. 15:3).

**REPROBATE.** Rejected because of lack of worth or being impure; not meeting the standard (Jer. 6:30; 2 Cor. 13:5).

**REPROOF.** Rebuke, correction (Prov. 1:23; 2 Tim. 3:16).

**REPROVE**. Rebuke, convict (Prov. 9:8; John 16:8).

**REQUITE**. Repay (1 Sam. 25:21; 1 Tim. 5:4).

**RESIDUE**. The rest; what's left over (Act 15:17).

**RESIST**. Oppose, stand against (Zech. 3:1; Matt. 5:39).

**RESOLVED**. Beginning to know (Luke 16:4).

**RESORT**. Come to, come together (Ps. 71:3; Mark 10:1).

**RESPECT**. Accept people by their appearance (2 Chron. 19:7; Rom. 2:11).
▼ Face-receiver *is a literal translation of a Greek word for respect. God looks on the heart of a person rather than the outward appearance, and He wants us to do the same (1 Sam. 16:7).*

**RESPITE**. Relief, rest (Ex. 8:15).

**RESTITUTION**. Restoration; something given back (Job 20:18; Acts 3:21).

**RESTORE**. Return (Gen. 20:7; Luke 19:8).

■ **RESURRECTION**. Raising to life after death (Matt. 22:23). God's raising of the dead in Christ to eternal life (Rom. 6:4-9). Because God raised Jesus from death, He will also raise Christians to eternal life (John 11:25; Rom. 6:5). Christ's resurrection is a foundation of the Christian faith (1 Cor. 15:12-21).
▼ *All people will experience a resurrection: Christians to life, non-Christians to condemnation (John 5:29; Acts 24:15). The resurrection gives Christians both power and hope (Phil. 3:10).*

**REUBEN** (RHOO ben), **REUBENITES** (RHOO ben ight). Oldest son of Jacob and Leah (Gen. 29:32). Reuben talked his brothers out of murdering their younger brother Joseph (Gen. 37:21-22). Reubenites were descendants of Reuben-one of the twelve tribes. They lived east of the Jordan.

■ **REVELATION**. Uncovering, revealing that which is hidden (Rom. 16:25). The Bible tells how God revealed Himself to people through nature, history, His actions, and supremely through His Son, Jesus (Gal. 1:12; Rev. 1:1).

**REVELATION, BOOK OF**. Last book in the NT. Traditionally the apostle John is credited with writing this book of prophecy. John recorded his vision from God while he was a prisoner exiled to the island of Patmos. The book opens with practical ethical and spiritual advice to seven churches John knew well. It then contains much vivid symbolism as God encourages the faithfulness of Christians and warns of the destruction of evil and the unfaithful.

**REVERENCE**. Fear, bow down, honor (Lev. 19:30; Matt. 21:37).

**REVILE**. Speak with insult or despising (Ex. 22:28; John 9:28).

**REVIVE**. Come to life, live again (Neh. 4:2; Rom. 14:9).

**REVOLT**. Rebel (2 Kings 8:20).

**REWARD**. Something given for good (Num. 18:31; Matt. 5:12) or bad actions (2 Pet. 2:13).
● *Standing-up for right has both hardships and rewards. How does focusing on the good reward help?*

**REZIN** (REE zin). King of Syria who fought

against the Judean king Ahaz (2 Kings 15:37). He was killed by Tiglath-pileser.

**RHODA** (ROH duh). A young girl at the home of John Mark's mother (Acts 12:13). Rhoda, either a servant or guest in the home, was sent to answer the door. She was so shocked at seeing the previously imprisoned Peter at the door that she forgot to let him in.

**RHODES** (ROHDZ). An island in the Mediterranean Sea where Paul stopped on a missionary journey (Acts 21:1).

■ **RIGHTEOUS.** Right or just, right with God (Mal. 3:18). A person is made right only through God in Christ (2 Cor. 5:21). See **JUSTIFICATION**.

■ **RIGHTEOUSNESS.** Rightness by God's standards (Isa. 41:10; 2 Cor. 5:21). Justice, fairness. Matching life with God's commandments, love, and purposes. Action based on love for God and a relationship with God.

**RIMMON** (RIM UHN). 1. City in Simeon, also En-Rimmon (Josh. 15:32; Neh. 11:29). 2. A rock in Benjamin (Judg. 20:45). 3. Father of Baanah and Rechab, the men who killed Saul's son Ishbosheth (2 Sam. 4:2). 4. A Syrian god (2 Kings 5:18).

**RITE.** Statute, rule (Num. 9:3).

**RIZPAH** (RIZ pah). Concubine (secondary wife) of Saul (2 Sam. 3:7).

*Temple ruins in the area of Lindos on the island of Rhodes.*

**ROBE.** An outer cloak or mantle (Jonah 3:6; John 19:2). The robe or mantle was often used for a covering at night.

**ROD.** A straight stick, also called a staff. Used for punishment (Ex. 21:20), measurement (Rev. 11:1), and defense (Ps. 23:4). God used a rod in a miraculous way to call Moses into service (Ex. 4:2-20) and to deliver the Israelites from the Egyptians (Ex. 14:16).

**ROE, ROEBUCK.** A small deer (Deut. 12:15).

**ROMANS, BOOK OF.** New Testament book Paul wrote to the Christians at Rome (Acts 20:2-3; Rom. 1:1; 15:25-28). Paul wrote the letter to tell of the world's need for salvation and God's provision of this salvation (Rom. 3:23; 6:23). It is as close to a summary of Paul's teaching as we have. Salvation comes by God's grace through faith and is not something

*Roman temple in the Corinthian style.*

humans can accomplish or earn (Rom. 10:9-10). Paul also wrote the letter to tell of his planned visit to Rome, to give guidance with some church problems, and to tell how Christians are supposed to live.

**ROME.** Capital of the Roman Empire and modern day capital city of Italy (Rom. 1:7).

*The famous Colosseum at Rome was built in the latter part of the first century A.D.*

Rome was founded about 753 B.C. and served the Roman Empire as a powerful city. Located on seven hills beside the Tiber River, Rome was the place of two imprisonments for Paul (Acts 28; 2 Tim. 4).

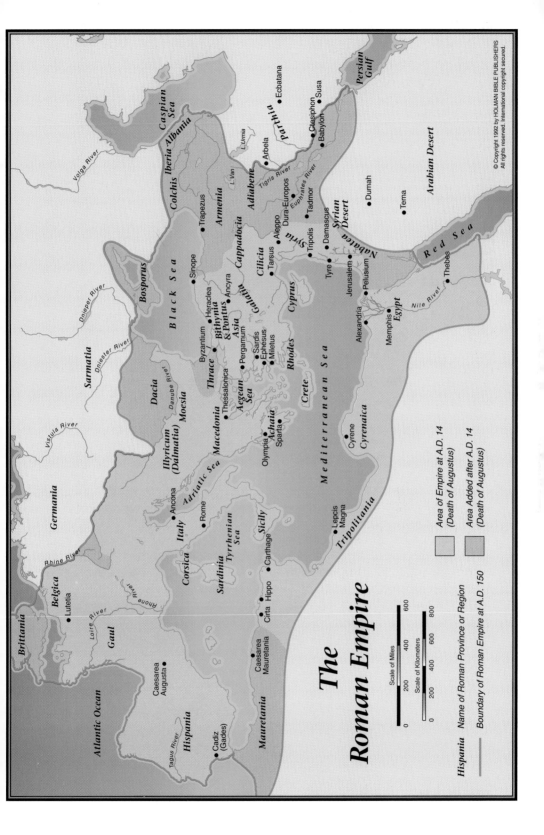

# The Roman Empire

Hispania  Name of Roman Province or Region

Boundary of Roman Empire at A.D. 150

Area of Empire at A.D. 14 (Death of Augustus)

Area Added after A.D. 14 (Death of Augustus)

Scale of Miles
0    200    400    600

Scale of Kilometers
0    200    400    600    800

*The Egnatian Way, shown here near Neapolis, was part of the extensive Roman road system.*

**ROOT**. Besides the usual meaning, it also symbolically means the source of a situation (1 Tim. 6:10); stability (Prov. 12:3); prosperity (Prov. 12:12). The Root of Jesse and the Root of David are terms used for the Messiah (Isa. 11:10; Rev. 5:5).

**RUDDY**. Reddish complexion (1 Sam. 16:12).

**RUSH**. A tall, slender plant that grows in water; reed (Isa. 9:14).

**RUTH**. Woman of Moab who married an Israelite (Ruth 1:4). Ruth's husband came with his family to Moab because of famine in their homeland. At his death, Ruth returned to Bethlehem with Naomi, her mother-in-law. Ruth was the great grand-mother of David and an ancestor of Jesus (Matt. 1:5).

**RUTH, BOOK OF**. Old Testament book that tells the story of Naomi and Elimelech who left their homeland in Bethlehem because of famine. They settled in the land of Moab. Elimelech died, and later his two sons died. Naomi was left with her two daughters-in-law, women of Moab. When Naomi decided to return to her homeland, she released the women of any obligation to her and urged them to remain in Moab. Ruth, full of devotion for Naomi, returned with her to Bethlehem. Ruth married Boaz, a kinsman, and became an ancestor of David and Jesus. The book shows the important role a foreigner played in God's plan of salvation.

**SABBATH.** (SAB buhth). Ceasing. God established the sabbath by ceasing the work of creation (Gen. 2:2-3). To keep, observe, or remember the sabbath means to do no work and to focus on worshiping God on the sabbath day. God commanded the sabbath observance (Ex. 20:8-11). Jesus practiced it and taught others about it (Luke 4:16; Mark 2:23- 28). Joy and blessings come from observing the sabbath (Isa. 58:13-14).

The sabbath is the seventh day of the week (Saturday) in the Jewish calendar. Christians observe this special day of rest on Sunday because of the resurrection of Jesus on that day and because the earliest Christians worshiped and gathered offerings on Sunday (Matt. 28:1,6; 1 Cor. 16:1-2).

▼ *The Pharisees interpreted "no work" too strictly (Matt. 12:2; Luke 6:7). They missed the intention of the sabbath (John 9:16): They felt that following rules was more important than caring about people. Jesus emphasized that the sabbath was made for people, not people for the sabbath (Mark 2:27).*

*Many rules about how to act on the sabbath are in the OT. Sincere religious people wrote rules and interpretations and put them in the Jewish books called the Mishna and the Talmud.*

● *The Pharisees were overly strict about the sabbath. Have we become too lenient? How do you spend Sunday?*

**SACKCLOTH.** Rough clothing worn as a sign of grief for the dead, repentance over personal sin, or sorrow over disaster (Gen. 37:34; Matt. 11:21). Sackcloth was made of goat or camel hair. It covered the middle of the body or the whole body.

■ **SACRIFICE.** Something offered in worship (Gen. 31:54; Mark 12:33). In the OT, sacrifices expressed repentance from sin and obedience to God. Jesus Christ became our Sacrificial Lamb so that we could receive God's gift of grace, which takes away our sin (John 1:29). Sacrifice can also be individual commitment to God (Rom. 12:1).

■ **SADDUCEES** (SAD joo sees). A group of Jewish people who believed only in the books of the Law; they did not believe in the resurrection (Matt. 22:23; Mark 12:18; Luke 20:27). They opposed Jesus and His ministry-as did the Pharisees. The Sadducees upheld the Law (priestly books); the Pharisees upheld the Prophets.
▼ *Jesus warned His disciples about the Sadducees and their teachings and explained the true nature of worship (Matt. 3:7; 16:1,11-12; John 4:22-24).*

■ **SAINTS.** Holy ones—set apart (Rom. 1:7; 1 Sam. 2:9). All true Christians are saints in the biblical sense of the word (Eph. 1:12-14; 1 Pet. 2:5,9). Not perfect people but those who have accepted Jesus as Lord and Savior (Phil. 1:1; 4:21).
● *Are you a saint?*

■ **SALVATION.** Safety, deliverance from evil, eternal life (Isa. 12:2; Luke 19:9). Salvation comes only by God's grace and through Jesus Christ when a person accepts Christ as Lord and Savior (Acts 4:12; Titus 2:11). It begins on earth and finds completion at death or at Christ's return.
● *Do you know you are saved?* See **REGENERATION**.

## SACRIFICIAL SYSTEM

| NAME | REFERENCE | ELEMENTS | SIGNIFICANCE |
| --- | --- | --- | --- |
| Burnt Offering | Lev 1; 6:8-13 | Bull, ram, male goat, male dove, or young pigeon without blemish. (Always male animals, but species of animal varied according to individual's economic status.) | Voluntary. Signifies propitiation for sin and complete surrender, devotion, and commitment to God. |
| Grain Offering Also called Meal, or Tribute, Offering | Lev 2; 6:14-23 | Flour, bread, or grain made with olive oil and salt (always unleavened); or incense. | Voluntary. Signifies thanksgiving for firstfruits. |
| Fellowship Offering Also called Peace Offering: includes (1) Thank Offering, (2) Vow Offering, and (3) Freewill Offering | Lev 3; 7:11-36 | Any animal without blemish. (Species of animal varied according to individual's economic status.) | Voluntary. Symbolizes fellowship with God. (1) Signifies thankfulness for a specific blessing; (2) offers a ritual expression of a vow; and (3) symbolizes general thankfulness (to be brought to one of three required religious services). |
| Sin Offering | Lev 4:1–5:13; 6:24-30; 12:6-8 | Male or female animal without blemish—as follows: bull for high priest and congregation; male goat for king; female goat or lamb for common person; dove or pigeon for slightly poor; tenth of an ephah of flour for the very poor. | Mandatory. Made by one who had sinned unintentionally or was unclean in order to attain purification. |
| Guilt Offering | Lev 5:14–6:7; 7:1-6; 14:12-18 | Ram or lamb without blemish | Mandatory. Made by a person who had either deprived another of his rights or had desecrated something holy. |

**SAMARIA** (suh MER ih uh). Important ridgetop city about forty-two miles north of Jerusalem and about twenty miles east of the Mediterranean Sea (2 Kings 3:1; John 4:4). Founded as the capital city of the Northern Kingdom of Israel, it was later controlled by many nations and partly destroyed many times.

Samaria came to refer also to the region around the city of Samaria and finally came to mean the entire Northern Kingdom of Israel (1 Kings 13:32; Jer. 31:5). In the NT Samaria was a region in central Palestine avoided by Jews (John 4:9).

**SAMARITAN** (suh MER ih tuhn). Originally, anyone living in Samaria. Later came to mean a race of persons formed when Jews married non-Jews. Jews intensely hated Samaritans and often refused to set foot in Samaritan territory. Jesus demonstrated that God loves Samaritans, just as God loves Jews (John 4:4-30).

**SAMUEL** (SAM yoo el). Prophet and the last judge of Israel. His birth was an answered prayer of his parents, Elkanah and Hannah (1 Sam. 1:20). Before Samuel's birth, his mother promised to give Samuel to God. She sent two-year-old Samuel to serve under Eli the priest. While Samuel was there, the Lord called him to lead Israel back to serve God.

Samuel warned the Israelite people not to

*Samuel blessing Saul.*

worship other gods or to ask for a king. They asked for a king anyway, and Saul became that king. Samuel anointed Saul, and later David, as the first two kings of Israel. Samuel's life was characterized by honesty and fairness.

**SAMUEL, 1, 2, BOOKS OF.** Two OT books of history named after Samuel the prophet. First Samuel tells about Samuel's life and death and Saul's life and death. It documents the change in Israel from rule by judges to rule by kings. It emphasizes faithfulness to God, no matter who rules. Second Samuel begins with David's anointing as king and includes most of his reign over Israel (2 Sam. 2:4; 5:3-4). The theme of both books is that faithfulness to God brings success and disobedience brings disaster (see 1 Sam. 2:30).

■ **SANCTIFICATION.** God's cleansing process to make a person whole and like Jesus (1 Cor. 1:30). It affects both character and conduct (Col. 3:1-17). Part of God's will and plan (1 Thess. 4:3; 2 Thess. 2:13).

■ **SANCTIFY.** Set apart (Gen. 2:3). Dedicate as holy and for God's use (Ex. 13:2). Sanctification is a process that begins when one becomes a Christian and concludes when Jesus returns or when we go to be with Him (1 Thess. 5:23). All Christians are sanctified (Eph. 5:26). See **SAINT.**

**SAPPHIRA** (suh FIGH ruh). Believer who died after lying about the selling price received for a possession-as did her husband (Acts 5:1-11). See **ANANIAS.**

■ **SATAN** (SAY tuhn). The devil, the evil one, the enemy (Matt. 4:10). Satan directly opposes God and hinders God's purposes (Zech. 3:1; Acts 26:18). He slanders God and His people (Job 1:6-12). He wants to control people and destroy them

and their devotion to God (John 10:10). Satan works through temptation, deception, and other subtle devices to take away the good God has given (Mark 4:15; 2 Cor. 11:14; 2 Thess. 2:9; Rev. 12:9). His power will one day be taken away, and he will be thrown in hell, where he will be forever (Rev. 20:10).

● *What circumstances make it easier for you to give into Satan? How might you avoid those circumstances?*

**SAUL** (SAWL). Name meaning *asked for.* 1. The first king of Israel (1 Sam. 9:15-17). He was tall, handsome, and initially a good leader. Samuel anointed Saul as king. Saul won several victories over Israel's enemies but later disobeyed God's commands (1 Sam. 15:11). He revealed himself unworthy to be a leader, displayed jealousy toward David, and showed anger toward his son Jonathan. He and his sons died in a battle against the Philistines (1 Sam. 31). David then became king (2 Sam. 2:4).

2. The Jewish name of the great Christian leader who was also known as Paul (Acts 13:9). Saul had persecuted Christians before his conversion (Acts 7:58).

■ **SAVED.** Rescued, brought to safety, delivered from the judgment of sin (Ps. 18:3; Acts 2:21). See **REGENERATION, SALVATION.**

■ **SAVIOR** (SAY vihawr). Deliverer, one who saves (2 Sam. 22:3; John 4:42). In the OT the word primarily referred to God but was also used of people (Neh. 9:27). In the NT the word refers primarily to Jesus but also to God (Luke 1:47).

**SCAPEGOAT.** A goat that symbolically bore the sins of the people. On the Day of Atonement, the priest symbolically transferred the sins of the people to the goat and drove it into the wilderness (Lev. 16:20-28).

*A young Jewish boy at his Bar Mitzvah with the Torah scroll reverently opened before him.*

**SCROLL.** A book made of flattened papyrus plant or animal skins rolled around sticks at both ends (Rev. 6:14). Also called a roll or book (Luke 4:17).

*This sepulchre, the Garden Tomb, is one site offered by tradition as the burial place of Jesus' body.*

■ **SECURITY OF THE BELIEVER.** Biblical teaching that those who are saved will continue to be saved. Though the phrase does not occur in the Bible, the concept appears in such references as Romans 8:38-39 and Philippians 1:6. Security of the believer is based on God's effort, not human effort.

● *Security of the believer is not an excuse for misbehavior or for ignoring God. What abuses have you seen of "security of the believer"?*

■ **SELAH** (SEE luh). A musical notation or cue for a pause or some other action (Ps. 85:2; Hab. 3:13).

**SEMITES** (SEM ights). People of Assyria and other groups of people believed to be descendants of Noah's son Shem (sometimes spelled Sem; Gen. 5:32; Luke 3:36). Though diverse as peoples, they speak similar languages, including Hebrew, Aramaic, Arabic, Canaanite, and Moabite.

**SEPULCHRE.** Grave, tomb, burial place (Gen. 23:6; Matt. 27:61). Sepulchres were cut out of rock, often carved in the

walls of existing caves (Mark 15:46). Many bodies were buried together. After a body decayed to the bones, these remains were often moved to a hole in the back of the cave to make room for the next body. *Sepulchre* is also used to describe empty religion and inner wickedness (Matt. 23:27; Rom. 3:13).

**SERAPHIM** (SER uh fim). Literally *the burning ones*. Winged angels who served as messengers for God. No one knows exactly what they looked like, but they had six wings (Isa. 6:2). See **CHERUBIM**.

**SERPENT**. Snake, especially a poisonous one (Ps. 58:4). Also a symbol for Satan or evil (Gen. 3:1; Matt. 23:33). God gave Moses a sign to show God's control over serpents (Ex. 4:3-5).

■ **SERVANT**. One who belongs to another (Rom. 1:1). Everyone is enslaved to something or someone, but choosing to be a servant of Jesus sets one free (Rom. 6:6-7; 8:2; John 8:34).

■ **SEXUALITY**. Maleness or femaleness. Sexual intercourse is a good gift from God intended for marriage (Gen. 1:27-28; 2:19-25). It is more than just physical; it is also an intimate means of expressing love through sharing mind and heart. Sexuality expressed through the union of marriage honors God and is blessed by Him.

**SHADRACH** (SHAD rak). New name given to Hananiah, friend of Daniel. He ate healthy food with Daniel and Meshach and Abednego and entered the Assyrian king's fiery furnace with the latter two (Dan. 1:6-15; 3:16-30).

**SHEKEL**. Unit of measure equaling about 11.5 grams or .4 ounce (Ex. 30:23-24). See **WEIGHTS AND MEASURES**.

**SHEMA** (SHEE mah). English writing of the first Hebrew word of Deuteronomy 6:4, meaning *hear*. The Shema came to include all of Deuteronomy 6:4-9, a confession of faith in the one true God and commitment to His commandments. Jesus quoted from the Shema in Mark 12:29.

▼ *Jewish worshipers later added other Scriptures to their Shema.*

**SHEOL**. OT name for place of the dead. See **HADES, HELL**.

■ **SIN**. Missing the mark of God's will by choice and because of human weakness (Jas. 1:14-15; Rom. 7:24-25). Action or attitude that disobeys God, betrays Him, or fails to do good (Rom. 3:23; Jas. 4:17). Sin always brings pain.

## THE SHEMA
### DEUTERONOMY 6: 4–9

4 Hear, O Ĭs´ra-el: the LORD our God *is* one LORD:

5 And thou shalt love the LORD thy God with all thine heart, and with all thy soul, and with all thy might.

6 And these words, which I command thee this day, shall be in thine heart:

7 And thou shalt teach them diligently unto thy children, and shalt talk of them when thou sittest in thine house, and when thou walkest by the way, and when thou liest down, and when thou risest up.

8 And thou shalt bind them for a sign upon thine hand, and they shall be as frontlets between thine eyes.

9 And thou shalt write them upon the posts of thy house, and on thy gates.

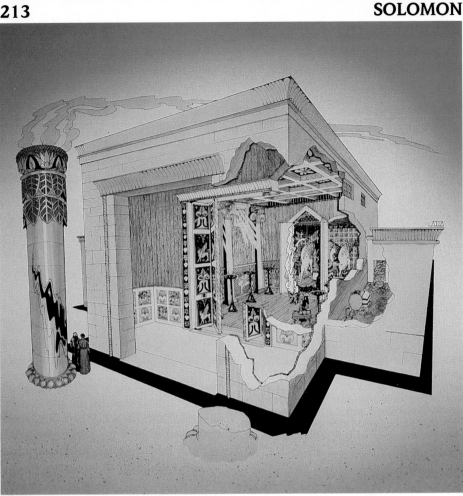

*Cut-away view of Solomon's Temple showing the porch, the holy place, and the holy of holies— where giant protecting cherubim and the sacred ark of the covenant were placed.*

▼ *The only unforgivable sin is unwillingness to accept God (Matt. 12:31).*

● *How can we keep from sinning? (See 1 Cor. 10:13; Phil. 4:13.)*

● *Give an example from your life which demonstrates the destructiveness of sin.*

**SIN OFFERING.** Any offering given after sin to reflect a repentant heart. Often, an offering given when someone sinned unintentionally (Lev. 4:2-35).

**SOLEMN ASSEMBLY.** A day to give full attention to God and to humble one's soul (Lev. 23:36). Solemn assemblies were religious events such as the one that occurred as part of the Day of Atonement. See the **Calendar Chart** pages 228 & 229.

**SOLOMON** (SAHL uh muhn). A son of David and the third king of Israel. Solomon was born to Bathsheba and David after their first son died. Solomon is best known for his wives, his wisdom, and for building the temple (1 Kings 3:12-28; 6:1). He also helped organize the nation, maintained peace most of the time, and built magnificent structures. Although Solomon was known for wisdom, he did not always act wisely, obey God, or lead well (1 Kings 11:9-10). Read about him in 1 Kings or 2 Chronicles.

*Reconstruction of Solomon's Temple (957–587 B.C.) at Jerusalem and its court. Shown are the ten lavers (five on each side of the Temple), the Molten Sea (lower, center), and the Altar of Burnt Offerings (center), Solomon's palace (left) stood immediately west of the Temple court, overlooking the Temple.*

**SONG OF SOLOMON, BOOK OF.** Old Testament book composed of six love songs from a husband to his wife and a wife to her husband. The book—celebrates love between a married couple-a tender, honest, delightful, and apprecia- tive love. Many Jews and Christians also see the book as representing the strength of the relationship between God and His people and the closeness between Christ and His church. Also called Song of Songs, the literal Hebrew name.

● *Read Song of Solomon to pinpoint the parts you consider most representative of true love.*

**SOUTHERN KINGDOM.** Same as Judah (but also contained the tribe of Benjamin). When Solomon died, rebellion divided the nation of Israel (1 Kings 14:19-30). The Northern Kingdom was made up of ten tribes that withdrew from King Rehoboam's rule about 922-912 B.C. and continued to be known as Israel. Judah was left as the Southern Kingdom. The Southern Kingdom continued until 587 B.C. when Babylonia conquered it. See the **King Chart** page 141.

■ **SOVEREIGNTY OF GOD.** Absolute authority and rule of God (see Isa. 45:5-6; Rom. 9:20-21). God alone has sovereign- ty.

**SPAN.** Linear measure equaling about nine inches (Ex. 28:16). Measured by the distance between the outstretched thumb and little finger or with three palms of a hand. A cubit is two spans. See **Weights and Measures** pages 244 & 245.

■ **SPIRIT.** Wind, breath, essence of being (Gen. 1:2; Luke 1:80). Often means the Holy Spirit (John 1:32). Sometimes refers to demons as unclean spirits or evil spirits (Matt. 8:16). See **HOLY SPIRIT.**

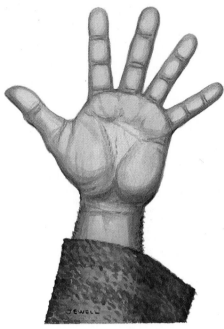

*A span.*

4:10). Stewardship is accountability for deciding how best to spend the time, talents, and possessions God has given to us (Luke 12:42). Failure to try to be a good steward is wickedness (Matt. 25:14-30).
● *Are you God's steward? How does this affect your actions and attitudes?*

**SUBJECT**. Obedient to (Luke 2:51). Under the control of, liable to (Heb. 2:15).

■ **SUBMISSION, SUBMIT**. Yield. Christian submission is to voluntarily yield in love and consider another's needs more important than one's own (Eph. 5:21; Jas. 4:7).

**SUFFER**. 1. Allow, let, permit (Mark 10:14). 2. Be in pain, go through troubles (Matt. 16:21).

■ **SUPPLICATION**. Plea or prayer (Job 8:5). Sincere and humble asking (2 Chron. 6:19; Esther 4:8; Eph. 6:18).

**SWADDLING CLOTHES**. A long piece of linen used to wrap babies (Job 38:9; Luke 2:7). Swaddling clothes were wrapped tightly to prevent movement. Perhaps this tightness made babies feel secure.

**SPIRITUAL**. Usually of God, like God (1 Cor. 2:15-16; Eph. 5:19). Occasionally refers to spirits against God (Eph. 6:12). True spirituality is obeying God in everyday life.

■ **SPIRITUAL GIFTS**. Abilities given to believers by the Holy Spirit (1 Cor. 12:7). Every Christian has at least one spiritual gift. We are to use spiritual gifts to build up other believers, create unity, express love, and reach new Christians (Eph. 4:13-16). For sample lists of these gifts see 1 Corinthians 12:1-11; Romans 12:4-8; Ephesians 4:11-13.
● *What are your spiritual gifts?*

**STATUTE**. Law or command (Ezek. 18:21).

■ **STEWARD, STEWARDSHIP**. One who manages money or possessions for another. In the OT a manager of a house (Gen. 43:19). In the NT a guardian (Gal. 4:2, RSV) or foreman (Matt. 20:8). Christians are stewards for God (1 Pet.

*Baby in swaddling clothes.*

*A sycamore tree in Jericho like the one into which Zaccheus climbed to see Jesus.*

**SYCAMORE.** Tree with wide spreading branches that were good for climbing (Luke 19:4). A cross between a fig and a mulberry tree, Bible sycamores were different from today's sycamore trees. Poor people ate their figs and used the wood (1 Kings 10:27). Sometimes spelled sycomore (KJV).

**SYNAGOGUE.** Jewish place of worship, study, and meeting (Ps. 74:8; Matt. 4:23) that arose after the destruction of the temple in 587 BC. Like the word *church* today, synagogue means both a community of believers and the place in which they meet. Men and women sat separately. The most important people sat in the front. There were several worship leaders. Competent members of the congregation were invited to read and explain the Scripture. When Jesus did this, people were amazed (Luke 4:16-22).

▼ *Synagogue services typically consisted of reciting the Shema (Deut. 6:4-9), prayers, Scripture readings from the OT, a sermon, and a benediction.*

*A typical synagogue of the first century A.D. showing the large inner room where the men gathered and its loft where the women gathered. This particular drawing is patterned after the synagogue at Capernaum.*

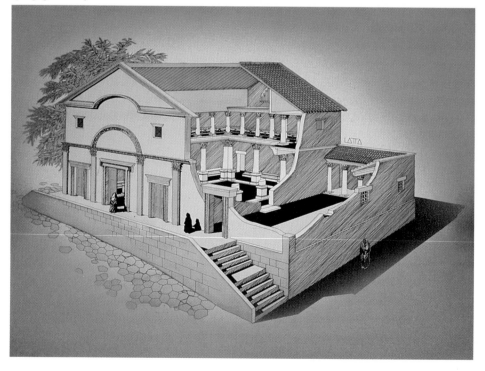

■ **TABERNACLE**. Tent, temporary dwelling place (Ex. 33:7; Matt. 17:4). Portable worship center Israel used until the temple was built. Symbolically, may refer to the physical body (2 Cor. 5:1-4).

**TABERNACLES, FEAST OF**. Annual Hebrew feast for the purpose of thanking God for the harvest (Lev. 23:34-36). Also

*Reconstuction of the Israelite Tabernacle and its court. The court was formed by curtains attached to erect poles. Before the tent was placed the Altar of Burnt Offerings and the Laver. The Tabernacle was always erected to face the east, so this view is from the northeast.*

called the Feast of Booths or the Ingathering. The people lived in booths during the feast as a reminder of their ancestors' nomadic life in the wilderness. The feast took place from the fifteenth to the twenty-second day of Tishri, a month approximately equivalent to our October. See the **Feast Chart** page 92 and **Calendar Chart** pages 228 & 229.

**TABITHA** (TAB ih thuh). Means *gazelle*. Another name for Dorcas. A follower of Jesus who did many good works in His name. When she died, God brought her back to life following Peter's prayer (Acts 9:36-42).

**TABLE**. Besides the usual meanings, can mean a writing surface or writing pad (Luke 1:63). The Ten Commandments were written on tables (Ex. 32:15-16).

**TABLET**. Bracelet, necklace, armlet, or buckle (Ex. 35:22; Isa. 3:20). Flat surface used for writing (NIV: Deut. 9:9; Luke 1:63).

**TALENT.** A unit of weight and money. As a weight, about seventy-five pounds (Ex. 25:39; Rev. 16:21). As money, it was equal to 3000 shekels in Palestine (but 3600 shekels in Babylon). Talents could be in gold or silver, with silver being worth about 1/15 of the gold. Whatever the exact comparison with our money, a talent was a huge sum of money that would require years of common labor to earn (Matt. 18:24; 25:15). See **MONEY**, and **Weights and Measures Chart** pages 244 & 245.

● *Whether talent refers to money or ability-as it does today—the Bibles teaches that the possessor has both opportunity and responsibility. How are you investing your talents?*

*The Cleopatra Gate at Tarsus commemorating Mark Antony's meeting of Cleopatra at this ancient city.*

**TAMAR** (TAY mahr). Means *palm*. 1. Wife of Er, the eldest son of Judah (Gen. 38:6). 2. Daughter of David. Her half-brother Amnon loved her deeply. He forced her to have sex with him and then despised her (2 Sam. 13:1-15).

**TANNER.** Dresser of animal hides (Acts 9:43). A tanner converts animal skin into leather by removing the hair and soaking it in a solution.

**TARRY.** Wait, stay behind, prolong, delay (Hab. 2:3; Heb. 10:37).

**TARSHISH** (TAHR shish). 1. Personal name given to a great-grandson of Noah, a Benjamite warrior, an official of King Ahaseurus of Persia, and others (Gen. 10:4; 1 Chron. 7:10; Esth. 1:14). 2. A wealthy Mediterranean trading port (Isa. 23:1; Jer. 10:9; Ezek. 27:12). Jonah sailed for Tarshish in an attempt to escape God (Jonah 1:3).

**TARSUS** (TAHR suhs). Birthplace of Paul the apostle and capital of Cilicia in Asia Minor (Acts 21:39). It was a learning center known for philosophy and literature and was about ten miles from the Mediterranean Sea.

**TASKMASTER.** Oppressive overseer (Ex. 1:11; 3:7). Taskmasters supervised forced labor projects. In the Book of Exodus, taskmasters forced Hebrew slaves to complete public works projects for Pharaoh.

**TASSEL.** Twisted cord fastened to the four corners of the outer garment worn by Jews to remind them of their covenant with God (NIV: Num. 15:38-39; Matt. 23:5; fringe or border in KJV).

▼ *The word translated tassel also means edge, border, hem; and it is the same word used when the woman touched the hem of Jesus' garment and was healed (Matt. 9:20; Luke 8:44).*

**TAX.** Verb: Register people or possessions (Luke 2:1,5; Acts 5:37); also set a value on something to determine what portion to charge for support of government or religion (2 Kings 23:35). Noun: Charges imposed by government or religious group (Matt. 17:24). For example, all Israelites paid half a shekel to support tabernacle worship (Ex. 30:13).

▼ *Jews were overtaxed in both the OT and the NT (1 Kings 12; Luke 19:2-8). In the NT tax collectors commonly collected more than was necessary and pocketed the excess. This unfair practice was one reason tax collectors were called sinners (Matt. 9:11, NIV). Some felt it was wrong to pay even fair taxes to Rome, but Jesus urged citizens to pay what was due to Caesar (Mark 12:14-17).*

**TEACH**. Cause to understand. Jesus was called Teacher (John 3:2).

*Reconstruction of Herod's Temple (20 B.C.–A.D. 70) at Jerusalem as viewed from the southeast. The drawing reflects archaeological discoveries made since excavations began in 1967 along the south end of the Temple Mount platform. The staircase (left), leads up from the lower city to a gateway (not shown) at Robinson's Arch. The monumental Herodian staircase also leads up from the lower city to the Double and Triple (Huldah) Gates. View provides an overview of the outer and inner courts of the Temple precinct atop the Temple Mount.*

Teaching is a spiritual gift (1 Cor. 12:28; Eph. 4:11).

**TEKOA, TEKOAH** (tih KOH uh). Town about six miles southeast of Bethlehem, best remembered as the home of Amos and a wise woman who sought help from David (2 Sam. 14:2).

**TEMPERANCE**. Self-control; use of a level head and sound mind (1 Cor. 9:25; Gal. 5:23; 2 Pet. 1:3-8).

**TEMPEST**. Violent storm, whirlwind,

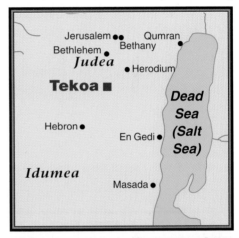

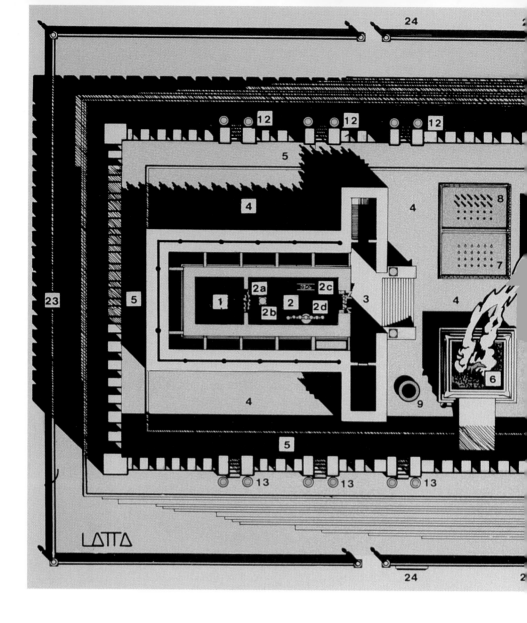

Herod's Temple (20 B.C.–A.D. 70) was begun in the eighteenth year of King Herod the Great's reign (37–4 B.C.). According to Josephus, first-century Jewish historian, Herod's Temple was constructed after removing the old foundations. The old edifice, Zerubbabel's Temple, was a modest restoration of the Temple of Solomon destroyed by the Babylonian conquest. The central building was completed in just two years — without any interruption of the Temple services. The surrounding buildings and spacious courts, considerably enlarged, were not completed until A.D. 64. The Temple was destroyed by the Romans under the commnd of Titus during the second Jewish revolt in A.D. 70.

1. Holy of Holies (where the ark of the covenant and the giant cherubim were once enshrined).
2. Holy Place
2a. Veil (actually two giant tapestries hung before the entrance of the holy of holies to allow the high priest entry between them without exposing the sacred shrine. It was this veil that was "rent" upon the death of Jesus).
2b. Altar of Incense

2c. Table of Shew Bread
2d. Seven-branched Lampstand (Great Menorah)
 3. Temple Porch
 4. Court of Priests
 5. Court of Israel (Men)
 6. Altar of Burnt Offerings
 7. Animal Tethering Area
 8. Slaughtering and Skinning Area
 9. Laver
10. Chamber of Phineas (storage of vestments)
11. Chamber of the Bread Maker
12. North Gates of the Inner Courts
13. South Gates of the Inner Courts

14. East (Nicanor) Gate
15. Court of Women
16. Court of Nazirites
17. Court of Woodshed
18. Lepers' Chamber
19. Shemanyah (possibly meaning "oil of Yah")
20. Women's Balconies (for viewing Temple
    activities)
21. Gate Beautiful (?)
22. Terrace
23. Soreg (three-cubit high partition)
24. Warning Inscriptions to Gentiles

hurricane, flood (Job 27:20; Matt. 8:24).

■ **TEMPLE.** House or place of worship (Ps. 11:4; Matt. 21:12). King Solomon built the first Temple, completed about 950 B.C. It was destroyed in 587 B.C. *Temple* can also refer to a Christian or a group of believers (1 Cor. 3:16-17; 6:19). This means a Christian is where God dwells; thus the Chrsitian must remain morally pure.

■ **TEMPTATION.** Enticement to do wrong (Jas. 1:13-14). Desire to do something bad that appeals to you. Temptation comes from Satan and is deceptive (Luke 4:1-13). God can help you avoid it and keep you from giving in to it (Luke 11:4; 1 Cor. 10:13). Temptation is not sin, but yielding to it is. Enduring temptation without giving in brings blessing and spiritual growth (Jas. 1:12).
● *What wrong actions or attitudes are most tempting to you? How does yielding to each bring harm, destruction, or bad consequences? How do you win victory over temptation?*

**TEMPTATION OF JESUS.** Forty days during which the devil tempted Jesus (Mark 1:12-13; Matt. 4:1-11; Luke 4:1-13). This time of temptation occurred at the beginning of Jesus' ministry, apparently to divert Jesus from God's plan. Jesus felt the temptations as strongly as we do, but He did not give in (Heb. 2:18; 4:15).
● *Examine Mark 1:12-13; Matthew 4:1-11; and Luke 4:1-13 to discover Satan's tempting strategies and Jesus' resisting strategies.*

**TEN COMMANDMENTS.** Ten basic rules for life that God gave the Israelites (Ex. 20:1-17). The Commandments reveal God's will for our relationship with Him and with others.
● *To understand the purpose of each Commandment, restate it in a positive way-what you are to do rather than what you are not to do. Notice that Exodus 20:8,12 do this.*
▼ *Deuteronomy 5:6-21 is another stating of the Ten Commandments.*

**TENDER EYED.** Soft, timid; possibly eye weakness or eye disease (Gen. 29:17).

**TERAH** (TEE ruh). Personal name meaning *turning, duration,* or *wandering.* Father of Abraham (Gen. 11:26-32). He lived to age 205 (Gen. 11:32).

**TERAPHIM** (TER uh fim). An idol used as a household god or for magic to try to tell the future (Judg. 18:14). They were kept in the house and possibly used as proof of inheritance rights. God condemned worship or use of teraphim (Gen 35:2; Ex. 20:4).

**TERRESTRIAL.** On or belonging to earth (1 Cor. 15:40).

**TERRIBLE.** Eliciting terror, awe, dread, fear, respect, or reverence (Dan. 7:7; Heb. 12:21).

**TESTAMENT.** Will (Heb. 9:16). Covenant, agreement between God and people (Matt. 26:28; Heb. 7:22). The Bible is divided into two divinely inspired Testaments that document covenants between God and people. The Old Testament was a covenant of promise, and the New Testament was a covenant of fulfillment (Gal. 3:8-29). Both covenants came as gracious gifts of God.
● *To see how the two Testaments relate to each other, read Galatians and Hebrews.*
▼ *Note that the word* **testament** *in the KJV appears only in the New Testament, but the word* **covenant** *is used in both the OT and the NT for the same purpose. Therefore, see* **COVENANT.**

# THE TEN COMMANDMENTS

| COMMANDMENT | PASSAGE | RELATED OLD TESTAMENT PASSAGES | RELATED NEW TESTAMENT PASSAGES | JESUS' TEACHINGS |
|---|---|---|---|---|
| You shall have no other gods before me | Exod 20:3; Deut 5:7 | Exod 20:23; 34:14; Deut 6:4, 13-14; 2 Kgs 17:35; Ps 81:9; Jer 25:6; 35:15 | Acts 5:29 | Matt 4:10; 6:33; 22:37-40 |
| You shall not make for yourself an idol | Exod 20:4-6; Deut 5:8-10 | Exod 32:8; 34:17; Lev 19:4; 26:1; Deut 4:15-20; 7:25; 32:21; Ps 115:4-7; Isa 44:12-20 | Acts 17:29-31; 1 Cor 8:4-6, 10-14; Col 3:5; 1 John 5:21 | Matt 6:24; Luke 16:13 |
| You shall not misuse the name of the Lord | Exod 20:7; Deut 5:11 | Exod 22:28; Lev 18:21; 19:12; 22:2; 24:16; Ezek 39:7 | John 5:12 | Matt 5:33-37; 6:9; 23:16-22 |
| Remember the Sabbath day by keeping it holy | Exod 20:8-11; Deut 5:12-15 | Gen 2:3; Exod 16:23-30; 31:13-16; 35:2-3; Lev 19:30; Isa 56:2; Jer 17:21-27 | Heb 10:25 | Matt 12:1-13; Mark 2:23-27; 3:1-6; Luke 6:1-11 |
| Honor your father and your mother | Exod 20:12; Deut 5:16 | Exod 21:17; Lev 19:3; Deut 21:18-21; 27:16; Prov 6:20 | Eph 6:1-3; Col 3:20 | Matt 15:4-6; 19:19; Mark 7:9-13; Luke 18:20 |
| You shall not murder | Exod 20:13; Deut 5:17 | Gen 9:6; Lev 24:17; Num 35:33; Exod 3:3 | Rom 13:9-10; Jas 5:21 | Matt 5:21-24; 19:18; Mark 10:19; Luke 18:20 |
| You shall not commit adultery | Exod 20:14; Deut 5:18 | Lev 18:20; 20:10; Deut 22:22; Num 5:12-31; Prov 6:29,32 | Rom 13:9-10; 1 Cor 6:9; Heb 13:4; Jas 2:11 | Matt 5:27-30; 19:18; Mark 10:19; Luke 18:20 |
| You shall not steal | Exod 20:15; Deut 5:19 | Lev 19:11,13; Exek 18:7 | Rom 13:9-10; Eph 4:28 | Matt 19:18; Mark 10:19; Luke 18:20 |
| You shall not give false testimony | Exod 20:16; Deut 5:20 | Exod 23:1, 7; Lev 19:11; Pss 15:2; 101:5; Prov 10:18; Jer 9:3-5; Zech 8:16 | Eph 4:25,31; Col 3:9; Titus 3:2 | Matt 5:37; 19:18; Mark 10:19; Luke 18:20 |
| You shall not covet | Exod 20:17; Deut 5:21 | Deut 7:25; Job 31:24-28; Ps 62:10 | Rom 7:7; 13:9; Eph 5:3-5; Heb 13:5; Jas 4:1-2 | Luke 12:15-34 |

*A small theater called an odeon at Thessalonica.*

**TESTIFY**. To tell about as an eyewitness, to state as true, to prove (Deut. 8:19; Acts 2:40).

● *To what can you testify? Has God given you a testimony? Who needs to hear it?*

■ **TESTIMONY**. Witness (Ruth 4:7; John 3:32). Sharing of experience. In the OT the word often referred to the Law or Ten Commandments (Ex. 25:21).

**TETRARCH**. Ruler of a small Roman territory in the early Roman Empire (Luke 3:1). Literally, *fourth part.*

**THADDAEUS** (THAD ih uhs). One of Jesus' twelve apostles (Mark 3:18). Same as Lebbaeus (Matt. 10:3). Possibly the same as Jude (short for Judas) who wrote the Bible book Jude. See **JUDE**.

**THANK**. Bless, declare blessed, profess, confess, praise (2 Sam. 14:22; Matt. 11:25).

**THANK OFFERING**. Offering to show thanks to God for a gift or for His help (2 Chron. 29:31; 33:16).

**THANKSGIVING**. Gratitude, especially toward God, for a gift or action (Jonah 2:9; 2 Cor. 4:15). Thanksgiving is an important element of Christian worship expressed in everyday life as well as during worship services. Many Psalms express thanksgiving.

● *How do you show thanksgiving in word? action? attitude?*

**THENCE**. From there (Gen. 11:8; Mark 1:19).

**THEOPHILUS** (thih AHF uh luhs). An early convert to Christianity to whom Luke addressed the Bible books of Luke and Acts (Luke 1:3; Acts 1:1). The name means *friend of God.*

**THESSALONIANS, 1, 2, BOOKS OF** (thess uh LOH nih uhns). New Testament books from Paul wrote to believers at Thessalonica. Paul began a church in Thessalonica, and then jealous Jews forced him to leave (Acts 17:4).

In response to Timothy's good report about the Thessalonians, Paul wrote 1 Thessalonians. In this first letter Paul encouraged and reassured the Thessalonian Christians, gave thanks for their expressed faithfulness and love, defended his motives, and answered questions about the return of Jesus Christ.

In 2 Thessalonians Paul used a more serious tone to address continuing confusion about the return of Christ, correct the mistaken belief that Christ had already returned, urge lazy Christians to go back to work, and emphasize the need for steady faith in the midst of suffering and trouble. Paul seemed to have a special affection for the Thessalonians.

**THESSALONICA** (THESS uh loh NIGH kuh). Both the largest city and Roman capital of Macedonia (Acts 17:11). It is now Thessaloniki in northern Greece. Thessalonica served as an important harbor and commercial center. Paul visited Thessalonica, began a church there, and later wrote two letters which became the Bible books 1 and 2 Thessalonians. Thessalonica was named for the daughter of Philip II and half sister of Alexander the Great.

**THICKET**. A thick growth of trees, shrubbery, or thorns (Gen. 22:13; Isa. 9:18; Jer. 4:7).

**THISTLE**. A prickly plant that existed in several varieties in Bible times (Gen. 3:18; Matt. 7:16). Used also as a symbol for trouble, judgment, or wickedness (2 Kings 14:9).

**THITHER**. There, to that place (1 Sam. 10:22; Matt. 2:22).

*This large thistle plant is one of many varieties that grow in Israel.*

**THOMAS** (TAHM uhs). One of Jesus' twelve apostles; also called Didymus, which means twin. He was eager and teachable. He went with Jesus to Judea at the risk of death (John 11:16). Thomas asked for evidence that Jesus had really risen from death. Jesus gave that evidence (John 20:24-28).

**THONGS**. Straps (Acts 22:25).

**THORN IN THE FLESH**. Paul's ailment which he did not identify except to say that it kept him humble (2 Cor. 12:7-10). Some think it was poor eyesight (Gal. 4:13-15).

**THRESH.** Separate grain from husks (Isa. 28:27; 1 Cor. 9:10). Done in these ways: by beating the sheaves with rod, by walking oxen or other animals over them, or by using a threshing sledge. Threshing took place on a threshing floor, a large flat rock, or piece of ground. Threshing floors were located where the wind could blow away the chaff (small pieces of husk).

**THRONG.** Squeeze, press, crowd together (Mark 5:31).

**THUMMIM** (THUHM im). Objects used at times along with **URIM** to help a seeker try to find the will of God (Ex. 28:30; Lev. 8:8). The objects of unknown shape and size were carried in the high priest's clothing. Urim and Thummim may have been stones, serving as a type of sacred lots. Perhaps users drew them from a bag and whichever came out first was the answer.

**THYATIRA** (thigh uh TIGH ruh). Hometown of Lydia, one of the first missionary converts to Christianity (Acts

16:14). A church grew there. The Lord praised the church at Thyatira for its works, love, service, faith, and patience. However, He condemned it for allowing Jezebel's followers to prosper (Rev. 2:18-24). Thyatira served as the center of sever-

al trade guilds, and Lydia was likely a member of one.

*The ruins of Thyatira in ancient Asia Minor (modern Turkey).*

**TIBERIAS, SEA OF** (tigh BIR ih uhs). A sea also known as Chinnereth and the Sea of Galilee (Num. 34:11; John 6:1). See **GALILEE, SEA OF.**
▼ *Also, the name of a city on the western shore of Galilee.*

**TIDINGS.** News (2 Sam. 4:10; Luke 2:10; Rom. 10:15).

**TIGLATH-PILESER** (TIG lath-puh LEE zur), **TILGATH-PILNESER** (TIL gath-pill NEE zur). King of Assyria from 745 to 727 B.C. (2 Kings 15:29). He conquered much of the Northern Kingdom of Israel and carried off its inhabitants to Assyria.

*The Tigris River flows through the country of Iraq (ancient Mesopotamia).*

**TIGRIS** (TIGH griss). One of two rivers of Mesopotamia, first cited in a description of the Garden of Eden (NIV: Gen. 2:14; Dan. 10:4). *Hiddekel* is the Hebrew name of the Tigris (KJV). Today the Tigris runs past Baghdad. See **EUPHRATES.**

**TILL.** Plow, plant, cultivate (Gen. 2:5).

**TIMBREL.** Percussion instrument-like a tambourine (Ps. 81:2).

**TIME.** Jews divided months into weeks of seven days ending with the sabbath (our Saturday; Ex. 20:11). The Hebrew day began at sunset. Hebrew months began with the new moon. See the **Jewish Calendar** on the next two pages.

**TIMOTHY.** A native of Lystra who learned the Scriptures from his Jewish mother Eunice and grandmother Lois (Acts 16:1; 2 Tim. 1:5). His father was a Greek. Timothy means *honoring God*, and that he did as he served alongside the apostle Paul, who was his father in the faith (1 Tim. 1:2). Timothy accompanied Paul on missionary journeys and was listed along with Paul in the sending of six letters: 2 Corinthians, Philippians, Colossians, 1-2 Thessalonians, and Philemon.

**TIMOTHY, 1, 2, BOOKS OF** (TIM uh thih). Books Paul wrote as letters to a young Christian coworker named Timothy. First Timothy warns against false teaching. It also gives instructions for church worship, presents characteristics of church leaders, and encourages Christian service. Second Timothy, apparently written near the end of Paul's life, gives encouraging advice to Timothy including how to endure and to serve Christ faithfully.

● *Read these Scriptures to see which verse most strongly applies to your life right now: 1 Timothy 4:12-16; 6:6-10; 2 Timothy 1:7,12; 2:15; 3:16-17; 4:18. Why?*

**TISHBITE** (TISH bight). Used to identify Elijah (1 Kings 17:1). The word appears to be a tribe or village name.

■ **TITHE.** One tenth; tenth of money or possessions (2 Chron. 31:5-6). To tithe is to give a tenth of one's money to God. Tithing is a way to obey and worship God (Deut. 14:22-29; Mal. 3:10). To fail to tithe is to rob God (Mal. 3:8).

▼ *In Bible times, tithes were managed by the Levites (Neh. 10:38; Heb. 7:5-9). Similarly, we give our tithe to our church and decide together how to spend it for God's ministries.*

● *Why do you think many Christians fail to tithe? What response does Malachi 3:8-10 give to these reasons?*

# THE JEWISH CALENDAR

| Year | | Month | English Months (nearly) | Festivals | Seasons and Productions |
|---|---|---|---|---|---|
| Sacred 1 | Civil 7 | Nison/Abib 30 days | April | 1 New Moon<br>14 The Passover<br>15-21 Unleavened Bread | Spring rains (Deut 11:14)<br>Floods (Josh 3:15)<br>Barley ripe of Jericho |
| 2 | 8 | Iyyar/Ziv 29 days | May | 1 New Moon<br>14 Second Passover<br>(for those unable to keep first) | **Harvest**<br>Barley Harvest (Ruth 1:22)<br>Wheat Harvest<br>Summer begins<br>No rain from April to Sept.<br>(1 Sam 12:17) |
| 3 | 9 | Sivan 30 days | June | 1 New Moon<br>6 Pentecost | |
| 4 | 10 | Tammuz 29 days | July | 1 New Moon<br>17 Fast for the<br>taking of Jerusalem | **Hot Season**<br>Heat increases |
| 5 | 11 | Ab 30 days | August | 1 New Moon<br>9 Fast for the<br>destruction of Temple | The streams dry up<br>Heat intense<br>Vintage (Lev 26:5) |
| 6 | 12 | Elul 29 days | September | 1 New Moon | Heat intense<br>(2 Kgs 4:19)<br>Grape harvest (Num 13:23) |

| # | Hebrew Month | Month | Festivals / Events | Season / Weather |
|---|---|---|---|---|
| 7 | Tishri/Ethanim 30 days | October | 1 New Year, Day of Blowing of Trumpet Day of Judgment and Memorial (Num 29:1) 10 Day of Atonement (Lev 16) 15 Booths 21 (Lev 23:24) 22 Solemn Assembly | **Seed time** Former or early rains begin (Joel 2:23) Plowing and sowing begin |
| 1 | Marchesran/Bul 29 days | November | 1 New Moon | Rain continues Wheat and barley sown |
| 2 | Chislev 30 days | December | 1 New Moon 25 Dedication (John 10:22,29) | **Winter** Winter begins Snow on mountains |
| 3 | Tebeth 29 days | January | 1 New Moon 10 Fast for the siege of Jerusalem | Coldest month Hail and snow (Josh 10:11) |
| 4 | Shebat 30 days | February | 1 New Moon | Weather gradually warmer |
| 5 | Adar 29 days | March | 1 New Moon 13 Fast of Esther 14-15 Purim | Thunder and hail frequent Almond tree blossoms |
| 6 | Veadar/Adar Sheni | March/April | 1 New Moon 13 Fast of Esther 14-15 Purim | Intercalary Month |
| 13 | Leap year | | | |

**Note 1** The Jewish year is strictly lunar, being 12 lunations with an average 29-1/2 days making 354 days in the year.

The Jewish sacred year begins with the new moon of spring, which comes between our March 22 and April 25 in cycles of 19 years.

We can understand it best if we imagine our New Year's Day, which now comes on January 1 without regard to the moon, varying each year with Easter, the time of the Passover, or the time of the full moon which, as a new moon, had introduced the New Year two weeks before.

**Note 2** Hence the Jewish calendar contains a 13th month, Veadar or Adar Sheni, introduced 7 times in every 19 years, to render the average length of the year nearly correct and to keep the seasons in the proper months.

**Note 3** The Jewish day begins at sunset of the previous day.

**TITTLE.** Could refer to any small mark-such as a dot or an accent mark over a word (Luke 16:17).

**TITUS** (TIGH tuhs). A Greek Christian coworker with the apostle Paul, who may have converted Titus to Christ (Titus 1:4). He traveled on missionary journeys with Paul and took Paul's first letter to the Corinthians with the assignment of helping the church correct its problems (see 2 Cor. 7:13-15).

**TITUS, BOOK OF** (TIGH tuhs). New Testament book Paul wrote as a letter to a Christian coworker named Titus. Paul wrote to encourage Titus in the face of opposition, to remind him to hold onto sound faith and sound doctrine, to urge him to seek Christian leaders with good character, and to show him how to teach.
● *God's ways are good and profitable for people (Titus 3:8). Give an example.*

**TOIL.** Labor, hard work (Gen. 5:29; Matt. 6:28).

**TOKEN.** Sign, proof, signal (Gen. 9:12; 2 Thess. 1:5).

**TOLERABLE, TOLERATE.** Bear, able to stand a hardship (Matt. 10:15).

**TOLL.** Tax, a measured amount (Ezra 4:13).

**TOMB.** Burial place (Job 21:32; Matt. 27:60). In NT times tombs were often caves or cut-out areas in stone because of the difficulty of digging in the rocky ground. Many tombs had shelves on which to lay the bodies. They also had heavy stone doors to seal the tomb. Jesus was buried in a tomb large enough for someone to sit inside (Mark 16:5). See **BURIED, SEPULCHRE.**

■ **TONGUES.** Besides the usual meaning, languages (Gen. 10:5; Acts 2:4). The gift of tongues is a spiritual gift that comes with cautions and restrictions about its use (1 Cor. 12-14). Speaking in tongues may refer to a foreign language or a unique utterance understood only by God or with

*A tomb.*

His help. (See Acts 2:4-11; 1 Cor. 14:1-33.)

**TORAH**. Hebrew word meaning *law* or *teaching* and used to refer to God's teachings. *Torah* came to mean the first five books of the OT (Genesis, Exodus, Leviticus, Numbers, Deuteronomy). The word does not appear in the KJV. See **PENTATEUCH**.

*Jewish rabbis conversing before a reverently opened and elaborately decorated scroll of the Torah.*

**TORMENT**. Torture; inflict pain (Heb. 11:37). Evil causes torment.

**TOW**. Short fibers of flax, easily broken and, therefore, used as a symbol for what is weak or temporary (Judg. 16:9).

**TOWER**. Tall structure that gave watchmen a vantage point for guarding cities, vineyards, pastures, and more. Towers ranged in size from a single room to a huge fortress. Used figuratively for God's salvation (2 Sam. 22:51).

● *Identify the specific towers in Genesis 35:21; Judges 9:46; Song of Solomon 4:4; Nehemiah 3:1.*

**TO WIT**. Namely, that is (Esther 2:12; Rom. 8:23).

**TRADITION**. Beliefs, teachings, practices, or rules handed down from the past (Matt. 15:2-3; 2 Thess. 2:15).
● *Ideally, traditions are accurate, good, and helpful; but some traditions are inaccurate, bad, and destructive. Give an example of each.*

**TRAIN**. Noun: Part of a long robe that trails behind the wearer (Isa. 6:1). Also, a procession of attendants (1 Kings 10:2). Verb: Teach (Prov. 22:6).

■ **TRANSFIGURATION**. Transformation, change of appearance (Matt. 17:2). This term described Jesus' appearance when He was glorified and shone with a heavenly brightness as He stood with Peter, James, and John.

**TRANSFIGURED**. Changed, transformed (Mark 9:2). During the transfiguration the disciples saw Jesus' glory and the brightness, splendor, and radiance of God's presence (Matt. 17:1-8; Mark 9:2-8; Luke 9:28-36).
● *What thoughts and emotions do you think you might have experienced at Jesus' transfiguration?*

■ **TRANSFORMED**. Changed outwardly or inwardly (Rom. 12:2; 2 Cor. 3:18, NIV). In the Bible, transformation often results from an encounter with God in Christ. See **REGENERATION**.

**TRANSGRESS**. Cross the line, step over from right to wrong, rebel, disobey God (1 Kings 8:50; Luke 15:29).

■ **TRANSGRESSION**. Lawlessness, sin,

rebellion against God (Prov. 12:13; 1 John 3:4).

**TRANSLATE.** Transfer, such as the transfer of a kingdom from one person to another (2 Sam. 3:10) or the transfer of believers into God's kingdom (Col. 1:13). Also change from life on earth to life in heaven without dying (Heb. 11:5).

▼ *Put into another language. The Bible was originally written in Hebrew and Greek. Bible scholars have translated it into English and many other languages. English translations of the Bible include the* King James Version, New International Version, New American Standard Version, and New Revised Standard Version.

**TRAVAIL.** Labor, very hard or painful work (Job 15:20; Isa. 53:11). Childbirth is a specific kind of travail (Isa. 23:4; John 16:21).

**TREACHEROUS.** Disloyal, unreliable, tricky, deceitful (Hos. 6:7).

**TREAD.** Trample. The past tense is *trodden* (Lam. 1:15).

**TREASON.** Betrayal, conspiracy (1 Kings 16:20).

**TREASURE.** What is valued (Matt. 6:20-21). Not limited to what you can see or touch.
● *Why are nonmaterial things greater treasures than material ones?*
● *What you treasure shows your priorities. Why?*

**TREE OF KNOWLEDGE OF GOOD AND EVIL.** Tree in the Garden of Eden used to demonstrate Adam's and Eve's obedience and loyalty-or lack of it-to God (Gen. 2:9). God commanded Adam and Eve not to eat from this tree. Satan said the tree would help Adam and Eve be like God. Both Adam and Eve ate from the tree. Rather than positive things, their actions brought shame, guilt, separation, and exclusion (Gen. 2:16-17; 3:1-24).
● *What leads people to sin? Wanting to be like God? Disobedience? Rebellion? Or what?*
● *The phrase "forbidden fruit" comes from this experience. Why do we want what we can't have?*

**TREE OF LIFE.** Tree in the Garden of Eden that symbolized eternal life. Adam and Eve had access to this tree until they chose to disobey God (Gen. 2:9,16-17; 3:22-24).

**TRESPASS.** False step, sin, violation of God's rights or the rights of a fellow human (Lev. 6:2; Matt. 6:14). The act of going beyond one's right and injuring another.

**TRIAL.** Event to try, prove, or test (Ezek. 21:13; Heb. 11:36). Being brought before a court to confirm or acquit a charge of wrongdoing (Mark 13:11, NIV).

**TRIBE OF ISRAEL.** Jacob, later called Israel, had twelve sons. The descendants of those twelve sons became the twelve tribes of Israel (Num. 13:4-15; Matt. 19:28). During the period of the Judges, each tribe had its own leaders and laws. David became king and moved Israel toward unity. Solomon became king after David. After Solomon's death, Israel divided into the Northern and Southern Kingdoms. (Judah and Benjamin formed the Southern Kingdom, and the remaining ten tribes formed the Northern Kingdom.)

■ **TRIBULATION.** 1. Troubles caused by an outside source (Acts 14:22; 1 Thess. 3:4; Rev. 2:10). Oppression. Can be physical, mental, or spiritual. Tribulation cannot separate Christians from God or destroy them (Rom. 8:35; John 16:33). God will

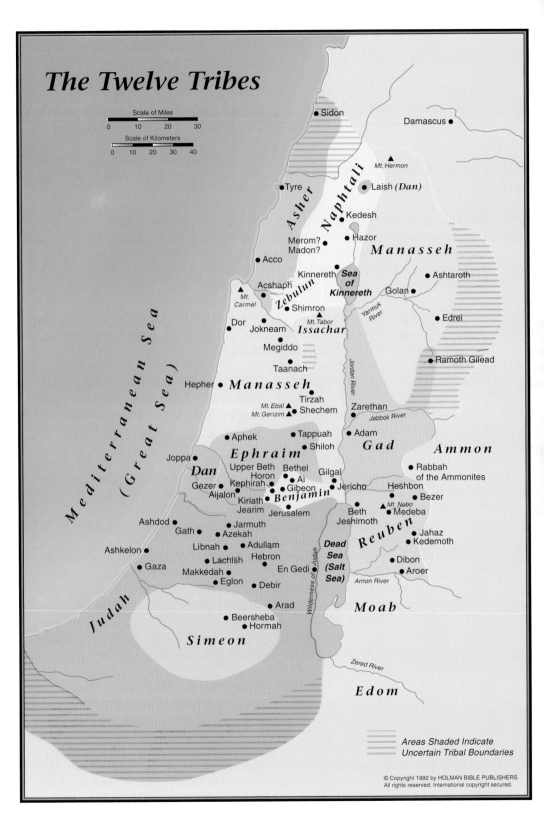

# The Twelve Tribes

Scale of Miles
0    10    20    30

Scale of Kilometers
0    10    20    30    40

Sidon

Damascus

▲ Mt. Hermon

Tyre

Laish (Dan)

Kedesh

*Asher*

*Naphtali*

Merom?
Madon?

Hazor

*Manasseh*

Acco

Ashtaroth

Kinnereth
Acshaph

*Sea of Kinnereth*

Golan

▲ Mt. Carmel

*Zebulun*

Shimron

Yarmuk River

Edrei

Dor

Joneam

▲ Mt. Tabor

*Issachar*

Megiddo

Ramoth Gilead

Taanach

Jordan River

Hepher

*Manasseh*

Tirzah

Mt. Ebal ▲
Mt. Gerizim ▲ Shechem

Zarethan

Jabbok River

Aphek

Tappuah

Adam

*Gad*

*Ammon*

Shiloh

*Ephraim*

Joppa

*Dan*

Upper Beth
Horon

Bethel
Ai

Gilgal

Rabbah
of the Ammonites

Gezer

Kephirah

Gibeon

Jericho

Heshbon

Aijalon

Kiriath
Jearim

*Benjamin*

Bezer

Jerusalem

Beth
Jeshimoth

▲ Mt. Nebo
Medeba

Ashdod

Jarmuth

*Reuben*

Gath

Azekah

Jahaz
Kedemoth

Libnah

Adullam

Ashkelon

Lachish

Hebron

*Dead Sea (Salt Sea)*

Dibon
Aroer

Gaza

Makkedah

En Gedi

Eglon

Debir

Arnon River

*Judah*

Arad

*Moab*

Beersheba
Hormah

Wilderness of Judah

*Simeon*

Zered River

*Edom*

*Mediterranean Sea (Great Sea)*

Areas Shaded Indicate
Uncertain Tribal Boundaries

comfort Christians through tribulation and deliver them from it (2 Cor. 1:3-4; Deut. 4:30-31; 1 Sam. 26:24). 2. The eventual result for persons who do evil (Rom. 2:9). 3. A period of excessive troubles near the end of the world or before the Lord's return (Mark 13:24; Dan. 12:1; Rev. 7:14).

● *Why do you think God allows people to go through tribulation?*

**TRIBUTE.** Tax forced upon a conquered people, a payment required by a superior (Ezra 4:20). Tributes required of conquered nations sometimes undermined the nation's economy.

**TRINITY.** Threefold. People's way of referring to the Godhead: God the Father, God the Son, God the Spirit (Matt. 28:19). The word *trinity* does not appear in the Bible, but references to the Godhead do (1 Cor. 12:4-6; 1 Pet. 1:2; Matt. 3:16-17).

● *The Trinity is God's mystery. Every attempt to illustrate the Trinity is inadequate. Some people think of the Trinity in this way: God is like water. The chemical compound (H2O) comes in solid (ice), liquid (water), and gas (steam). Each has specific functions. Ice cools, water quenches thirst, and steam cooks and cleanses. Others picture three separate matches brought together as one flame and suggest that this illustrates God the Father, God the Son, and God the Holy Spirit. The Bible teaches that only one God works with His creation in the three persons of Father/Creator, Son/Savior, and Spirit/Comforter. The Trinity shows God has personal relationships and expresses love within His own Being. How do you evaluate these pictures? What picture helps you understand the Trinity?* See *GOD, HOLY SPIRIT, JESUS.*

**TRIUMPH.** Rise above, cry aloud, sing, shout, be victorious over (Ex. 15:1; Ps. 47:1; 2 Cor. 2:14; Col. 2:15).

**TRIUMPHAL ENTRY.** Jesus' entrance into Jerusalem on the Sunday before His crucifixion (Matt. 21:1-9; Mark 11:1-10; Luke 19:29-38; John 12:12-16). It is called Palm Sunday because palm branches were laid in Jesus' path. The triumphal entry is important because during that event Jesus as the Messiah was publicly recognized. Until then Jesus refused public recognition of Himself as Messiah and ministered outside Jerusalem. His riding into Jerusalem on a colt fulfilled Messianic prophecy (Zech. 9:9).

**TROAS** (TROH az). An important city and seaport in the Roman province of Asia a few miles south of ancient Troy (Acts 20:5). Paul visited Troas on two missionary journeys.

**TROPHIMUS** (TRAHF ih muhs). Gentile (non-Jew) who became a Christian in Ephesus and later accompanied Paul (Acts 21:29).

**TROUGH.** Structure that holds animal feed or water (Ex. 2:16). Can also hold bread dough (Deut. 28:17, NIV).

**TROW.** Think (Luke 17:9).

**TRUE, TRUTH.** Genuine, honest, sincere, actual, reliable, able to be trusted (Ps. 33:4; Matt. 22:16). Actual fact rather than pretense, appearance, or claim. God is the one Source of truth, and Jesus is called the Truth (John 14:6).

**TRUMPETS, FEAST OF.** An annual Hebrew feast that celebrated the new civil year with a blast of trumpets (Lev. 23:23-25; Num. 29:1). It occurred on the first day of the seventh month, Tishri, which is approximately our month of October. See the **Feast Chart** page 92 and the **Calendar Chart** pages 228 & 229.

*A section of the ruins of the theater at Troas.*

▼ *This feast is now Rosh Hashanah, the second most holy day in the Jewish calendar.*

**TRUST.** Depend on, put one's confidence in (Prov. 3:5; 2 Cor. 1:9). A confident hope (2 Cor. 1:10). Belief (1 Thess. 2:4).

**TUMULT.** Uproar, confusion, rowdy assembly (Ps. 83:2; Matt. 27:24).

**TUNIC.** Loose fitting, knee-length, shirt-like garment worn by men and women under their outer clothes (Mark 6:9, NIV).

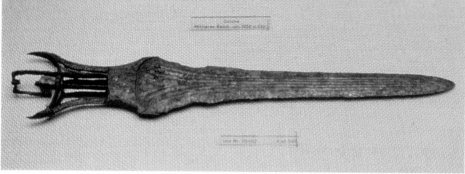

*An ancient two-edged sword.*

**TURBAN** (NIV). Brimless headdress formed by winding cloth around the head (Job 29:14). The high priest wore a special one (Lev. 8:9). Removing one's turban symbolized mourning (Ezek. 24:17).

*Modern Arab man wearing typical head cloth (called kaffiyeh) worn by Middle Easterners for millennia.*

**TURTLEDOVE**. Dove. Bird used by poor people for sacrifice (Lev. 12:6-8; Luke 2:24).

**TWAIN**. Two, both (Isa. 6:2; Matt. 5:41).

**TWILIGHT**. A specific boundary between sunset and complete darkness (1 Sam. 30:17; 2 Kings 7:5). Also, some usages appear to refer to darkness (Job 3:9; 24:15; Ezek. 12:6).

**TWINED**. Two or more strands twisted together; interlaced (Ex. 26:1).

**TWO-EDGED**. Sharp on both edges (Heb. 4:12).

**TYCHICUS** (TIK ih kuhs). Christian and fellow minister with Paul. Tychicus accompanied Paul to Jerusalem. Later Paul sent him to Ephesus and Colosse (Acts 20:4).

**TYRE** (TIRE). Ancient Phoenician seaport city famous for wealth, wickedness, independence, and boldness (2 Sam. 5:11; Luke 6:17). It was north of Carmel and south of Sidon. Enemies found it difficult to capture Tyre because it was well protected by breakwaters and stood on a rocky island half a mile off the coast.

In the OT David and Solomon had friendly alliances with Tyre. Jezebel, a daughter of the King of Tyre, promoted Baal worship. Old Testament prophets denounced Tyre. In the NT Jesus preached in Tyre, and Paul spent a week there. See **PHOENICIA, SIDON**.

**UNBELIEF**. Lack of faith or trust (Matt. 13:58). Unbelief often means to be disobedient to God—in other words, to be an unbeliever (Rom. 11:30; Heb. 4:11).

**UNCIRCUMCISED**. Males who had not had a circle of skin cut off at the front end of the penis (as a ceremonial procedure; Gen. 17:14). Uncircumcision was also used to refer to Gentiles or unbelievers (Eph. 2:11).

**UNCLEAN**. Defiled, impure, polluted (Lev. 5:2; Rom. 14:14). Under Jewish law a person became ceremonially unclean by eating certain food, having contact with the dead, having leprosy, having a bodily discharge, or having undergone childbirth. The unclean person had to go through a ceremony of purification. In the NT, uncleanness for Christians was primarily spiritual impurity in one form or another (Eph. 5:5).

**UNDEFILED**. Clean, pure (Ps. 119:1; Heb. 7:26).

**UNFAITHFUL**. Deceitful (Prov. 25:19).

**UNGODLY**. Godless, wicked, irreverent (Ps. 1:6; Rom. 5:6).

**UNHOLY**. Not set apart for God (Lev. 10:10; Heb. 10:29); wicked (1 Tim. 1:9; 2 Tim. 3:2).

**UNLEAVENED**. Food prepared without yeast (Gen. 19:3; Mark 14:1).

**UNLEAVENED BREAD, FEAST OF**. The Feast of Unleavened Bread, also called the Passover, was celebrated to help the Israelites remember their deliverance from the hands of the Egyptians (Ex. 12). God instructed the Israelites to omit leaven (yeast) from their bread because of the need for a hasty departure from Egypt. Leavened bread requires time to rise. See **PASSOVER** and the **Feast Chart** page 92.

■ **UNPARDONABLE SIN**. Sin that is beyond forgiveness; blasphemy against the Holy Spirit or hardness of heart (Matt. 12:31-32; Ex. 8:32). To blaspheme the Holy Spirit is persistently to ignore or discredit His work in one's life.

The person who blasphemes the Holy Spirit chooses to reject Christ. That person's heart becomes so hard that it is dead to God. Obviously, the person who has a concern about a personal relation to God has a heart that is still alive and not beyond repentance and God's forgiveness.

● *Many think they have done something so bad that God could never forgive them. If you are worried about God's forgiveness, that is an indication that you have not committed the unpardonable sin. You can be forgiven. How might you convince someone that God wants to forgive him or her?*

**UNRIGHTEOUS**. Opposite of being right and acceptable to God (Isa. 55:7; 1 John 1:9). Unjust (Heb. 6:10). See **JUSTIFICATION**.

**UNSEARCHABLE**. Cannot be understood or traced (Job 5:9; Eph. 3:8).

**UNTIMELY**. Not the natural or proper time-early or late (Job 3:16; Rev. 6:13).

**UNWITTINGLY**. Without knowing, unintentionally, by mistake (Lev. 22:14; Josh. 20:3).

**UPHOLD**. Support (Ps. 51:12; Heb. 1:3).

**UPPER ROOM**. Second floor room where Jesus met with His disciples shortly before His arrest, trial, and crucifixion (Mark 14:15). It was here that Jesus prepared His disciples for His death, the Holy Spirit's coming, and their ministry of reconciliation.

**UPRIGHT**. Having strong moral character and integrity (1 Sam. 29:6); to stand straight or erect (Lev. 26:13; Acts 14:10).

**UPROAR**. Loud noise, riot (1 Kings 1:41; Matt. 26:5).

**UR**. Ancient city of Mesopotamia, located southeast of Babylon (Gen. 11:31). It was a prosperous city and the hometown of Abraham.

**URIAH** (yoo RIGH uh). 1. Husband of Bathsheba (2 Sam. 11:3). Because of King David's adulterous affair with Bathsheba and her resulting pregnancy, David sent Uriah to the front lines of battle so he would be killed. 2. Priest in Jerusalem (2

Kings 16:10). 3. A prophet and another priest by this name.

**URIM** (YOO rim) and **THUMMIM** (THUHM im). Objects used by the high priest to try to find the will of God (Ex. 28:30; 1 Sam. 28:6-25). The objects of unknown shape and size were carried in the high priest's clothing. Urim and Thummim may have been stones, serving as a type of sacred lots. Perhaps users drew them from a bag and whichever came out first was the answer. See **THUMMIM**.

**USURY**. Interest charged for a loan (Ex. 22:25; Matt. 25:27). Jews were not allowed to charge other Jews interest, but it was all right to charge a non-Jew (Deut. 23:19-20).

*The excavations at Ur showing the palace foundations with a ziggurat in the distance.*

▼ *In the KJV,* usury *is not used in the modern sense of charging excessive or illegal interest. In contemporary translations the word* interest *is usually used.*

**UTTER.** Verb: Speak (Prov. 23:33; Matt. 13:35). Adjective: Complete, total (1 Kings 20:42).

**UTTERANCE.** Speech (Acts 2:4).

**UZZAH** (UHZ zuh). Son of Abinadab who died while touching the ark of the covenant (2 Sam. 6:3-8). There were also other OT men called by this name.

**UZZIAH** (uz ZIGH uh). Also known as Azariah (see 2 Chron. 26:1; 2 Kings 15:1). King of Judah, the Southern Kingdom (2 Kings 15:1-13). He was a strong and successful king who reigned for fifty-two years. However, he came to a sad end. He was afflicted with leprosy after he tried to assume the priestly duty of offering incense in the Temple (2 Chron. 26:16-23). Uzziah is also the name of other OT men. See **King Chart** page 141.

**VAIN.** In the KJV, usually empty or futile (Ps. 73:13; 1 Cor. 15:14). The word is used to translate a number of Hebrew words that have different meanings. *Falsehood* is often the meaning of vain in the KJV (Ex. 20:7). In the KJV *vain* never means conceited.

**VALIANT.** Brave, strong (Jer. 46:15; Heb. 11:34).

**VANITY.** Emptiness, that which is without value or meaning (Eccl. 1:2; Acts 14:15). In the KJV, never in the sense of conceit.

**VARIANCE.** Separate (Matt. 10:35). Dispute, strife (Gal. 5:20).

**VASHTI** (VASH tigh). Wife of Ahasuerus, king of Persia (Esther 1:9). When Vashti refused to parade her beauty in front of the king's guests, Ahasuerus removed Vashti as queen and replaced her with Esther.

**VEIL.** (Spelled VAIL in some KJV Bibles.) Covering (Gen. 24:65; 2 Cor. 3:13). Curtain (Ex. 26:31; Matt. 27:51). The temple veil or curtain separated the holy place from the holy of holies. Only the high priest was allowed to pass through this veil, and only on the Day of Atonement. When Christ was crucified, the temple veil tore in two. This symbolized that Christ's death provided personal, individual access to God.

**VENGEANCE.** Justice, revenge, repayment (Ps. 94:1; Heb. 10:30).

**VENTURE.** At random, innocently, without specific aim (1 Kings 22:34; 2 Chron. 18:33).

**VESSEL.** Container, utensil (Ex. 25:39; Matt. 25:4).

**VESTMENT, VESTURE.** Clothing, garment (2 Kings 10:22; Matt. 27:35).

**VEXATION.** Sadness, wrong (Eccl. 1:14). Trouble (2 Chron. 15:5). Anguish (Isa. 65:14).

**VILE.** Despised, filthy, dishonored (Ps. 12:8; Jas. 2:2).

**VINE, VINEDRESSER.** A creeping or climbing plant that produces melons, cucumbers, or grapes. Usually in the Bible the word refers to a grapevine (Gen. 40:10; Matt. 26:29). Grapes were a staple food in Bible times, eaten either fresh, dried as raisins, or used in wine-making. Those who took care of the vines were called vinedressers. Symbolically, *vine* referred to Israel (Hos. 10:1). Jesus

*Grapes growing on the vine.*

referred to Himself as the true vine and His disciples as the branches (John 15:1,5).

**VINEGAR.** Sour liquid produced from fermentation of grain or fruit (Num. 6:3; Matt. 27:34). Nazarites were not to drink vinegar. Jesus refused a vinegar mixture offered to ease His pain at the crucifixion.

**VINEYARD.** A field where grapes are grown, usually enclosed by a wall for protection against animals and thieves (Gen. 9:20; Matt. 20:1). Vineyards also had watchtowers for lookouts to give added protection. During harvesttime some grapes were left in the vineyard for gleaning (collection) by the poor and strangers (Lev. 19:10). See **GLEAN.**

**VINTAGE.** Harvest or yield of grapes (Lev. 26:5).

**VIOLATE.** Do violence to (Ezek. 22:26).

**VIPER.** Poisonous snake (Job 20:16; Acts 28:3). John the Baptist and Jesus used the term to refer to the wickedness of the religious leaders (Matt. 3:7; 12:34).

**VIRGIN.** A person who has not had sexual intercourse (Gen. 24:16; Matt. 25:1).

● *What standards of sexuality do you have? How do they reflect God's standards revealed in the Bible?*

**VIRGIN BIRTH.** The birth of Jesus produced through the miraculous intervention of God's Spirit and without human intercourse (Matt. 1:18-25).

**VISAGE.** Face, form, or appearance (Isa. 52:14; Dan. 3:19; Lam. 4:8).

**VISION.** A special message or revelation from God (Dan. 2:19; Acts 9:10). A vision could contain instructions or interpretations of present-day or future occurrences. God often gave visions to OT prophets.
● *In a modern-day sense, God plants His will in the lives of those who look for it. What do you feel God's will is for you? How can you find that will?*

**VOID.** Empty, lacking (Gen. 1:2; Prov. 7:7; Rom. 4:14).

**VOW.** A personal, voluntary promise. In the Bible, the vow is almost always to God (Gen. 28:20; Acts 18:18). Sometimes the vow was conditional on God's action or response; sometimes it was simply a dedication of devotion to God.

**WAGES.** Payment for services, reward (Gen. 29:15; Luke 3:14). Also used as payment or judgment for sin (Rom. 6:23).

**WAIL.** Cry or beat the chest as a sign of grief or repentance (Esth. 4:3; Rev. 1:7).

**WALK.** Used literally (Ex. 2:5; Matt. 4:18). Also used to refer to a person's complete life-style (Gen. 5:24; Rom. 8:4; Eph. 2:2,10).
● *How might God evaluate your lifestyle?*

**WALL.** Literally, a wall of any kind (Prov. 24:31). Walls of sun-baked clay surround-ed and protected houses and cities in bibli-cal times (Ezra 5:8; Acts 9:25). Symbolically, wall was used to indicate sal-vation (Isa. 26:1), truth and strength (Jer. 15:20), and protection (Zech. 2:5). The "wall of partition" referred to the worship practice of separating the Jew and the Gentile (Eph. 2:14).

**WANTON.** Looking with lustful eyes, lewdness (Rom. 13:13; 2 Pet. 2:18).

**WARD.** A prison or a guarded place (Gen. 42:16-19; 2 Sam. 20:3).

**WARE.** Utensils, things for sale (Neh. 13:16).

**WASTE.** Place of desolation or drought (Lev. 26:31).

**WATCH.** A time of guard duty (Neh. 4:9; Matt. 14:25).

**WATCHMAN.** A person who keeps guard, a lookout (2 Kings 9:17). Watchmen were stationed on the walls of a city to warn of approaching enemies.

*An ancient watchtower remains relatively unchanged in an open field in Israel.*

They were also placed in the fields and vineyards during the time of harvest to watch for thieves.

**WATCHTOWER.** A high structure where a lookout could watch for approaching danger (Isa. 21:8).

**WAX.** Become, grow (1 Chron. 11:9; Luke 1:80).

**WEAN.** Cause a child to become independent of the mother's nourishment (1 Sam. 1:23).

**WEDDING.** Marriage of a man and woman-festive occasion of singing, dancing, and feasting that lasted one or two weeks (Matt. 22:31).

**WEEKS, FEAST OF.** Celebrated a successful barley harvest and came seven weeks after the Passover (Lev. 23:15-21). Same as Pentecost. Second of three annual festivals (Deut.16:16). No work was to be

*Roman bronze balance scale.*

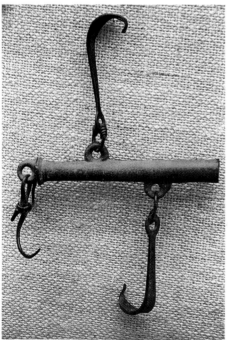

done, and every male went to the sanctuary (Lev. 23:21). Sin and peace offerings were made. See **PENTECOST** and the **Feast Chart** page 92.

**WEIGHTS AND MEASURES.** See pages 244 and 245.

**WELFARE.** Peace, completeness, prosperity (Gen. 43:27; Neh. 2:10).

**WELL.** A hole or pit dug in the ground to get water (Gen. 16:14; John 4:11). In the arid Bible lands, wells were very important. Dispute over the ownership of a well was a frequent source of strife (Gen. 26:15ff.).

*A chaduf for raising well water near ancient Lystra in south central Asia Minor (modern Turkey).*

*Well at modern Beersheba thought by some to be Abraham's well.*

**WHEAT.** The basic grain of the ancient Near East (Ezra 7:22; John 12:24). Wheat was ground between stones to make flour. Many varieties of wheat existed, but it is difficult to identify the specific grain referred to in Scripture. The KJV often

*A small whirlwind in the desert of the Wadi Arabah.*

refers to wheat or grain as corn, the more general British term (Mark 4:28). Wheat is sometimes used as a symbol of true commitment to God (Matt. 3:12, 13:24-30; Luke 3:17). Wheat harvest was celebrated with the Feast of Weeks, later called Pentecost. See **FEAST OF WEEKS** and **PENTECOST**. Also see **feast chart** following **FEAST**.

**WHELP**. Lion's cub, dog's pup, or other young animal (Nah. 2:11-12). Used figuratively of Judah and Dan (Gen. 49:9: Deut. 33:22).

**WHENCE**. From where (Gen. 16:8; Phil. 3:20).

**WHEREAS**. Because, since (Isa. 60:15; Jas. 4:14).

**WHIRLWIND**. Hurricane, tempest, violent wind (Isa. 66:15).
▼ *Some of the Hebrew words translated* whirlwind *could refer to any kind of strong wind-not just one that whirled.*

**WHITEWASHED**. Covered with thin coat of white paint. Looks white or fine on the outside but is unclean and corrupt on the inside (Matt. 23:27, NIV). Translated *whited* or *untempered* mortar in KJV (Ezek. 13:11).

**WHITHER**. Wherever, where (Gen. 28:15).

**WHOLE, WHOLESOME**. Complete, perfect, entire, healthy, or well (Prov. 15:4; John 5:6).

**WHORE, WHOREDOM**. Prostitute, one who had sexual intercourse with someone besides a marriage partner for money or profit (Lev. 21:9). Used symbolically in Revelation 17:1. Whoredom was considered a crime punishable by death (Gen. 38:24). Used figuratively for idolatry (Hos. 1:2). See **PROSTITUTE**.

**WICKED**. Sinful, evil, bad, worthless, without value, wrong, cruel, malignant (Ps. 9:16; 2 Thess. 3:2).
● *Wickedness is also doing nothing with*

# TABLE OF WEIGHTS AND MEASURES

## WEIGHT

| Biblical Unit | Language | Biblical Measure | U.S. Equivalent | Metric Equivalent | Various Translations |
|---|---|---|---|---|---|
| Gerah | Hebrew | 1/20 shekel | 1/50 ounce | .6 gram | gerah; oboli |
| Bekah | Hebrew | 1/2 shekel or 10 gerahs | 1/5 ounce | 5.7 grams | bekah; half a shekel; quarter ounce; fifty cents |
| Pim | Hebrew | 2/3 shekel | 1/3 ounce | 7.6 grams | 2/3 of a shekel; quarter |
| Shekel | Hebrew | 2 bekahs | 2/5 ounce | 11.5 grams | shekel; piece; dollar; fifty dollars |
| Litra (Pound) | Greco-Roman | 30 shekels | 12 ounces | .4 kilogram | pound; pounds |
| Mina | Hebrew/Greek | 50 shekels | 1 1/4 pounds | .6 kilogram | mina; pound |
| Talent | Hebrew/Greek | 3000 shekels or 60 minas | 75 pounds/ 88 pounds | 34 kilograms/ 40 kilograms | talents/talent; 100 pounds |

## LENGTH

| Biblical Unit | Language | Biblical Measure | U.S. Equivalent | Metric Equivalent | Various Translations |
|---|---|---|---|---|---|
| Handbreadth | Hebrew | 1/6 cubit or 1/3 span | 3 inches | 8 centimeters | handbreadth; three inches; four inches |
| Span | Hebrew | 1/2 cubit or 3 handbreadths | 9 inches | 23 centimeters | span |
| Cubit/Pechys | Hebrew/Greek | 2 spans | 18 inches | .5 meter | cubit(s); yard; half a yard; foot |
| Fathom | Greco-Roman | 4 cubits | 2 yards | 2 meters | fathom; six feet |
| Kalamos | Greco-Roman | 6 cubits | 3 yards | 3 meters | rod; reed; measuring rod |
| Stadion | Greco-Roman | 1/8 milion or 400 cubits | 1/8 mile | 185 meters | miles; furlongs; race |
| Milion | Greco-Roman | 8 stadia | 1,620 yards | 1.5 kilometer | mile |

| Biblical Unit | Language | Biblical Measure | U.S. Equivalent | Metric Equivalent | Various Translations |
|---|---|---|---|---|---|
| Xestēs | Greco-Roman | 1/2 cab | 1 1/6 pints | .5 liter | pots; pitchers; kettles; copper pots; copper bowls; vessels of bronze |
| Cab | Hebrew | 1/18 ephah | 1 quart | 1 liter | cab; kab |
| Choinix | Greco-Roman | 1/18 ephah | 1 quart | 1 liter | measure; quart |
| Omer | Hebrew | 1/10 ephah | 2 quarts | 2 liters | omer; tenth of a deal; tenth of an ephah; six pints |
| Seah/Saton | Hebrew/Greek | 1/3 ephah | 7 quarts | 7.3 liters | measures; pecks; large amounts |
| Modios | Greco-Roman | 4 omers | 1 peck or 1/4 bushel | 9 liters | bushel; bowl; peck-measure corn-measure; meal-tub |
| Ephah [Bath] | Hebrew | 10 omers | 3/5 bushel | 22 liters | bushel; peck; deal; part; measure; six pints; seven pints |
| Lethek | Hebrew | 5 ephahs | 3 bushels | 110 liters | half homer; half sack |
| Cor [Homer]/Koros | Hebrew/Greek | 10 ephahs | 6 bushels or 200 quarts/ 14.9 bushels or 500 quarts | 220 liters/ 525 liters | cor; homer; sack; measures; bushels/sacks; measures; bushels; containers |

## LIQUID MEASURE

| Biblical Unit | Language | Biblical Measure | U.S. Equivalent | Metric Equivalent | Various Translations |
|---|---|---|---|---|---|
| Log | Hebrew | 1/72 bath | 1/3 quart | .3 liter | log; pint; cotulus |
| Xestēs | Greco-Roman | 1/8 hin | 1 1/6 pints | .5 liter | pots; pitchers; kettles; copper pots; copper bowls; vessels of bronze |
| Hin | Hebrew | 1/6 bath | 1 gallon or 4 quarts | 4 liters | hin; pints |
| Bath/Batos [Ephah] | Hebrew/Greek | 6 hins | 6 gallons | 22 liters | gallon(s); barrels; liquid measure/ gallons; barrels; measures |
| Metretes | Greco-Roman | 10 hins | 10 gallons | 39 liters | firkins; gallons |
| Cor [Homer]/Koros | Hebrew/Greek | 10 baths | 60 gallons | 220 liters | cor; homer; sack; measures; bushels/sacks; measures; bushels; containers |

*what you have (Matt. 25:24-26). Evaluate your life in light of this definition.*

**WIDOW.** Woman whose husband has died (Ex. 22:24; Luke 2:37). Widows were protected by law and given help (Deut. 27:19; Acts 6:1). Because they did not inherit their husband's property, they were poor and helpless.

**WILDERNESS.** Barren and rocky desert or an uncultivated land suitable for nomads and grazing (Deut. 1:19; Matt. 15:33). Wilderness areas were often rocky

deserts with little rainfall-not necessarily sandy areas. Other wilderness areas had considerable growth.

▼ *Because the Hebrews rebelled against God after He freed them from Egypt, they wandered in the wilderness for forty years. The NT warns present Christians not to make the same mistake (1 Cor. 10:1-12).*

**WILT.** Second person singular of *will*; be willing, want to (Judg. 1:14; John 5:6).

**WIMPLE.** A covering, cloak, shawl, mantle (Isa. 3:22).

*The Wilderness of Judea (Wilderness of Judah).*

*An ancient Pompeii wine shop where wine was served from pottery containers sunk into the bar counter.*

**WIND**. Besides its usual meaning, the word in the original languages was used for wind, breath, spirit, or Holy Spirit (Gen. 6:17; Ps. 51:10-17; John 3:5-8; Gal. 5:16-23).

Both Hebrew and Greek have only one word for wind, breath, and spirit.

**WINE**. Juice pressed out of grapes and then fermented (Num. 6:3; Matt. 9:17).

Wine was part of meals, a medicine, and a disinfectant (Matt. 26:29; Luke 10:34; 1 Tim. 5:23). The Bible warns against drinking much wine (Prov. 23:29-30). Part of the Nazarite vow included abstaining from drinking wine (Num. 6:1-4; see also Luke 1:15).

▼ *Wine could refer to juice, wine diluted with water, or undiluted wine.*

● *What is involved in deciding whether to drink wine or alcoholic beverages? See Romans 14:13-23 and 1 Corinthians 10:31 for important considerations.*

*Reconstruction of a first-century wine press, showing the pressing basin with drain leading to the lower collecting basin.*

**WINEBIBBERS**. Persons given to drinking wine (Prov. 23:30; Matt. 11:19).

**WINEPRESS**. The device used to make

*Arabs winnowing grain in the ancient way with wooden winnowing forks.*

wine from grapes (Neh. 13:15). In large stone vats juice was pressed from grapes, often by walking on them. The juice left the winepress through a small drain at one end, was collected in large jars or wineskins, and then was allowed to ferment (become alcoholic). The winepress is used in images of God's judgment (Rev. 14:19-20).

**WINESKIN.** Container for wine, made from a whole animal skin (Mark 2:22). The skins stretched as the wine fermented, so old, brittle skins would not do.

▼ Bottle *translates the Greek word for wineskin in Matthew 9:17; Luke 5:7-38.*

**WINNOW.** Process of removing threshed grain from its uneatable parts (Ruth 3:2; see Matt. 3:12). A person would pick up wheat stalks with a winnowing fork and shake or toss them into the breeze. The heavy grain would fall to the ground, and the chaff would blow away. Winnowing could also occur before a fan.

■ **WISDOM.** Understanding, knowledge gained by experience (2 Chron. 9:23; 1 Cor. 1:17), a gift of God (Jas. 1:5). Wisdom is a characteristic of God. The Bible books of Job, Proverbs, and Ecclesiastes along with some Psalms such as 1, 119, are called Wisdom Literature. Sometimes people include James in the NT as Wisdom Literature.

**WISE.** One who applies knowledge to real life, understands, decides skillfully (Prov. 10:5; Eph. 5:15). Not all who are called wise are truly wise (Gen. 41:8; Rom. 11:25). The truly wise obey God.

**WISE MEN.** 1. An educated class of persons who were responsible for preserving and transmitting learning and counselling rulers (1 Chron. 27:32). 2. The men who came from the East to see Jesus (Matt. 2:1). They appear to have been astrologers. We don't know their names or number.

**WIT, WIST, WOT.** Old English for know (Gen. 24:21; Luke 2:49).

**WIT, TO.** Namely, that is (Esther 2:12; Rom. 8:23).

**WITHER.** Dry up, fade, wear away, weaken (Ps. 102:4; 1 Pet. 1:24).

**WITHSTAND.** Resist, strengthen self, stand up against an opponent (2 Chron. 13:7; Eph. 6:13).

■ **WITNESS, WITNESSING.** Testify, tell what you have seen or experienced (Gen. 31:44; John 1:7). The NT usage is from the Greek word *martyr*. A Christian is to be a witness by sharing personal experience of what Jesus has done in and for him or her (Acts 1:8; Mark 5:19).

**WIZARD.** Knowing one, magician or sorcerer, one who speaks to the dead (Isa. 8:19). Wizards were readily available but unreliable (1 Sam. 28:3-19). The Bible strictly forbids seeking advice from wizards, also called mediums (Lev. 19:31).
● *Why does God forbid seeking advice from wizards?*

**WOE.** Deep sorrow, grief, misery, or trouble (Num. 21:29; Prov. 23:29; Ezek. 2:10; 1 Cor. 9:16; Rev. 9:12). Also used in denouncing (Isa. 5:8-22; Matt. 23:16).

**WOMAN.** Human being created in the image of God to be the counterpart of man (Gen. 1:26-27). See **MAN.**
▼ *God created man and woman to reflect His image in creation and to complete each other (1 Cor. 11:11-12).*

**WOMB.** Uterus, site of an unborn baby's growth until birth (Gen. 25:24; Luke 1:15). *Fruit of the womb* means children (Deut. 7:13).

**WONDER.** Miracle, astonishing or amazing event (Ex. 4:21; Matt. 24:24). Also a feeling of amazement (Acts 3:10) or the act of marveling or being amazed (Luke 2:18). Wonders and signs often appear together to refer to miracles from God and their meaning (Acts 15:12).

● *What do you find wonderful about God?*

**WONT**. Accustomed, in the habit of (Num. 22:30; Luke 22:39).

**WORD**. Expression, statement, communication, speech (Deut. 32:1; Matt. 8:8). May be a single word or an entire message. In addition to the usual meanings, the word can be God's revelation to people (Matt. 4:4). God's Word includes His directions, purpose, will, and plan. God's Word comes through the person Jesus Christ (who is the Word; John 1:1-5,14), through prophets and teachers (Mic. 1:1), and through personal revelation (2 Sam. 23:2; Rev. 1:1-2). The Bible is God's Word (2 Tim. 2:15; 3:16-17).

▼ *Words have great power for good or evil. In the Bible one's spoken word was frequently seen as something that could not be canceled (Gen. 27:33). However, only God's Word has absolute power (Gen. 1:3,6,9,11,14,20,24,26; Isa. 55:11).*

● *What power does God's Word have in your life?*

**WORK**. Action that leads to results (Job 34:25). God works to create, save, guide, care for, and sustain (Ps. 8:6; Phil 1:6). Human works may be vain efforts to do good to others or to obey religious rules in an effort to earn or win salvation. We are saved by God's gift of grace and faith and not by our works (Eph. 2:8-9). However, we are God's work created for the purpose of good works (Eph. 2:10). Such works are motivated by love for God and for others not by self-interest. Although works do not save, they reflect whose child we are and whether we are obedient to our Father (1 John 3:1-10). Works also reflect the nature of the kind of faith that saves (Jas. 2:14-26). Though our salvation comes through Jesus, our works will be judged (1 Cor. 3:13-15).

● *What kind of work is your faith producing? What do you goals show about your commitments?*

**WORLD**. Earth, universe, era or age (Isa. 64:4; Matt. 12:32; Acts 17:24). Can also mean the present life on earth (Gal. 1:4) or life in heaven (Luke 18:30).

**WORM**. Creeping, spineless creature used as an image of lowliness or weakness (Job 17:14; Ps. 22:6; Isa. 41:14).

**WORMWOOD**. Bitter nonpoisonous plant that symbolized a bitter, sad experience (Lam. 3:19).

▼ *The OT pictures wormwood as the opposite of justice and righteousness (Jer. 23:15). In Revelation 8:11 a destructive star is called by this name.*

■ **WORSHIP**. Adore, obey, reverence, focus positive attention on (Ex. 34:14; John 4:23). Enjoy the presence of God. Any action or attitude that expresses praise, love, and appreciation for God. Worship can be expressed through obedience (Mic. 6:8) and the way we treat people (Matt. 25:37-40). Worship can be private or public (Matt. 6:6; Heb. 10:24-25).

● *Name at least three ways you worship God.*

■ **WRATH**. Anger, God's consistent attitude and response to sin (Rom. 1:18). God's wrath is grief that expresses itself in correcting us and motivating us to do right (1 Thess. 5:9; Rom. 13:4; Rev. 16:1).

● *How do you feel about God's wrath?*

**WREST**. To turn aside or distort (Ex. 23:6; 2 Pet. 3:16).

**WROTH**. Angry (Gen. 4:5; Rev. 12:17).

**WROUGHT**. Done, worked (Ps. 45:13; 2 Cor. 12:12).

● *In Bible times this name for God was considered too sacred to pronounce. Why do people take God's name so lightly today?*

**XERXES** (ZURK seez). King of Persia from 486-464 B.C. (NIV: Ezra 4:6; Esther 1:1; Dan. 9:1. KJV: Ahasuerus). He was the son of Darius and grandson of Cyrus the Great. He battled against the Greeks in revenge over a previous loss.

◆

■ **YAHWEH** (YAH weh). Name for God. English pronunciation of the Hebrew consonants YHWH. Usually translated "the LORD" (Ex. 3:15). Communicates that God both exists and is present with His people as a personal God. See **GOD**.

*The tomb of Xerxes located in the modern country of Iran.*

**YEA.** *Yes* is the basic meaning (Deut. 33:3; Matt. 9:28). However, the word sometimes has one of the following meanings: also, even if, truly, but. Sometimes used to emphasize that the answer to a question is yes: translated truly or indeed (Gen. 3:1).

**YEAR OF JUBILEE.** The fiftieth year after seven cycles of seven years (forty-nine years). In the year of Jubilee, servants were freed; and possessions were returned to the original owners (Lev. 25:9-14). The year of Jubilee gave a new start to those who had had to sell themselves or their land to escape poverty.

**YEARN.** Feel deeply for (Gen. 43:30; 1 Kings 3:26).

**YOKE.** A wooden frame that joins and enables two animals to work together (Deut. 21:3; Phil. 4:3). Often used in the Bible as a symbol of oppression, slavery, or

*The gate building of Xerxes at Persepolis which led to a mammoth terrace built by Darius the Great.*

burden (2 Chron. 10:4; Gal. 5:1). However, Jesus described His yoke as easy, meaning well-fitting (Matt. 11:29-30).

● *Second Corinthians 6:14 warns against being yoked together with an unbeliever. Why?*

**YONDER.** Beyond; there (Num. 16:37; Matt. 26:36).

———◆———

**ZACCHEUS** (za KEE uhs). Chief tax col-

*An ox and a donkey yoked together and pulling a wooden plow.*

*A tomb in Jerusalem which is said by local tradition to be Zacharias' tomb.*

lector who climbed a sycamore tree to see Jesus (Luke 19:2-9). Jesus called him down and went to his house. That day, Zaccheus repented of his dishonest practices and was saved.

● *In response to Jesus, Zaccheus righted past wrongs. What response to Jesus do you need to make?*

**ZACHARIAH** (zak uh RIGH uh). Alternate spelling of Zechariah.

**ZACHARIAS** (zak uh RIGH uhs). Greek form of Hebrew name *Zechariah*. Priest who was the father of John the Baptist (Luke 1:5). Another Zacharias was the son of Barachias who was stoned to death by the Jews (Matt. 23:35).

**ZADOK** (ZAY dahk). Name means *righteous*. A priest in the days of David (2 Sam. 8:17). Two other Zadoks were the father of Jerusha (2 Kings 15:33) and a person who sealed the covenant with Nehemiah (Neh. 10:21).

**ZEAL**. Enthusiasm; eagerness (Isa. 59:17). The word can mean eagerness to make the desires of God become reality (Num. 25:10-13; Acts 22:3). Zeal can be inaccurate or misdirected (Rom. 10:2). A person with zeal is described as zealous.

**ZEALOT** (ZEHL uht). One who acts with great zeal or enthusiasm for a cause, often militantly (Matt. 10:4, NIV). *Zealot* came to designate a member of a Jewish political group who tried to overthrow Roman oppression.

**ZEBEDEE** (ZEB uh dee). Father of James and John, who were disciples of Jesus and husband of Salome (Matt. 27:56; Mark 1:19, 15:40).

**ZEBULUN** (ZEB yoo luhn). Jacob's tenth son; also, the tribe named for Zebulun (Gen. 30:20; Judg. 4:6). This tribe of Israel lived between the Sea of Galilee and Mount Carmel.

**ZECHARIAH** (zek uh RIGH uh). Means *Yahweh remembered*. Can be spelled Zachariah. Among the many Zechariahs are these: 1. A king of Israel who reigned for six months in 746 B.C. and then was assassinated. He was the son of Jeroboam II (2 Kings 15:8). See **King Chart** page 141. 2. The prophet Zechariah, active from 520-518 B.C., who urged the Israelites to rebuild the Temple after the Exile. His prophecies are recorded in the

Bible book of Zechariah. 3. Grandfather of Hezekiah (2 Kings 18:2). 4. A gatekeeper in the temple (1 Chron. 9:21). 5. One of Josiah's overseers in repairing the temple (2 Chron. 34:12). 6. Musician who helped Nehemiah (Neh. 12:35). 7. Godly advisor of King Uzziah (2 Chron. 26:5). 8. Son of Jehoshaphat the king; his brother Jehoram killed Zechariah when Jehoram became king (2 Chron. 21:2-4).

**ZECHARIAH, BOOK OF.** Old Testament book in the minor prophets sections. It records the rebuilding of the temple after the Babylonian captivity (sometime after 538 B.C.). Even more than the rebuilding, the prophet Zechariah emphasized the relationship to God that the building represented (Zech. 10:6). Zechariah 1-8 prophesies the restoration of Jerusalem, rebuilding of the temple, and purification of God's people. Zechariah 9-14 focuses on the awaited Messiah and the final judgment.

**ZEDEKIAH** (zed uh KIGH uh). Means *Yahweh is my righteousness* (or *my salvation*). 1. A false prophet who wrongly encouraged Ahab to attack the Syrians at Ramoth-Gilead (1 Kings 22:11-12). 2. The last king of Judah, who reigned from 596-587 B.C. (2 Kings 24:17-18). Nebuchadnezzar, king of Babylon, made Zedekiah king of Judah. When Zedekiah rebelled, the Babylonians destroyed Jerusalem and removed Zedekiah from power. Four other Zedekiahs appear in Scripture.

**ZEPHANIAH** (zef uh NIGH uh). Bible Zephaniahs include: 1. Prophet and author of the book of Zephaniah (Zeph. 1:1). 2. The priest who requested prayer for Israel, reported false prophecy from Babylon to Jeremiah, and was later executed by Nebuchadnezzar (Jer. 29:25).

**ZEPHANIAH, BOOK OF.** Old Testament book in the minor prophets, written before the Babylonian captivity. The book contains a prophecy of doom for Judah's worship of other gods, a promise of punishment for other nations, and a picture of the restoration of Jerusalem with a faithful remnant of God-honoring citizens.

**ZERAH** (ZEE ruh). Also, **ZARA** and **ZARAH**. Means *sunrise*. Zerah was a twin born to Tamar and her father-in-law, Judah. Zara is named in the genealogy of Jesus Christ (Gen. 38:30; Matt. 1:3).

**ZERUBBABEL** (zuh RUHB uh buhl). Means *descendant of Babel*. Grandson of King Jehoiachin who, after being held captive in Babylonia, returned to Jerusalem as governor. He led in both the initial failed attempt to rebuild the temple and then the later successful one (Ezra 3:2-4:4; 5:2).

**ZEUS** (ZOOS). Greek name for the ruler of the gods, corresponding to the Roman name, Jupiter (Acts 14:12, NIV; Jupiter in KJV). Followers of Zeus believed that Zeus controlled the weather. Much to Barnabas' dismay, he was called Zeus after a man was healed. Paul and Barnabas used this as an opportunity to teach about the true God (Acts 14:8-18).

**ZION** (ZIGH uhn). Fortress, name for Jerusalem or a part of Jerusalem (Ps. 2:6; Rev. 14:1, NIV). Originally *Zion* referred to the oldest part of Jerusalem, a southeastern hill. Later it also included the northeastern hill on which the temple was built; and finally it referred to the entire city. *Zion* can also refer to the whole nation of Israel (Isa. 1:27), the city of God in the age to come (Isa. 28:16), or heaven (Isa. 59:20).

**ZIPPORAH** (zip POH ruh). Wife of Moses and daughter of Jethro, also called Reuel, priest of Midian (Ex. 2:16-21; 3:1).

# KEY TO PRONUNCIATION

| Sign | Example | Results |
|---|---|---|
| ay | day, name | DAY, NAYM |
| a | hat, cat | HAT, CAT |
| ah | rah, far | RAH, FAHR |
| e, eh | care, fare | KEHR, FEHR |
| u, uh | about, around | uh BOWT, uh ROWND |
| aw | awl, call | AWL, CAWL |
| u, uh | afraid | uh FRAYD |
| ee | daemon, demon | DEE muhn |
| uh | Elijah | ih LIGH juh |
| ay | mail, hail | MAYL, HAYL |
| igh | aisle | IGHL |
| uhm | adam's apple | A duhms |
| uhn | roman | ROH muhn |
| k | cord, chorus | KAWRD, KOH ruhs |
| s, ss | city | SIH tih |
| ee | mete, Crete | MEET, KREET |
| e, eh (uh) | met, let | MEHT, LEHT |
| u, uh | term | TUHRM |
| i, ih | elastic | ih LASS tihk |
| g | get | GEHT |
| gh, j | germ | JUHRM |
| igh | high, sign | HIGH, SIGHN |
| ih | him, pin | HIHM, PIHN |
| ee | machine | muh SHEEN |
| u, uh | firm | FUHRM |
| o, oh | note, rode | NOHT, ROHD |
| ah | not, rot | NAHT, RAHT |
| uh | amok | uh MUHK |

| Sign | Example | Results |
|---|---|---|
| aw | or, for | AWR, FAWR |
| f | alpha | AL fuh |
| z | his, muse | HIHZ, MEWZ |
| ss | kiss | KISS |
| yoo, ew | tune, mute | TYOON, MEWT |
| uh | huh, tub | HUH, TUHB |
| u, uh | hurl, furl | HUHRL, FUHRL |
| oo, ew | truth | TREWTH |
| th | thin | THIHN |
| t | Thomas | TAHM uhs |
| sh | attraction | uh TRAK shuhn |
| i, ih | city | SIH tih |

## Seldom Used Marks

| Sign | Example | Results |
|---|---|---|
| uh | Balaam | BAY luhm |
| ih | Colossae | koh LAHS sih |
| oh | Pharaoh | FAY roh |
| aw | author | AW thuhr |
| ee | sea | SEE |
| eh | zealous | ZEH luhs |
| ee | gee | JEE |
| oo, ew | brew | BREW |
| uh | legion | LEE juhn |
| yaw | Savior | SAYV yawr |
| oy | boil | BOYL |
| uhn | onion | UHN yuhn |
| uhr | author | AW thuhr |
| ow | out | OWT |
| uh | zealous | ZEH luhs |

# ART CREDITS

The publishers express deep gratitude to the following persons and institutions for the use of art materials in this book.

## Photographs and Artifacts

**Arnold, Nancy, Nashville, TN.** Pp. 57; 73, left; 191; 216.

**The Baptist Sunday School Board, E. C. Dargan Research Library, Fon H. Scofield, Jr., Collection, Nashville, TN.** Pp. 31; 44; 59; 67; 73, top right (Rockefeller Museum, Jerusalem, Israel); 98, bottom; 99; 100; 104; 112; 144; 159; 181; 183, bottom right; 189, bottom; 194; 198; 199; 203; 236, middle left; 240; 241; 248; 251; 252, both; 253.

*Biblical Illustrator,* **Nashville, TN. David Rogers:** pp. 37 (The Louvre, Paris, France); 61; 114; 117 (The Archaeological Museum, Ankara, Turkey); 150; 158, top (The Archaeological Museum, Ankara, Turkey); 163, bottom (Museum of the Ancient Orient, Istanbul, Turkey); 171, top; 184; 218; 225; 242, top right; 242, bottom right. **Ken Touchton:** pp. 49; 55; 58; 73, bottom right; 111, top; 113; 124; 125, top; 137; 158, bottom; 163, top; 185; 188, top; 204; 211, top; 231.

**Brisco, Thomas V., Fort Worth, TX.** Pp. 162, 183, top; 211, bottom.

**Couch, Ernie, Nashville, TN.** Pp. 94; 173; 189, top.

**Holman Pictorial Collection of Biblical Antiquities, Holman Bible Publishers, Nashville, TN.** P. 34 (Oriental Institute, Chicago).

**Ellis, C. Randolph, Malvern, AR.** Pp. 125, bottom; 134; 177.

**Langston, Scott, Fort Worth, TX.** Cover photo; and pp. 86; 111, bottom; 169, bottom; 180, both; 206; 246.

**Smith, Marsha A. Ellis, Nashville, TN.** P. 40.

**Stephens, Bill, Nashville, TN.** Pp. 20; 75 (Augst Museum, Augst, Switzerland); 118, top (Roman Museum, Malta); 118, bottom (Beersheba Museum, Beersheba, Israel); 131; 139; 140; 148; 151; 155; 169, top (Museum of Guilia Villa, Rome, Italy); 171, bottom; 187; 188, bottom; 224; 235; 236, top (Glyptothek Museum, Munich, Germany); 242, left; 247.

**Tolar, William B., Fort Worth, TX.** Pp. 82-83; 98, top; 161; 165; 197; 226; 227; 238; 243.

## Paintings and Illustrations

© **Baptist Sunday School Board (The Sunday School Board of the Southern Baptist Convention), Nashville, TN. Bill Latta:** pp. 32; 53; 70; 85; 115; 116; 122-23; 126-27; 198; 204; 213; 214; 216; 217; 219; 220-21; 248. **Ben Stahl:** pp. 147; 186.

© **Broadman Press, Nashville, TN. Don Fields:** pp. 27; 29; 51; 52; 93; 215, bottom. **Ben Stahl:** pp. 69; 129; 133; 136; 152.

© **Holman Bible Publishers, Nashville, TN. Jack Jewell:** pp. 79; 178; 215, top; 230.

© **Dover Pictorial Archives. Gustave Doré:** pp. 23; 33; 50; 66; 68; 84; 86; 131; 135; 159; 164; 195; 209.

## Charts

© **Holman Bible Publishers, Nashville, TN.** Pp. 9-16; 21; 30; 46-47; 48; 54; 78; 92; 103; 106; 109; 130; 132; 138; 141; 142; 157; 166; 168; 174-75; 187; 190; 193; 208; 212; 223; 228-29; 244-45.

## Maps

© **Holman Bible Publishers, Nashville, TN.** Pp. 19; 25; 35; 37; 39; 43; 53; 56, both; 62; 67; 71; 72; 76; 82; 85; 89; 97; 100; 101, both; 105; 111; 117; 119; 124; 128; 134; 139; 145; 149, both; 153; 154; 162; 164; 172; 173; 176; 177; 179; 180; 182; 183; 184; 198; 200; 203; 205; 208; 218; 219; 225; 226, both; 227; 233; 235; 236; 238.